HIKING TRAILS I
Victoria and Vicinity

Covering the Capital Regional District,
including:
Saltspring, Portland, and Sidney Islands;
the Saanich Peninsula, core municipalities,
and the Western Communities;
Sooke west to Port Renfrew;
the West Coast Trail;
and north to Spectacle & Oliphant Lakes

TWELFTH EDITION, 1997

Published by the Vancouver Island
Trails Information Society

compiled and edited by
Susan Lawrence

Original copyright © 1972 Outdoor Club of Victoria
Trails Information Society

Twelfth Edition © 1997 by the Vancouver Island Trails Information Society
(name change only)

First published as HIKING TRAILS, Victoria and Southern Vancouver Island
December 1972;
compiled and edited by Jane Waddell

Fifth printing February 1974
Revised, expanded and retitled November 1975
Revised February 1977
Revised April 1979
Revised and expanded October 1981
Revised and expanded January 1987
Reprinted with revision notes June 1990
Revised and expanded November 1993
Revised and expanded June 1997

Printed by Hemlock Printers Ltd., Burnaby, BC

Distributed by
Orca Book Publishers
1030 North Park St.
Mail: PO Box 5626, Stn. B, Victoria, BC V8R 6S4

Maps by A. N. Fraser Drafting Services

Cover photo by Irene Lawrence:
View south from the Ridge Trail near Jocelyn Hill in Gowlland Tod Park.
Mount Finlayson, centre; Sawluctus Island in Finlayson Arm, right.

Illustrations by Judy Trousdell

ISBN 0-9697667-2-6

CONTENTS

	Page
Legend	6
Editor's Notes	7
Hints and Cautions	10
⟨1⟩ Outer Gulf Islands	19
⟨2⟩ Saltspring Island	24
⟨3⟩ Sidney area	38
⟨4⟩ North Saanich area	41
⟨5⟩ Central Saanich area	56
⟨6⟩ Highlands area	68
⟨7⟩ Saanich area	85
⟨8⟩ Oak Bay area	122
⟨9⟩ Victoria area	128
⟨10⟩ Esquimalt area	143
⟨11⟩ View Royal area	146
⟨12⟩ Langford and Colwood areas	155
⟨13⟩ Metchosin area	166
⟨14⟩ East Sooke area	180
⟨15⟩ Sooke area	188
⟨16⟩ Sooke to Port Renfrew	194
⟨17⟩ Port Renfrew / San Juan area	203
⟨18⟩ West Coast Trail	210
⟨19⟩ Malahat area	214

CONTENTS, continued

Trail systems and greenways 217

Club addresses 221

Useful addresses 222

Acknowledgements 223

Index 223

Bus information .... appendix

List of maps .... inside back cover

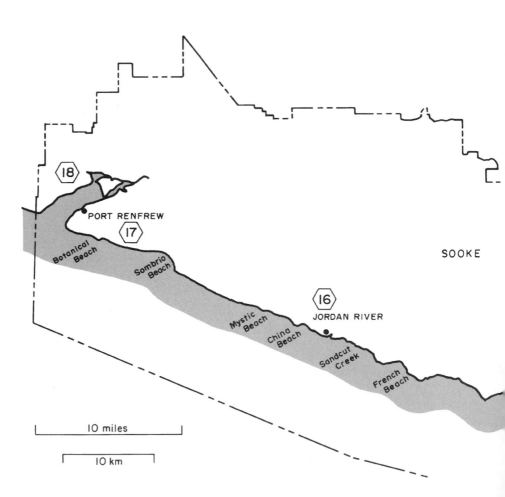

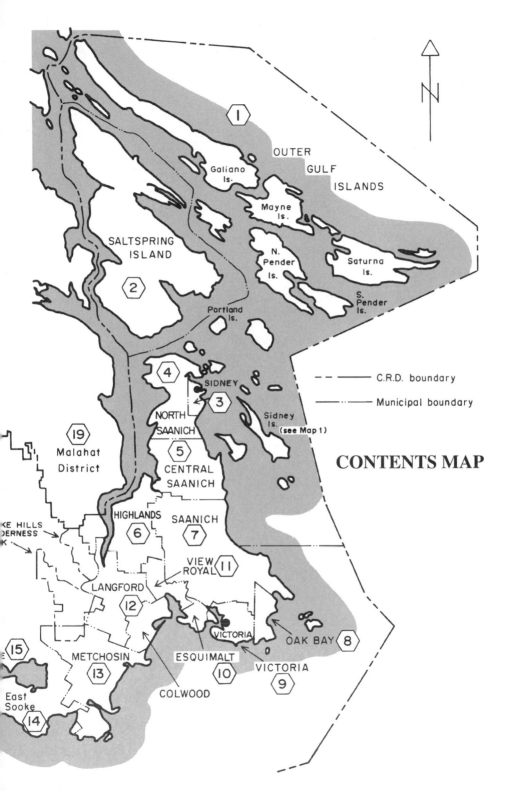

OUTER GULF ISLANDS

Galiano Is.

Mayne Is.

SALTSPRING ISLAND

N. Pender Is.

Saturna Is.

S. Pender Is.

Portland Is.

SIDNEY

NORTH SAANICH

Sidney Is. (see Map 1)

- - - C.R.D. boundary

- · - Municipal boundary

CONTENTS MAP

Malahat District

CENTRAL SAANICH

HIGHLANDS

SAANICH

KE HILLS
DERNESS

VIEW ROYAL

LANGFORD

VICTORIA

OAK BAY

METCHOSIN

ESQUIMALT

VICTORIA

East Sooke

COLWOOD

N

5

Legend

—⑰—	highway
———	other roads
—— ——	gravel or dirt road
– – – – –	trail
··············	rugged trail
• • • • • •	horse trail
—+— —+—	abandoned railway right-of-way
——— – –	CRD boundary
—— – ——	park boundary
——·· ——	municipal boundary
——· ——	DND property, Greater Victoria Water District
——··· ——	other boundary (cemetery, golf course)
P ▪	parking
Ⓟ	limited parking
✻	beach access
Ⓥ	view
㉘	km posts on Galloping Goose Trail
– –C– –	cycling permitted
—— ○ ——	power line

Inset diagrams show how the maps interrelate. See page 70.

Note that maps are not all at the same scale.

Picnic tables and toilet facilities are not shown on maps. These are termed "park facilities" and will usually be found near the main parking area.

EDITOR'S NOTES

What is new:
So just what *is* new, you ask, in our Twelfth Edition? The answer: plenty. We completed our last revision of this volume in the winter of 1993, for distribution in the spring of 1994. That particular year had great significance for Victorians, as we hosted the 1994 Commonwealth Games from August 18 to 28. That year also marked an unprecedented increase in the number of parks in British Columbia, including the Commonwealth Nature Legacy Parks in the Capital Regional District: Glencoe Cove, Haro Woods, Panama Hill, Gowlland Tod, Mount Finlayson (added to Goldstream) and Juan de Fuca with its Marine Trail. We've included all of the above, and also added a smattering of new trails and hikes such as Rithet's Bog, Boulderwood Knoll, Quarry Park and Butterworth Park. We have also included much new material in the Port Renfrew/San Juan Valley area. Because some of these new areas take you into fairly rugged country (and because we keep encountering people who are shockingly ill-prepared) we have also expanded our Hints and Cautions section.

What is comfortably the same:
As is apparent from the Table of Contents and the Contents Map, all of the destinations described in this book, except for Spectacle Lake Provincial Park, are within the Capital Regional District (CRD). We have clustered the hike descriptions within each municipality or area, and ordered the areas from north to south, and then to the west. Our hikes are suitable for a variety of abilities and interests, ranging all the way from short neighbourhood outings for parents pushing strollers, right up to week-long backpacking trips in remote areas.

A note about our past:
The **Vancouver Island Trails Information Society** is a non-profit society dedicated to providing accurate information to the public about trails and parks on Vancouver Island. Originally, VITIS was formed as the Outdoor Club of Victoria Trails Information Society. O.C.V. members, especially Dr. Jim Fiddess and Ted Fairhurst, had long dreamed of producing a book about the trails known and used by the club. Their dreams were realized in 1971 with the formation of a hard-working

committee. The new editor was to be Jane Waddell, ably assisted by Bill Burroughs, John Harris, Dave Birch and Jane Toms among others. The group incorporated as a non-profit society and produced its first book in December of 1972, so this year we are proud to be celebrating our 25th anniversary. That very first volume, *Hiking Trails: Victoria and Southern Vancouver Island*, contained only 32 pages and 18 destinations, and had an initial print run of only 2000 copies. Hand-drawn maps and delightful sketches by Laurie Rossiter illustrated the text. Several of the original supporters of the project had promised to underwrite the printing costs, should the project fail, but by the time the invoice for printing was received from Morriss Printing, the book had hit Eaton's best-seller list and the printing costs were already recouped. By 1975 it had been reprinted five times and already revised, expanded and retitled; separate volumes on central and northern Vancouver Island had also been produced. In 1993, in an effort to better describe the scope of our work, and to eliminate long-standing confusion, the name of the Society was changed to the Vancouver Island Trails Information Society. Any profits made from the sale of our books are donated to like-minded worthy projects.

What the future holds:
As I look forward to the new millennium, I see two major factors affecting parks and trails in our Capital Region. The first factor is population growth, so we have included the population figures for each area, by way of reminding our readers of the pressures we place on our natural environment by our just being here. The land area included in the CRD is 2,427 square kilometres (937 square miles). The population has already risen from 182,189 in 1966 to 326,010 in 1996. All of Vancouver Island, including our southernmost portion, is a beautiful, and therefore popular, place to live. How we deal with the inevitable population growth will depend on what value we place on the very elements that create that beauty.

A second factor is the emergence of the linear concept in parks planning by all levels of government. The factor has always been there, especially as a vision of the Regional Trails committee, who have been meeting regularly since the 1970s. It has also been present in more rural communities such as North Saanich and Metchosin, where equestrians have sought longer, loop rides. Now it is embodied in the trail systems and the greenspace corridors described at the end of the book. We moved toward the linking concept in our eleventh edition and continue it in this, our twelfth.

Expanding your horizons:

As you visit the various destinations described in this volume, you may find your explorations enriched by one of the following: a current street map, one of the better bird guidebooks, and the Victoria Natural History Society's *The Naturalist's Guide to the Victoria Region* (which has a further extensive bibliography). Should you wish to explore further afield, we can recommend our own *Hiking Trails II*, which covers the Gulf Islands and the southeastern portion of Vancouver Island, from Koksilah River Park to Mount Arrowsmith (revised and expanded 1993 by Richard K. Blier). Our *Hiking Trails III* covers central and northern Vancouver Island including Strathcona Park (revised and expanded 1995 by James Rutter).

The Concise Oxford Dictionary defines a hike as "a long tramp in the country undertaken for pleasure or exercise". Be it long or short, in the country or in town, we encourage all users of this book to "take a hike!" Get out there and tramp about for pleasure and exercise. See you on the trail!

Susan Lawrence
Editor, twelfth edition
May, 1997

With special thanks to the Editorial Committee: Joyce Folbigg, John W. E. Harris, George Kelly, Jane Toms and Ron Weir and to the other Society members: Betty Burroughs, Irm Houle and Aldyth Hunter. John and Jane were both members of the original committee, and Betty continues in the place of her late husband, Bill.

HINTS AND CAUTIONS

Trails. While only some of the well-established, better-known trails are described here, they may lead to other opportunities which can be pursued by the more experienced and hardy. Most of the trails are footpaths; a few can be used by horses where permitted by park regulations. Stay on the **bridle trails** and off picnic areas and beaches. The CRD Parks that include bridle trails are: Bear Hill, Devonian, Elk/Beaver Lake (equestrian training facilities off Beaver Lake Road), Francis/King, Horth Hill, Thetis Lake (fire roads only), Witty's Lagoon and the Galloping Goose Regional Trail. Riders should avoid disturbing the full width of trails at muddy spots. When approaching other trail users, steady your mount and explain how you would like hikers and cyclists to proceed. Pass at a walk. Ensure the trail is clear before trotting or cantering. When riding on roadways, be aware that section 116(c) of the Motor Vehicle Act treats a horse as a vehicle: "A person riding an animal or driving an animal-driven vehicle on a highway has the rights and is subject to the duties of the driver of a vehicle...." **Motorized bikes** are prohibited off-road in all parks. In the limited park areas where cycling is permitted (chiefly the Galloping Goose Trail and the V & S Trail in Elk/Beaver Lake Park), **cyclists** are asked to observe not just the rules of the road, but also rules of courtesy: keep to the right and warn other trail users ("Passing on your left!") as you approach from the rear. In all circumstances, cyclists must yield to horse riders and hikers.

Dress for the activity. Experienced hikers dress in layers and choose their clothing carefully (natural fibres, yes; denim jeans, no). Wear or carry raingear for the upper and lower body. A large waterproof poncho with grommets can be your shelter in an emergency; waterproof pants or gaiters will keep your legs and feet dry when bushwhacking in the wet. Most of these trails can be hiked in good walking shoes or even runners; the Juan de Fuca Marine and West Coast Trails are the most obvious exceptions. You will always be safer and more comfortable, however, in well-fitted over-the-ankle boots. By the very nature of our west coast weather and topography, trails may sometimes be muddy or steep in places, and even on a dry day on a level, open trail, it's easy to turn an ankle on a stick or stone.

Carry the essentials. Take along a day's supply of drinking water, even on short outings, and drink often to avoid dehydration. More and more people are distrustful of water from creeks and lakes. Even in the "wild" the risk of water contamination is high. If you must use creek water, boil it or use water purification tablets. A parasitic infection of the intestines, giardiasis (known as "beaver fever"), is spread by animal and human waste and is increasing. A small packsack, or "day pack", is a good way to carry lunch (pack extra for emergencies), water, maps, compass, extra sweater for warmth, long-sleeved shirt (sun protection), sunhat or rainhat or toque, gloves, raingear, sunscreen and sunglasses (even in winter, for bright days in snow), toilet paper or paper tissues, insect repellent, whistle, flashlight (with spare batteries), waterproof matches (or full lighter), pocket knife, twine, and any essential first aid requirements. None of these articles, apart from the clothing items, are bulky or heavy, but each has its purpose in an emergency. Articles placed in an orange-colored plastic garbage bag inside your packsack will remain dry in the wettest weather. The plastic bag can be pressed into service as a sit-upon (stuffed with your extra sweater) or, in an emergency, as a shelter or a distress signal. Even for day-hikers, a compass and knowledge of how to use it is useful, since one can lose direction easily (especially in fog) and even on a trail it can be difficult to tell which way to turn. An altimeter is not necessary for any of these hikes, but it could be fun and useful on some of the climbs, such as Bruce Peak, especially in foggy weather. Topographic maps and aerial photographs can be useful companions if you decide to strike off from the trails shown. To prevent your book from becoming damaged on the trail, it is a good idea to carry with you only a photocopy of the area in which you are interested.

Make room for the extras. A camera and a pair of binoculars can enhance your enjoyment of an outing. When your destination includes the option of a swim, pack your swimsuit. Outdoors outfitters can also supply a special sponge-like towel that takes up practically no room in your backback but absorbs an incredible amount of water when you're drying off.

Check the weather forecast before setting out. The weather can change quickly and dramatically here on the west coast; be prepared for the unexpected. A combination of wet and wind can quickly lead to hypothermia, a potentially fatal condition. You do not want to get caught in a treed area if high winds blow up after you have set out. The Victoria Weather Office at Victoria International Airport was closed in March, 1997. From now on, the phone numbers for recorded forecasts will be listed in the blue pages of the telephone book. You can dial free to 656-3978 for a recorded forecast from Environment Canada, or go on-line at: http://www.ec.gc.ca, or: http://www.weatheroffice.com. To make detailed inquiries of a real person, the pay-per-call number is 1-900-565-4555; cost: $1.95 per minute with a two-minute minimum. Marine forecasts are available at 656-7515 or 656-2714. Weather radio is available on 162.4 megahertz.

Do not push the limits of daylight. Always leave a margin of time to allow for the unexpected. The flashlight in your backpack is meant for emergency use (or a bit of spelunking) but it could mean the difference between getting out safely after nightfall or having to spend the night in the bush.

Do not hike alone. The greatest danger is probably from slipping on loose rocks on moss- covered hillsides, or on logs. From August on, dry arbutus leaves on steep slopes are extremely slippery. The wise hiker travels with a friend in case of an accident. Keep together; do not split up. A whistle is useful for communication if accidentally separated. If you are lost, logging roads generally lead out if one follows them downhill. Conversely, following streams downhill, especially on our rugged west coast, can lead you to gullies, cliffs and waterfalls. Make for higher, more-open ground. Cross-country scrambling is difficult, so stay on trails unless absolutely certain where you are going. Leave information on your plans, including the expected time of return, with someone who is reliable. Remember that searches in our rough terrain are difficult and expensive. If you do become lost, stop hiking (you'll only get further away from where you are expected to be). Remain calm. Gauge the amount of daylight remaining and prepare to spend the night outdoors if necessary. Come daylight, move to open ground where air or ground searchers can spot you; signal your position by blowing your whistle; light a fire if it is safe to do so. The Provincial Emergency Program has a Trip Plan form prepared by Search and Rescue volunteers. You fill out half to take with you, and half to leave behind with a responsible person.

Be careful with fires, especially during dry weather. Fires are not permitted in many areas, or permits may be necessary from local fire departments. Above all, put out fires thoroughly! Clear an area free from flammable materials around your fire to a distance of at least one metre and do not establish a fire within at least three metres of any log, bush or tree. Pour water on the fire afterwards and sort through the ashes with your bare hands to be certain there are no hot spots left which could flame up again. Smoke only at rest stops, never when walking, and be sure that cigarettes and matches are completely extinguished. Carry out your butts. Report forest fires at once; do not assume that someone else has already done so. Phone the operator and ask for Zenith-5555, or dial direct to 1-800-663-5555.

Hunting season. Be aware of the danger of being mistaken for a wild animal during hunting season and wear bright clothing. Carry a whistle or horn to warn hunters of your presence. Avoid heavily hunted areas.

Mosquitoes and other pests. These can be a serious nuisance and you may need to carry a repellent. Wasps should be avoided; they nest in the ground and in bag-like nests in trees. Many people are allergic to the stings of insects and plants, so pack any necessary antidotes. There are no wild poisonous snakes on Vancouver Island.

Wild animals. Although our resident **black bears** are rarely encountered on southern Vancouver Island (we have 13,000 black bears on the Island, but no grizzly bears), the number of reported bear sightings did increase dramatically when the public first started using the western-most portion of the new Juan de Fuca Trail in the summer of 1995. Those who did not actually see a bear did report seeing bear "sign". A parks representative commented at the time that the trail was "paved blue" with bear scat after the bears feasted on ripe blue salal berries. Always use discretion in the woods of Vancouver Island, particularly in areas where food, such as berries, is available. Remember they are not the intruders, we are, and bears defend their personal space, their food, and their cubs. Even so, bears will generally do their best to avoid you if they hear you coming, so talking loudly and making other noises when hiking in suspicious areas is advised. Bears have an excellent sense of smell and of hearing, and, contrary to popular belief, very good eyesight. It is likely the bear sees you but you remain unaware of his presence. If you do see or hear bears, give them a wide berth and leave the area immediately; if you are actually approached, act large and make lots of noise. Move slowly away and avoid eye contact. A bear can run as fast as a horse, uphill or down, and black bears are good tree-climbers. When camping, store food away from camp, never in your tent. Don't sleep in the clothes you wore to cook food. It is best not to take children or dogs into bear country. Because BC is home to about 160,000 black bears, the Wildlife Branch of the BC Ministry of Environment, Lands and Parks has produced two pamphlets: *Safety Guide to Bears in the Wild* and *Safety Guide to Bears at Your Home.* In 1996, the Wildlife Branch issued a province-wide bear alert: by mid-July of that year, there had been one death and three maulings by bears in BC. In just one week in that July, the following bear sightings were reported within the CRD: a sow and her two cubs at Thetis Lake; two adult bears roaming between Willis Point and Prospect Lake; two adults on Wright Road, and three on Otter Point Road, in Sooke. This is black bear country.

Vancouver Island is also **cougar country**, though you can live your whole life here and never see one. (Though tourists did see one in the Empress Hotel parking lot some years ago.) Sightings are rare and confrontations are extremely rare. Even so, in the last century there have been two dozen attacks on humans by cougars on Vancouver Island, with four fatalities. Generally, these attacks have been on children. Cougars are big animals, with males weighing 60-90 kg and females, 40-50 kg. They are fast and strong and they are predators. Their prey is primarily deer, but includes other animals, large and small. Children are probably the most common human target because their size, sounds and movements resemble those of other prey animals. Cougars are most active at dawn and dusk, but will roam and hunt during any time of the day or night. They may be encountered at any time of the year, but the likelihood of contact increases in late spring and summer when yearlings leave their mother to establish their own territory. Avoidance is the best defence. Hike in groups and make your presence known. Keep children in the centre of your group, never running ahead or trailing behind. If you come across cougar prints, scat, or a buried food cache, leave the area immediately. If you actually encounter a cougar, **do not run.** Stay put and stay calm. Allow the cougar an escape route. Gather up and protect children. Face the animal, maintain eye contact, and make yourself look and sound large. Stand tall, wave branches; do not crouch or turn your back. If the cougar acts agressive, stand your ground and make yourself look and sound strong, more like a threat than a meal. If you are attacked, fight back with any means at your disposal. A cougar sighting is a rare and treasured event, one to be reported to friends and family; a cougar confrontation is a serious event, one to be reported to a Conservation Officer. The BC Ministry of Environment, Lands and Parks has produced a pamphlet, *Safety Guide to Cougars.*

Traversing private property. Ask permission. Close gates if found closed; leave them open if found open. If you are unsure if land is private or public, avoid trespass. When travelling the Galloping Goose Regional Trail, keep in mind that it is just a narrow corridor; adjacent land is privately owned. Respect logging company signs; in this area most of their holdings are owned by them, not leased public lands. Do not damage equipment and report those you see doing so.

Do not litter the trails. Don't drop gum wrappers, orange peel, lunch bags or soft drink cans. Carry them out in your packsack. Use sanitation facilities where they exist; elsewhere be considerate of your fellow hiker. Take nothing and leave nothing.

Do not chop "blazes" into trees. They are unsightly and lead to infection by a variety of insects and diseases. If for some reason you wish to mark a trail with plastic tape, keep use of it to a minimum as it deteriorates slowly. A more temporary marker is toilet paper, easily seen and useful in any packsack.

Flowers and plants. Particularly in parks, but in other places too, leave wild flowers where you find them. Unlike garden varieties, they seldom last long when picked, and uprooted specimens rarely can be transplanted to city gardens. Poison oak is rare. While there are many edible plants, there are some poisonous ones. Eat wild berries and mushrooms only if you are certain they are edible. The stinging nettle and devil's club may be encountered on southern Vancouver Island but contact with these is only irritating.

Ecological reserves are fragile areas of Crown land administered by BC Parks (assisted by volunteer wardens) under the BC Ecological Reserves Program. They are not parks. They are set aside for scientific research, outdoor classroom use, and to preserve rare, endangered, or representative native plants, animals, ecosystems, or geological formations. Although most ecological reserves are open to the public for passive enjoyment, active hiking is discouraged. (A few sites, principally seabird nesting colonies, are so sensitive that human intrusion is banned.) Over time, the Vancouver Island Trails Information Society has eliminated from its volumes some of the earlier hike descriptions that are now in or near ecological reserves. BC Parks has a brochure giving the name, location, and special features of BC's 135 ecological reserves, totalling nearly 160,000 ha of land and marine waters.

Hikers in Capital Regional District Parks should be prepared to observe a number of specific rules, subject to additional rules posted in the parks. Watch for and observe these signs. Many of these rules apply in provincial parks, and most should be observed everywhere as a matter of good sense, courtesy, and conservation. The rules basically are designed to allow users and surrounding landowners quiet, peaceful enjoyment.

Most parks are open from sunrise to sunset. Some parks permit "special uses" for which "park use permits" are required. These allow group activities which can be planned and organized ahead of time with the confidence that space will be available. Commercial activities and advertisements are not allowed except by permit. No natural or park features or structures may be removed, damaged or polluted.
Model airplanes and alcohol are not permitted. Keep dogs off beaches and picnic areas between June 1 and September 15. Dogs are not allowed where signs indicate they are prohibited. Elsewhere, dogs must be on a leash or under control. Dog handlers are required to pick up dog droppings and need to carry their own plastic bags for this purpose. People and their animals are encouraged to stay on park trails, as off-trail use damages sensitive ecosystems. Firearms (except under special permit such as for retriever trials using blank ammunition), bows and crossbows are prohibited. No hunting is permitted in Capital Regional District Parks. Do not camp or sleep overnight in CRD parks.

Particularly observe signs for boating and swimming; no swimming in posted boating areas and vice versa. Boaters should be aware of and follow the Canada Shipping Act and Regulations. Boating is permitted on the following lakes: no power boats on Prior Lake; electric motors only on Matheson, Durrance, and Thetis Lakes; 10 horsepower maximum on Elk and Beaver Lakes (over 10 horsepower in yellow buoyed area only of Elk Lake).

Motor vehicles may only be parked in designated areas and may only travel on roadways. Vehicles left unattended over 48 hours, and vehicles parked in No Parking and Tow Away zones are subject to being towed away.

Visitors to Provincial Parks should be aware of two sections of BC Provincial Park Regulations:

18. No person shall have a horse or other draught or riding animal in a park or recreation area except
    (a) in an area or on a trail as permitted by a sign or other device, or
    (b) as authorized by a park officer.
25. No person shall ride a cycle in a park or recreation area except
    (a) on a park road
    (b) in an area or on a trail as permitted by a sign or other device, or
    (c) as authorized by a park officer.

BC Parks has a **campground reservation service** available from March 1, covering March 15 to Sept.15. Phone 1-800-689-9025 from 7 am to 7 pm weekdays, 9 am to 5 pm weekends. The non-refundable reservation fee is $6 per night (maximum fee $18), plus GST, payable by Visa or MasterCard at the time of booking. The Vancouver Island campgrounds included, as of 1997, are: Bamberton, Beaumont, Englishman River Falls, French Beach, Goldstream, Gordon Bay, Montague Harbour, Miracle Beach, Prior Centennial, and Rathtrevor Provincial Parks, plus Pacific Rim National Park (Green Point campground). Maximum stay is 14 nights (Pacific Rim, only 7); bookings accepted from 2 days to 3 months in advance. Camping fees: $9.50 to $20 per night, payable by Visa or MasterCard when booking. There are limits on the number of people and vehicles per campsite.

One final word of caution: leave your valuables at home or pack them with you. Lock the doors and trunk of your vehicle.

Conditions of the parks and trails that we describe in this book will constantly be changing, so we add a caution and a request: **we cannot be held responsible for errors or discrepancies in the text or maps**; and, we ask that you help us to keep our books current and useful. You may write to us in care of our distributor, Orca Book Publishers (address on title page), or e-mail us at **ahunter@vanisle.net.** All of our books are revised regularly. In the meantime we encourage you to keep yourself updated on current conditions in these regional, provincial and municipal parks by contacting CRD Parks or BC Parks (see page 222), or the local jurisdiction (see relevant pages of this text).

⟨1⟩ THE OUTER GULF ISLANDS AREA (see CONTENTS MAP)
   est. 1995 pop.: 4,280

In 1791, Lieutenant Eliza of the Spanish navy named the waters between the mainland and what is now Vancouver Island "Gran Canal de Nuestra Senora del Rosario la Marinera". A year later, on June 4 (King George III's birthday), Captain George Vancouver renamed this "inlet" the Gulf of Georgia in honour of "His Britannic Majesty". Captain Richards amended the name to Strait of Georgia in 1858, but the misnomer, Gulf, lingers as applied to the string of islands within the strait. As you continue to read this volume, notice how strongly the influences of earlier Spanish and British visitors are reflected in our local place names.

Wallace Island Provincial Marine Park; **Mount Norman** (South Pender Island); **Mount Parke** (Mayne Island); **Bluffs Park, Bodega Ridge** and **Dionisio Point Provincial Park** (all Galiano Island), are described in another book in our series: ***Hiking Trails II: Southeastern Vancouver Island***. The seventh edition, revised and expanded by Richard K. Blier, was published in 1993. The Outer Gulf Islands are serviced by passenger/vehicle ferries operated by the British Columbia Ferry Corporation (BC Ferries). In the Victoria area, phone (250) 386-3431 for information on schedules and fares; or call toll-free from within BC: 1-888-BCFERRY (223-3779). Sailings depart year-round from the Swartz Bay ferry terminal, shown on Maps 6 and 9. Telephone listings for the Outer Gulf Islands of North and South Pender, Galiano, Mayne, and Saturna are found at the end of the white pages of the BC Tel Victoria Area telephone directory. (Long distance charges apply.) Charles Kahn's *Hiking the Gulf Islands* (Orca Book Publishers, 1995) and Bruce Obee's *The Gulf Islands Explorer-The Outdoor Guide* (Whitecap Books, 1990) both offer additional information (climate, accommodations, government, other recreation, etc.) and further bibliographies.

SIDNEY SPIT PROVINCIAL MARINE PARK (MAP 1)

See our Contents Map, page 5, for the location of Sidney Spit at the northern tip of Sidney Island, about 5 km off-shore from the Town of Sidney. Access is by boat or kayak, or as a foot-passenger on the "little ferry" service provided, under a 5-year contract to BC Parks, by Able II Charters Inc, from the foot of Beacon Avenue, Sidney (see Map 5). In 1997, service is available daily May 15 to September 7; weekdays, hourly 9 am - 5 pm; weekends, hourly 10 am - 7 pm. From September 8 to October 15, 1997, service is available every day at 10 am, 12 noon, 2 pm and 4 pm. Cost in 1997: adult $7, senior $6, children 12 and under $5. Reservations are accepted for groups of 10 or more. Call Able II Charters at 727-7700 for further information. On your trip over to the island watch for marine mammals, Rhinoceros Auklets and Heerman's Gulls.

The 400-ha park is open year-round (fees collected from May 1 to October 15) and has full marine park facilities. Moorage, 1997: $6.00 per boat per night at the buoys, $1.50/metre/night at the dock. Fees, 1997, for group camping at the covered group picnic shelter: $50/night. For reservations phone RLC Enterprise Ltd (under contract with BC Parks), 474-1336. Camping is permitted only in the large field near the private wharf: $9.50/party (on a first-come basis). No camping is permitted on the spit or the hook spit (claw).

MAP 1: SIDNEY SPIT PROVINCIAL MARINE PARK

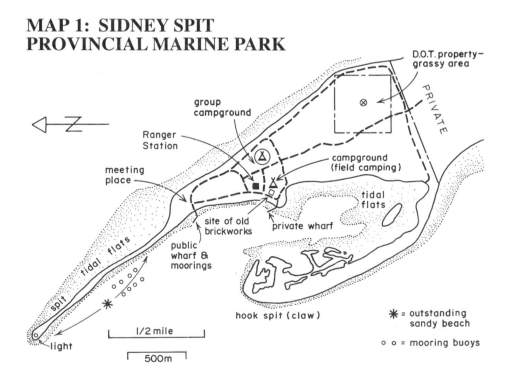

At low tide one can hike for miles along the spit or claw, with year-round opportunities for the enjoyment of hikers, naturalists and birdwatchers. Fallow deer are a common sight in the open grassy fields within the park. Originally imported to nearby James Island from England at the turn of the century, they swam here in the 1960s. The bricks for the Empress Hotel in Victoria were produced at the site of the old brick-works, where the Sidney Island Brick and Tile Company was in operation from 1906 to 1915. The portion of the island south of the lagoon is privately owned. Sidney Island was earlier named Sallas Island, but Captain Richards of the survey ship *Plumper* renamed it in 1859 after Frederick W. Sidney, a fellow naval surveyor.

The forest is very dry in summer and fire poses a great hazard. No fires are permitted in the park, so bring your own campstove if you are camping. Be prepared to "pack in and pack out", as there are no garbage facilities in the park. Potable (but salty) water is available; you may want to bring your own fresh water.

A BC Parks brochure (see page 222), details the human and natural history of the island and provides current information on camping, moorage, and schedules/fares for the "little ferry". The ferry trip and the undeveloped nature of the park itself make it unsuitable for wheelchair access.

PRINCESS MARGARET PROVINCIAL MARINE PARK (PORTLAND ISLAND) (MAP 2)

The whole of Portland Island is Princess Margaret Provincial Marine Park (194 ha). Ferry service to the island is available from the foot of Beacon Avenue, Sidney (see Map 5), landing at Princess Bay. Provided by Able II Charters Inc, 727-7700, scheduled service is from June 15 to September 15: Friday 5 pm; Saturday and Sunday 10 am and 2 pm. Reservations accepted for groups of 10 or more. Cost: adult $12, senior $8, children 12 and under $8.

There are park facilities at Princess Bay and at Royal Cove, both good seasonal anchorage for boats. Otherwise, the island is largely undeveloped. The broad trails have existed for many years, and the Youth Crew Program has constructed other trails for BC Parks. Best swimming is at the shell beach and at Princess Bay. Camping is permitted in designated areas only. No fires are permitted in the park. The smaller islands around the marine park are privately owned, with the exception of Brackman Island, which is Ecological Reserve 121, valued for its ungrazed Gulf Island vegetation. BC Parks (see page 222) distributes a brochure on Princess Margaret Park.

Portland Island was presented to Princess Margaret in 1958 and she graciously returned it in 1967 "for the benefit of the people of the province". The island was officially named in 1858 after HMS *Portland,*the flagship of Rear Admiral Fairfax Moresby, commander in chief of the Pacific Station from 1850 to 1853. Records show that in 1875 a John Palau from the Sandwich Islands (now Hawaii) pre-empted land here. This may account for the names Kanaka Bluff and Pellow Islets, as his name was spelled in a variety of ways. Kanakas (Hawaiians) were numerous among the early HBC workers all along our coast, with one being the ancestor of a colorful character nicknamed "King Freezy" on account of his frizzy hair. A local leader whose real name was Chee-al-thluk, he had the distinction of being painted by Paul Kane, who labeled the portrait "Cheaclach, Head Chief of the Clal-lums at Esquimalt". As Chee-al-thluk, he had the distinctive flattened head that was an admired characteristic among his group, and as many as fifteen wives at one time,

Chads
Island
(private)

Royal Cove

Arbutus
Point

Turnbull
+
+ Reef

PORTLAND

ISLAND

Kanaka
Bluff

Pellow
Islets

orchard

orchard

G. B. Church –
Artificial Reef

Shell Beach

Princess Bay

private

Tortoise
Islets

Brackman
Island
(Ecological Reserve 121
– No public access)

Hood
Island
(private)

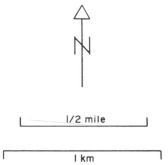

N

1/2 mile

1 km

LEGEND

⚓ primary anchorage

⚓ temporary anchorage

T small pier

Ⓦ water

△ campsite

□ information board

Ⓣ toilets

+ rocks

rocks

✳ navigation light

✕ Park Host Float

MAP 2: PRINCESS
MARGARET PROVINCIAL
MARINE PARK
(PORTLAND ISLAND)

though he later gradually reduced their numbers through decapitation. As "King Freezy", he drowned in a canoe accident while under the influence of alcohol. The history of early Hawaiian settlement is chronicled in Tom Koppel's book *Kanaka: The Untold Story of Hawaiian Pioneers in British Columbia and the Pacific Northwest.*

In the late 1920s "One-armed Sutton", a colourful character who had served at Gallipoli, China, South America and Mexico, won a Derby Sweep Stake and bought the island, with ambitious plans. He built a stable for racing horses, planted an orchard of apple and plum trees near Princess Bay and had pens built for Chinese pheasants. The 1929 Wall Street crash wrecked his plans and though he tried to recoup his fortunes by returning to Manchuria, he forfeited Portland Island and, after many vicissitudes, died destitute in a Japanese prison camp in Hong Kong in 1944. His colorful story is told in *General of Fortune,* a biography by Charles Drage.

② SALTSPRING ISLAND (CONTENTS MAP and MAP 3)
   est. 1995 pop.: 9,270

Saltspring or Salt Spring (the preferred local name) gets its current name from the salt springs located on private land at the north end of the island. Earlier, in a Salish dialect, it was called Tuam, which may mean "facing the sea", or "one on each end" (referring to the Bruce and Tuam peaks). In 1854, James Douglas referred to it as Chuan, Captain Grant, in 1856, as Saltspring. Captain Richards named it Admiral Island in 1859, after Rear Admiral Baynes (see page 33, Mount Maxwell), but local usage prevailed and the name Saltspring was officially adopted in 1910. Captain Richards also named Ganges Harbour after the Admiral's flagship, HMS *Ganges*, and Fulford Harbour after its captain, Admiral John Fulford. Ganges was Admiralty Bay until renamed by Captain Richards in 1859. Burgoyne Bay was named by Richards after Captain Hugh Talbot Burgoyne, also of the *Ganges*; Southey Point, after James Lowther Southey, RN, secretary to the Admiral; Mount Bruce after Admiral Henry William Bruce, commander in chief of the Pacific Station at Esquimalt 1854-1857; and Cape Keppel after Rear Admiral the Hon. Sir Henry

Keppel, KCB, a friend and associate of Admiral Baynes. Captain Richards (1820-1900) ended his distinquished naval career as Admiral Sir George Henry Richards, KCB, FRS. He served in all quarters of the globe, including the Arctic (in search of Sir John Franklin.) A measure of his Victorian modesty is revealed in the few local geographic features that bear his name: Richards Channel (named by Captain Walbran in 1903), and Mount Richards, near Duncan (named by Captain Parry of HMS *Egeria* in 1905). Captain John T. Walbran's *British Columbia Coast Names, 1592-1906, Their Origin and History*, from which much of this information is gleaned, is much more than a recitation of etymologies; it captures the life and times of earlier explorers along our coast.

Three Saltspring destinations, **Bruce Peak**, **Mount Maxwell Provincial Park** and **Mount Erskine,** are described in *Hiking Trails II* (see page 19). Because the principal ferry access to Saltspring Island is from the Swartz Bay terminal of BC Ferries, these three hikes are now also included in *Hiking Trails I*, along with **Beaver Point Provincial Park, Ruckle Provincial Park** and a new Saltspring Island CRD park, **Mill Farm**. We've also included several walks in CRD Community Parks.

See Section ⟨1⟩, page 19, for information on BC Ferries routes from Swartz Bay (in North Saanich) to Fulford Harbour (Saltspring Island) and from Crofton (on Vancouver Island, near Duncan) to Vesuvius Bay (Saltspring Island). For information on accommodations, studio tours and cycle routes, the Saltspring Island Information Centre, at 121 Lower Ganges Road, can be reached at 250-537-5252 (e-mail to chamber@saltspring.com; Web site is http://www.vacations.bc.ca/chamber). Telephone listings for Saltspring Island are at the end of the white pages in the BC Tel Victoria Area telephone directory. (Long distance charges apply.) Walk-in campsites are available at **Ruckle Provincial Park**. Fifteen drive-in and eleven walk-in campsites (tents only) are available at **Mouat Provincial Park**, at the end of Seaview Road, a five-minute walk south of Ganges (on the hill). Mouat Park (22 ha) also has walking trails and a picnic area. **Centennial Park** in "downtown" Ganges has a playground and picnic area; it's a waterfront park, but there is no actual beach access, so you must be content to enjoy the views of the harbour.

For further information on hikes on Saltspring Island, please contact:

Salt Spring Island Parks, Arts and Recreation Commission
145 Vesuvius Bay Road (Portlock Park)
Salt Spring Island, BC V8K 1K3
phone: 250-537-4448; fax: 250-537-4456

The Commission offices are located at **Portlock Park**, Saltsprings's largest recreation park (4 ha), with outdoor swimming pool, tennis courts, soccer fields, baseball and 400-m track. The park was donated to the community by the Salt Spring Lions Club in 1974.

REGINALD HILL (MAP 3)

As you arrive on Saltspring Island via BC Ferries' Swartz Bay - Fulford Harbour route, take the first right turn past the ferry slip, and take Morningside Drive for 1 km to its dead end. Park here, not within the private residential development. Do some diligent leg-stretches in this ample parking area, then walk about 100 m past the subdivision entrance gate to the first driveway on the left. Follow the trail markers as they lead you up a steep forested ascent to the summit. At 241 m, this is only a "Hill" on an island of many "Mounts", but your efforts are well rewarded, with a fine view of Fulford Harbour. There's a small loop at the summit, then you return the way you came. Note that while the trail itself is on public parkland, the surrounding properties are privately owned. No trespassing, please. Time: about 50 minutes up; 40 down. Length: 3 km return.

Notes:
- The following five hikes require that you travel **Musgrave Road** to the trailheads. Musgrave Road is a rough, twisting, dirt/gravel road that climbs sharply above Fulford Harbour to about 600 m elevation and then descends just as precipitously to Musgrave Landing at sea level. Chose your season to visit, your vehicle, and your driver accordingly.
- If your group includes people with varying interests and abilities, **Drummond Children's Park** might make a good alternative destination for some while others follow more energetic pursuits. It's just

a five-minute drive from the Fulford ferry terminal. From the Fulford-Ganges Road, turn south on Isabella Point Road; the park is just 600 m along. There's a children's playground and a picnic area right beside the sandy low-bank beach. The park is wheelchair accessible.

HOPE HILL TRAILS (MAP 3)

From Fulford Harbour on the Fulford-Ganges Road drive 1.3 km to Isabella Point Road. Turn left for 0.5 km and then right onto Musgrave Road. Travel a further 3.4 km to the trailhead. It's on your left, 0.5 km past the hairpin bend. You start off on an old logging road, then climb, sometimes steeply, to above 500 m in elevation. Red metal markers, cairns and ribbons mark the many loop trails. Keep to these marked circular routes, as any spurs head out into private property. The trails shown on Map 3 are all on Crown Land, but Hope Hill itself, at just under 650 m, is private. Please avoid trespass.

BRUCE PEAK (MAP 3)

Access as above, but follow Musgrave Road for 6.3 km past the Isabella Point Road junction. Take the right fork here for Bruce Peak and continue 0.3 km to limited parking at a road junction. (If you thought Musgrave Road was rough, this road is rougher.) Continue on foot up the rough jeep road to the summit and installations, where the views at 711 m are magnificent. For an equally pleasant hike, take the old road to your left leading southwest. After walking about 10 minutres, turn right at the intersection ①. Soon you will come to a fork. Go right onto a major trail with good viewpoints westward. Whenever there is a choice, take the left fork until you can see the lesser peak, "Brucey" and its transmitter tower on your right. The open area ② has an especially fine viewpoint. An old road, scoured by motorcyclists, continues north from here but you should take the minor trail close by. Hike east up to the transmitter site and continue on to the main lookout. Our map shows other roads, mostly overgrown. You could extend your hike considerably by taking the left fork after ① with excellent views. A rough sheep track heads back up to "Brucey". (See notes p. 30.)

MAP 3: SALTSPRING ISLAND

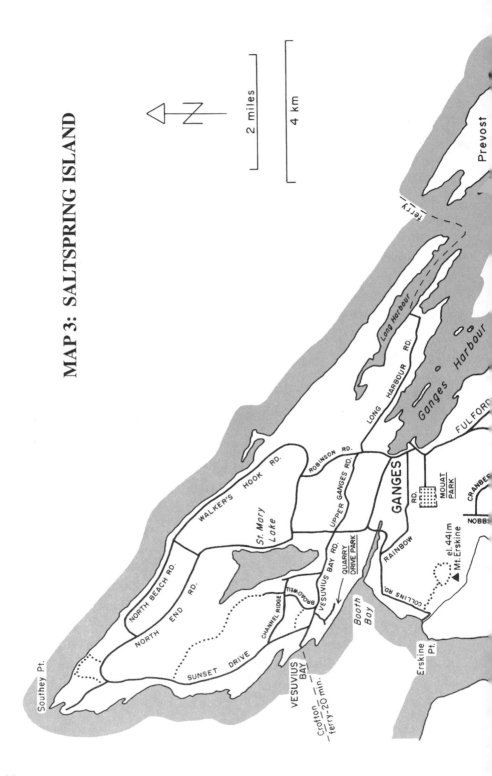

N

2 miles

4 km

Southey Pt.

NORTH BEACH RD.

NORTH END RD.

WALKER'S HOOK RD.

St. Mary Lake

ROBINSON RD.

UPPER GANGES RD.

BROADWELL

CHANNEL RIDGE

SUNSET DRIVE

VESUVIUS BAY RD.

QUARRY DRIVE PARK

VESUVIUS BAY

Crofton ferry–20 min.

Booth Bay

GANGES

RAINBOW

COLLINS RD.

el. 441m Mt. Erskine

Erskine Pt.

MOUAT PARK

RD.

CRANBE

NOBB

LONG HARBOUR RD.

Long Harbour

ferry

Ganges Harbour

FULFORD

Prevost

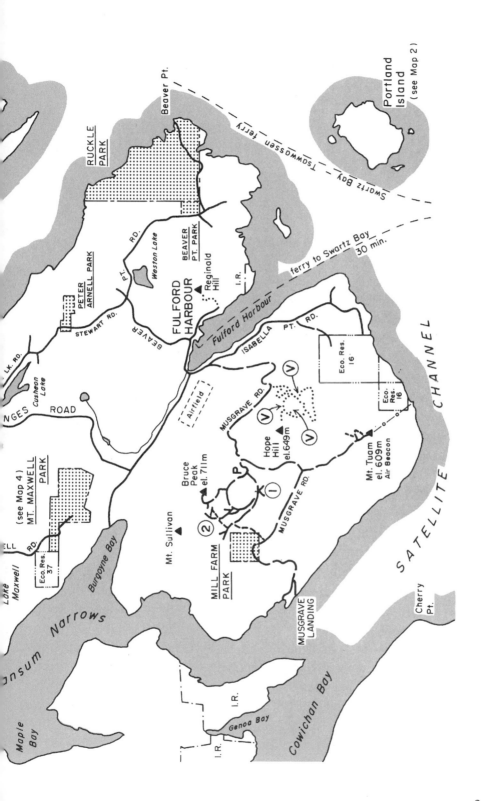

RUCKLE PARK

Beaver Pt.

Tsawwassen ferry

Swartz Bay

Portland Island (see Map 2)

PETER ARNELL PARK

RD.

Weston Lake

BEAVER PT. PARK

FULFORD HARBOUR

Reginald Hill

I.R.

ferry to Swartz Bay 30 min.

STEWART RD.

BEAVER PT. RD.

Fulford Harbour

ISABELLA PT. RD.

LK. RD.

Cusheon Lake

GES ROAD

Eco. Res. 16

MUSGRAVE RD.

Airfield

V

V

V

Hope Hill el.649m

Mt. Tuam el. 609m Air Beacon

Eco. Res. 16

(see Map 4) MT. MAXWELL PARK

Bruce Peak el.711m

P

1

MUSGRAVE RD.

SATELLITE CHANNEL

ELL RD.

Lake Maxwell

Eco. Res. 37

Burgoyne Bay

Mt. Sullivan

2

MILL FARM PARK

MUSGRAVE LANDING

Cherry Pt.

nsum Narrows

Maple Bay

I.R.

I.R.

Genoa Bay

Cowichan Bay

29

Notes:
- Responsible agent - BC Forest Service, Duncan
- Do not take your dog. There are many sheep and goats on Saltspring Island and the other Gulf Islands.
- Do not light fires. Fire is a very serious hazard on all the Gulf Islands.
- Hunters frequent some areas in the fall. Wear bright colours so you can be easily identified.

MOUNT TUAM (MAP 3)

Access as above but continue left at the Bruce Peak fork for a further 1.8 km. The road to Mount Tuam is gated at Musgrave Road and again about 2 km in, not far from the open summit. The walk in is along a dirt road (so, muddy or dusty, according to season) but the easy grade makes for ready access to sweeping views as far as Cowichan Bay, the Saanich Peninsula and the Outer Gulf Islands, with Satellite Channel glistening below. Keep to the summit (after all, you're here for the view) where the Department of National Defence owns about 15 ha. Do not descend the slopes in any direction, as you will soon be trespassing on private property. In previous editions of our Hiking Trails II we included a southeast access to Mount Tuam via Isabella Point and Mountain Roads, but we have ceased to do so because access was through Mount Tuam Ecological Reserve #16 (actually two separate parcels), valued for its arbutus/Douglas-fir forest. (See page 15.)

MILL FARM REGIONAL PARK (MAP 3)

Access as above but continue along Musgrave Road past the Mount Tuam turnoff. The park reserve boundaries are posted along the road. Although this 65-ha site was purchased in a court-ordered sale in November, 1996, with combined funds from the CRD, the Saltspring Island Conservancy and the province, it is classified as park reserve and it will be some time before the park is open for visitors. It is the site of a former commune, so the current residents are permitted to stay on as tenants until the end of 1999. The farm is just one part of a much larger federal/provincial proposal to protect 2800 ha in the Mount Tuam - Mount Bruce - Satellite Channel area under the Pacific Marine Heritage Legacy (PMHL). Mill

Farm has one of the large stands (26 ha) of old growth Douglas-fir valued by the PMHL group, which has also identified 30 threatened and vulnerable wildflower species; three endangered plant species (phantom orchid, yellow montane violet, and scalepod); two endangered butterfly species (Propertius Dusky Wings, Zerene's Fritillary); the largest Garry oak tree in BC; expanses of intact Garry oak meadow habitat; large stretches of continuous second-growth forest; eagle nests; and 10 km of pebble beaches, stretching from Musgrave Point to Cape Keppel (below Mt. Tuam). Protection could take the form of park status (the area includes 243 ha of Ecological Reserve, 728 ha of Crown Reserve, 931 ha of private Forest Reserve) or conservation covenants on private lands (eligible for income tax credits). The PMHL Fund has earmarked $60 million in federal and provincial funds for acquisition of land in this coastal region. Boundaries of a new national park are expected in about five years.

MUSGRAVE GREENBELT (MAP 3)

Access as for Bruce Peak and Mount Tuam, but continue about 7 km past the Bruce Peak fork. When you are close to the bottom of the hill, keep left to the 35-ha park. The greenbelt area, a former farm, was purchased in 1974 as a day-use recreation park. Following one of the old farm roads takes you to a lovely waterfall, best viewed in the rainy season; another overgrown road takes you down to a beach and a large rock, dubbed "Musgrave Island". For the Musgrave Greenbelt, getting there is all the work; once there, you'll find the trails are easy, pleasant rambles.

BEAVER POINT PROVINCIAL PARK,
RUCKLE PROVINCIAL PARK (MAP 3)

After arriving at Fulford Harbour via BC Ferries, watch for Beaver Point Road and the directional signs at the top of the hill. After about 6 km you'll find the Beaver Point Community Hall (the old one-room Beaver Point School, built 1885), and the entrance to 16-ha Beaver Point Provincial Park, through which you can hike into adjoining 486-ha Ruckle Provincial Park, which was transferred from the Ruckle family to the province in 1974. Present-day members of the family continue to farm the lands that Henry Ruckle began clearing in 1872. Beaver Point, named after the Hudson's Bay Company's ship *Beaver*, which once ran aground there, was the earlier site of the main wharf, built and maintained originally by Henry Ruckle. Later the ferry terminal was moved to Fulford Harbour.

BC Parks has erected numerous interpretive signs giving the historical background of the park. Don't miss the old farmstead near the park entrance. It doesn't take much imagination to flesh out the scene with the sounds of poultry and livestock (and maybe the rustle of a taffeta petticoat nearer the house). For natural history buffs, the land features range from cultivated fields and hedgerows to thick forest and wild ocean shoreline, producing a great diversity of wildlife. One unwelcome visitor is carpet burweed, a sharp-spined visitor from South America that is currently being given its eviction notice. Beaver Point is popular for SCUBA shore dives. Day-use park facilities include picnic tables, with the choicest locations toward the point, where every picnic site seems to have its own private cove. The point itself reveals a spectacular near-360-degree marine panorama. Walk-in field camping and a park Meeting Place welcome overnighters. Fires, when permitted, are in fire rings only, never on the beaches. Use only the firewood provided. A BC Parks brochure, which includes a detailed history of the Ruckle family, is available. The Victorienteers (see page 221) have produced a colour map of Ruckle Park; price: $5.00 to non-members. Only the less-rugged areas of the park are wheelchair accessible.

PETER ARNELL PARK (MAP 3)

Access as above, but at the junction of Beaver Point Road and Stewart Road, turn left and watch for the park sign about 2 km along, near the top of a rise. (If you come to the sharp bend, you've missed it.) To the left side of the road, the park has a picnic area and a monument to Peter Arnell, a young surveyor who was accidentally killed on Galiano Island in 1968. He was born in England, but his family had connections to Saltspring. Across the road is a signed trail that roughly follows the perimeter of the park through a young forest. Although the park is on a ridge, sadly it has no viewpoints, though one does catch tantalizing glimpses of vistas beyond. The trail is suitable for a range of abilities, but is not wheelchair accessible.

Note: In this park and elsewhere, use extreme caution when descending slopes littered with fallen arbutus leaves. For slipperiness, they are August's equivalent to January's black ice.

MOUNT MAXWELL PROVINCIAL PARK, BAYNES PEAK (MAPS 3 and 4)

Mount Maxwell (Class "A") Provincial Park (199 ha) takes its name from the mountain that was officially named Mount Baynes (in 1858) after Rear Admiral Robert Lambert Baynes, commander of the Royal Navy's Pacific Station from 1857 to 1860. Through local usage it became known as Maxwell's Mountain after the family that farmed the valley below it from the 1860s on. This was disputed by the Baynes family. In 1912 the matter was resolved by retaining the name Mount Maxwell, while remembering the admiral by naming its finest viewpoint Baynes Peak (594 m). Here you'll find a spectacular Gulf Island vista over Burgoyne Bay, Sansum Narrows, Maple Bay and the surrounding mountains.

On Fulford-Ganges Road, either 11.2 km from Fulford Harbour or 1.6 km from Ganges, turn southwest onto Cranberry Road and continue up Maxwell Mountain Road for 9 km to the main parking lot. The pavement ends at the 4 km mark.

Notes:
- You may see signs along the way pointing to water but do not rely on it as drinkable. Some sources may dry up in summer.
- The road to Mount Maxwell is not plowed in the winter.
- The road to the park passes through the Mount Maxwell Ecological Reserve #37. (See page 15.)
- See also notes for Bruce Peak.

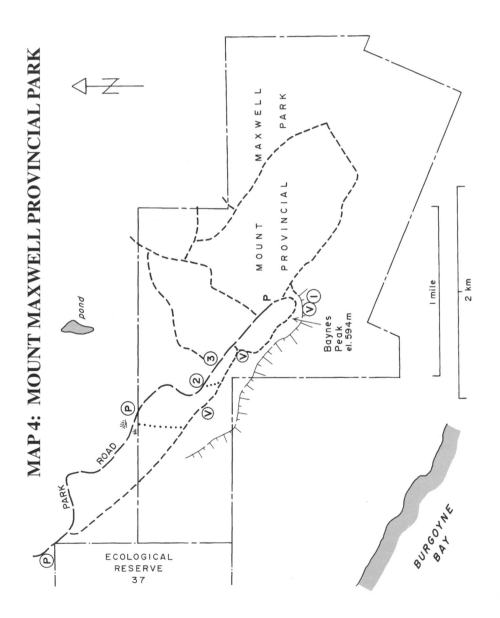

MAP 4: MOUNT MAXWELL PROVINCIAL PARK

At Baynes Peak ①, the best viewpoint, there are park facilities but no camping is permitted. The main viewing area at the sheer drop-off is fenced. The view walk is clearly marked from the south end but becomes less clear going north. You can pick a route through open forest to ② where there is limited roadside parking. Follow the road east about 300 m and find a minor, sometimes indistinct, trail ③ which leads you through salal mainly along the north boundary. Ignore a trail leading off to the north and continue around the park boundary. (There are no boundary markers. You can estimate the boundary by the larger trees within the park.) Return by trail to the main parking lot. Trails are unmarked and mostly overgrown with salal. One trail starts just outside the ecological reserve and follows below the ridge.

If you are wondering why the Garry oaks and Douglas-firs in this area are dying, the answer is: *lambdina fiscellaria somniara* (western oak looper in plain English), a moth larva that eats leaves. The looper has killed about 200 Douglas-firs and several Garry oaks in a 50-ha area that includes Mount Maxwell Provincial Park, the adjoining Mount Maxwell Ecological Reserve (whose main feature is the Garry oaks), and private land. This naturally dry area has suffered above-normal temperatures and below-average rainfall for a decade, making the trees more susceptible to the 15-year infestation of loopers. In the cycle of nature, the death of the Douglas-firs should give Garry oak seedlings a better chance to grow, but the hand of man has introduced feral goats into the equation. About 100 wild descendants of domestic goats are ranging through this area, munching on the oak seedlings.

MOUNT ERSKINE (MAP 3)

Mount Erskine, about 4 km north of Mount Maxwell Provincial Park, has several fine views from its 441-m summit. Vancouver Island, Thetis, Kuper, Galiano, Valdes and the Shoal Islands near Crofton are visible.

From Fulford Harbour travel 14 km to Rainbow Road in Ganges; from Vesuvius Bay ferry, 7 km to Rainbow Road. From Ganges, go west onto Rainbow Road, which becomes Collins Road, and travel 4.9 km. Look for a red diamond-shaped marker on a roadside tree, indicating the trailhead. The trail is steep in spots, but well-marked and easily followed. You may have to skirt fallen trees. Allow about an hour to approach the summit (which, as private property, is off-limits).

Notes:
- Carry an adequate supply of water.
- There is very limited roadside parking.
- Respect the rights of the private property owners near Erskine Point and at the summit.
- The Mount Erskine trail described is on Crown Land.
- See also notes for Mount Maxwell.

CHANNEL RIDGE (MAP 3)

Access 1: From Vesuvius Bay Road, ascend Broadwell Road to its intersection with Channel Ridge Road. Head east past Cormorant Crescent and turn right onto Canvasback Place. The marked trailhead is on the right, just behind the second of two square concrete water reservoirs. The best viewpoint on the route is about 5 min. from this south end of the trail, and overlooks Saint Mary Lake toward Wallace and Galiano Islands. The forest here includes many arbutus trees (*Arbutus menziesii*, also known as Madrone), the only native broadleaf evergreen in Canada. (See Note with Peter Arnell Park.)

Access 2: From Vesuvius Bay Road, head north on Sunset Drive. The marked trailhead is at the gap in the fence opposite 1110 Sunset Drive. The ascent is steep here, but the trail levels out more as you approach the top of the ridge. The trail is marked with red metal flashes on the trees, and takes you through young forestland with some water views through the trees. Trail, one way: length: 4.5 km; time: 1½ hr.

QUARRY DRIVE PARK (MAP 3)

From Vesuvius Bay Road, just west of Broadwell Road, turn south on Chu-An Road, then turn right onto Quarry Drive. The trailhead is signposted on the south side of the road near the end of Quarry Drive. A steep rugged trail leads down to a sandy beach. Allow 15 minutes each way. Beach walks are possible, both northwest toward Vesuvius Bay (named in 1859 after HM paddle sloop *Vesuvius*), and southeast toward Booth Bay. Please respect the rights of the private landowners nearby.

DUCK CREEK (MAP 3)

From Vesuvius Bay Road head north on Sunset Drive. After 0.4 km watch for a bank of mailboxes on the left near 208 Sunset Drive. The trail starts on the opposite side of the road, behind the map board. A BC 21 Environmental Youth Team, the Salt Spring Salmonid Enhancement Society, and the Salt Spring Island Parks and Recreation Commission worked together to create this community park, a restful spot for fish and humans alike. The creekside trail is suitable for walkers of all abilities, but numerous steps prevent wheelchair access. Trail length, one way to Broadwell Road: 1.5 km; time: 45 min.

JACK FOSTER TRAIL, Southey Point (MAP 3)

Take either Sunset Drive or North End Road and turn north onto Southey Point Road. (There's a fir tree in the middle of the intersection.) The marked trailhead is immediately to your right where a plank crosses the ditch. There's limited parking across the road. Be careful not to block driveways. The trail itself is on public land, but narrowly skirts private property, so keep to the trail. Don't be put off by the steep descent near the outset; the rest of the walk is easy, taking you through woods and out to the beach. It's best to plan your visit at low tide, so you can walk south (right) along the beach for about 1 km. Your view is across Trincomali Channel to Galiano Island. (The channel is named for the sailing frigate HMS *Trincomalee*, launched in Bombay in 1817, and in turn named after the port of Trincomalee on the Indian Ocean.) You could return the way you came, or complete a loop route by heading inland just before the breakwater. Scramble up the bank and follow a public path between two private properties to emerge on North End Road. Head north (right) for about 1 km to your setting-out point. If you do the loop route you will cover close to 4 km and take about an hour plus time to explore the beach.

⟨3⟩ SIDNEY AREA (MAP 5)   1996 census: 10,701

Lovely Sidney-by-the-Sea has so much to offer residents and visitors alike, so allow yourself plenty of time to be pleasantly distracted when you visit one of the three mini-hikes included here, or when you set off on one of the "little ferries" to **Sidney Island** or **Portland Island** (see pages 19 and 22). In particular, naturalists will appreciate the Roberts Bay federal bird sanctuary with its handsome interpretive centre and abundant opportunities to view marine life and other wildlife. The sanctuary is one of the oldest in Canada, having been established in 1931 as Shoal Harbour Bird Sanctuary. It's managed by the local Citizens Coalition for Conservation, with support from the township. This is a good place to spot a Bufflehead Duck, adopted as Sidney's official bird. He's a handsome and distinctive little fellow, with a large white head patch and white sides. The Port of Sidney waterfront promenade is fully wheelchair accessible and takes you past the Historical and Marine Mammal Museum and the Centennial Bandstand. The BC Aviation Museum is off Canora Road. Nearby, Brethour Cemetery is now a heritage site, preserving thirty-five graves of Brethour family members and farm workers who once lived and worked on the original 200-ha farm. The private burial ground was started in 1875 when a pair of twins died at birth. Star Marine Services (655-5211), which operates scheduled ferry service to Piers Island (privately owned) and on-call water-taxi service to Portland Island, also offers Sidney Harbour cruises. The Town of Sidney took its name from the large island offshore; earlier the area was known as Tseteenus ("sticking out").

For more information on the Sidney area please contact:

> **Town of Sidney**, 2440 Sidney Avenue
> Sidney, BC   V8L 1Y7
> phone 656-1184; fax 655-4508

LOCHSIDE DRIVE PROMENADE:

Tulista Park, near the intersection of Weiler Avenue and Lochside Drive, is your setting-off point for the new seaside walkway extending south to the Sidney/North Saanich border. Pick a clear day to make the most of fantastic views. The promenade is wheelchair accessible and offers wheelchair access to the beach. Just be sure you are able to climb any access that you can descend. When you reach the southern municipal border, you are welcome to continue your walk along the beach, but be advised that the land between the beach and Lochside Drive is private property. **Iroquois Park**, across Fifth St. from Tulista Park, has playing fields and tennis courts.

RESTHAVEN PARK:

From the town centre, head north on Resthaven Drive to its intersection with Bowerbank Road. From the park, follow a paved promenade that

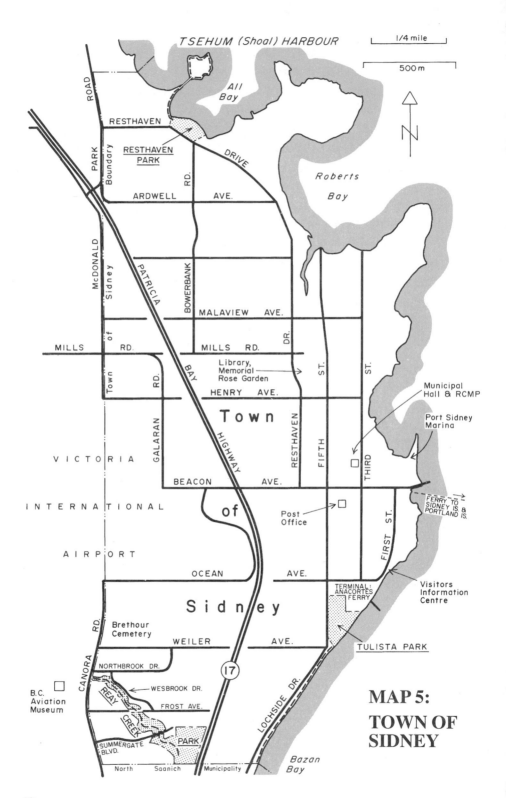

TSEHUM (Shoal) HARBOUR

1/4 mile

500 m

N

All Bay

Roberts Bay

ROAD

PARK

Boundary

RESTHAVEN

RESTHAVEN PARK

DRIVE

RD.

ARDWELL AVE.

McDONALD

Sidney

PATRICIA

BOWERBANK

of

MALAVIEW AVE.

DR.

MILLS RD.

Town

MILLS RD.

BAY

Library, Memorial Rose Garden

RESTHAVEN ST.

FIFTH ST.

HENRY AVE.

Town

Municipal Hall & RCMP

GALARAN RD.

HIGHWAY

Port Sidney Marina

VICTORIA

BEACON AVE.

THIRD

INTERNATIONAL

of

Post Office

FERRY TO SIDNEY IS & PORTLAND IS.

FIRST ST.

AIRPORT

OCEAN AVE.

Sidney

TERMINAL: ANACORTES FERRY

Visitors Information Centre

CANORA RD.

Brethour Cemetery

WEILER AVE.

TULISTA PARK

NORTHBROOK DR.

17

B.C. Aviation Museum

REAY CREEK

WESBROOK DR.

FROST AVE.

LOCHSIDE DR.

MAP 5: TOWN OF SIDNEY

SUMMERGATE BLVD.

PARK

Bazan Bay

North   Saanich   Municipality

40

hugs the shoreline out to and around the small island that was once home to Resthaven Hospital, run by the Seventh Day Adventists. Note that the adjacent land is private property. Wheelchair accessible.

REAY CREEK PARK:

This little park is an oasis surrounded by residential development and the traffic of the Victoria International Airport. But a true oasis it is, quiet and peaceful, with lush native vegetation and a tranquil stream which is home to coho salmon and cutthroat trout. Access is off Wesbrook Drive via Northbrook Drive, or where Frost Avenue deadends on both sides of the creek. As you make your way south-east toward the open parkland you will cross Summergate Boulevard, access to Summergate Village (private property). This park is not wheelchair accessible.

In the 1930s or 40s an earthen dam was built on the creek, creating an artificial pond that became home to waterfowl and fish stocks. The following decades saw the degradation of the stream due to neglect and toxic run-off from nearby industrial lands. In 1982, commercial fisherman Stan Levar, along with the Sidney Anglers Association, began reclamation of the stream. Then, in 1997, heavy rains caused a break in the earthen dam, creating a flow of silt downstream to threaten sensitive fish-rearing areas. Commercial and sports fishermen, the town of Sidney, and the federal government through its South Islands Streams initiative joined forces to make emergency repairs to the dam; the project will be completed during the dry months of summer 1997.

〈4〉 **NORTH SAANICH AREA (MAP 6)**   1996 census: 10,411

Following are descriptions of the three major parks in North Saanich: **Coles Bay, Horth Hill** and **John Dean**. In each case we suggest opportunities for you to strike off into the surrounding countryside for longer rambles. New in this edition are some of the smaller parks: **Nymph Point**, **Blue Heron**, **Quarry**, **Bazan Bay** and **Patricia Bay** Parks, and new, too, is a map showing the trail network and beach accesses in the **Deep Cove** area. You may wish to call in at the North Saanich Municipal

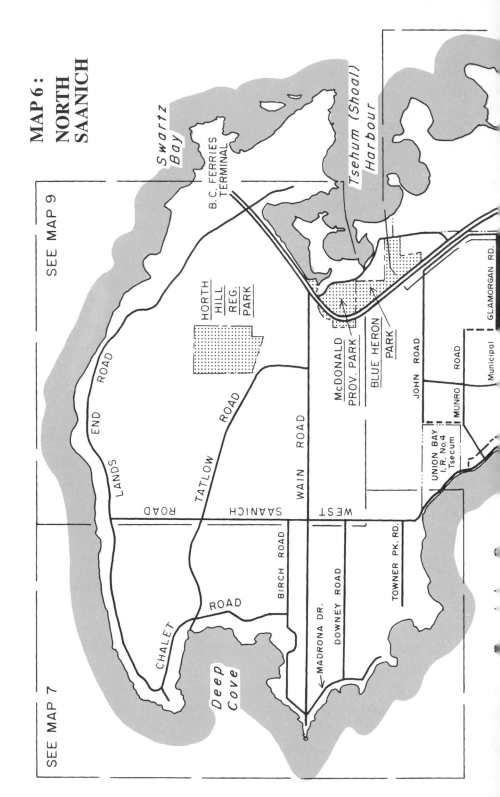

MAP 6:
NORTH
SAANICH

Swartz Bay

SEE MAP 9

B.C. FERRIES TERMINAL

Tsehum (Shoal) Harbour

HORTH HILL REG. PARK

McDONALD PROV. PARK

BLUE HERON PARK

GLAMORGAN RD.

JOHN ROAD

Municipal

MUNRO ROAD

UNION BAY I.R. No.4 Tsecum

END ROAD

LANDS

TATLOW ROAD

WAIN ROAD

WEST SAANICH ROAD

TOWNER PK. RD.

BIRCH ROAD

DOWNEY ROAD

MADRONA DR.

CHALET ROAD

Deep Cove

SEE MAP 7

42

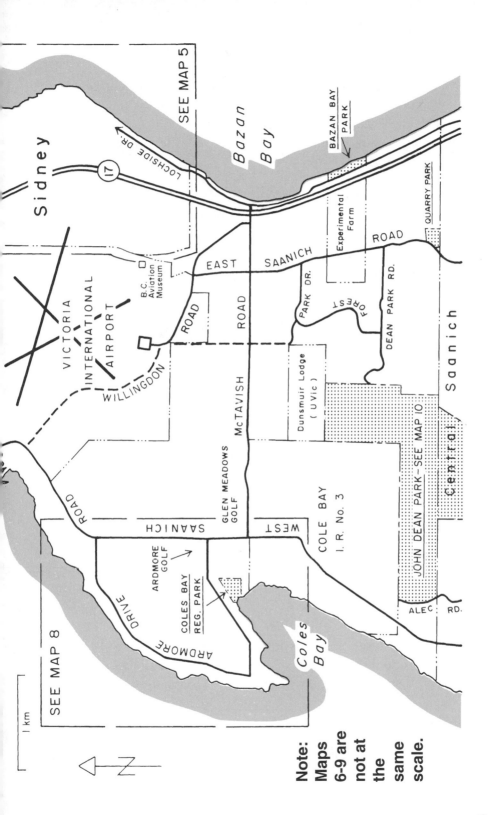

Note: Maps 6-9 are not at the same scale.

43

Hall to pick up copies of half-a-dozen hand-drawn maps covering these and other areas such as **Cloake Hill**, **Patricia Bay** and **Curteis Point**. These maps are current to 1992 and show the many bridle trails developed throughout the municipality. **Denham Till Park** (forest, orchard and children's playground), and **Wain Park** (sports fields) both have trails that could facilitate loop hikes.

North Saanich Municipal Hall
1620 Mills Road   Mail: Box 2639
phone 656-0781   Sidney, BC V8L 4C1

NYMPH POINT PARK (MAPS 6 and 9)

From Highway 17, north of Sidney, turn right at the Wain Road exit onto McDonald Park Road. Almost immediately, turn left onto Marina Way at the sign for the North Saanich Marina (Sidney North Saanich Yacht Club). Just before the entrance to the Yacht Club, look for the carved wooden sign marking the start of the chip trail out to Nymph Point.

BLUE HERON PARK (MAP 6)

Exit from Highway 17, as above, but continue on McDonald Park Road for a short distance. Just past the entrance to **McDonald Provincial Park** (see Maps 6 and 9), which is a very attractive wooded campground facility, turn right at the handsome wooden sign marking the entrance to Blue Heron Park (gate open sunrise to sunset). Ahead and to your right are 10 picnic tables (wheelchair accessible) and a water tap. Please, no camping or fires. The park is held in trust for the community by the Sidney and North Saanich Memorial Park Society and is managed by the North Saanich Parks Committee. The central portion of the park is developed for outdoor sports in connection with adjacent Parkland Secondary School and the Panorama Leisure Centre (656-7271). A walk past the ball diamond, heading south parallel to the highway, brings you to a rough natural area and the wooded section beyond. This very pleasant area of interconnecting trails can also be accessed directly from McDonald Park Road, south of the school. Look for the East Trail sign opposite house #10559.

BAZAN BAY PARK (MAP 6)

Heading north from Victoria on Highway 17, turn east (right) onto Mount Newton Cross Road and then left (north) onto Lochside Drive; or, from Highway 17 turn east on McTavish Road, then immediately right onto Lochside Drive and head south for a short distance. The numerous picnic tables along the bluff are wheelchair-accessible, but the trail and stairs down to the beach are not. Across Lochside Drive, there is an open grassy area where dogs are free to romp, but in the park itself dogs are banned from April 1 to September 30. This popular sea-side 3.48-ha park was granted to North Saanich in 1994, under the BC Lands Free Crown Grant Policy. Bazan Bay and Valdez Island are both named after Cayetano Valdes y Bazan, a Spanish naval officer who explored this area along with Dionsio Alcala Galiano in 1792.

COLES BAY REGIONAL PARK (MAP 8)

Acquired in 1966, Coles Bay Regional Park (4 ha), is about 23 km from Victoria. Travel north on Highway 17 and West Saanich Road (17A). Turn left on Ardmore Drive (signposted) and left again on Inverness Road (signposted) to the gated park entrance (open sunrise to sunset). A 10-minute walk along any of the woodland trails takes you through a mixed forest of Douglas-fir, broadleaf maple and western red cedar, out to a rocky, pebble and mud beach, which is best visited at low tide. As you gaze across the bay, try to imagine life as it was for the Saanich people (Pauquachin, Tsecum, Tsawout and Tsartlip) before European contact, when, in winter, they retreated to permanent cedar dwellings at Coles, Patricia, Saanichton and Brentwood Bays. John Coles first visited this area in 1851 as a midshipman aboard HMS *Thetis,* but it was as a local pioneer farmer from 1857 to 1866, and later as Saanich's representative in the first Legislative Assembly, that he lent his name to the bay. The Paquachin (meaning "drop-off") reserve nearby is correctly spelled as Cole Bay Reserve.

Washrooms (wheelchair accessible) and picnic facilities are available at the group picnic area. Trails (hilly) and beach (stairs down) are not suitable for wheelchairs.

MAP 7: DEEP COVE AND ENVIRONS

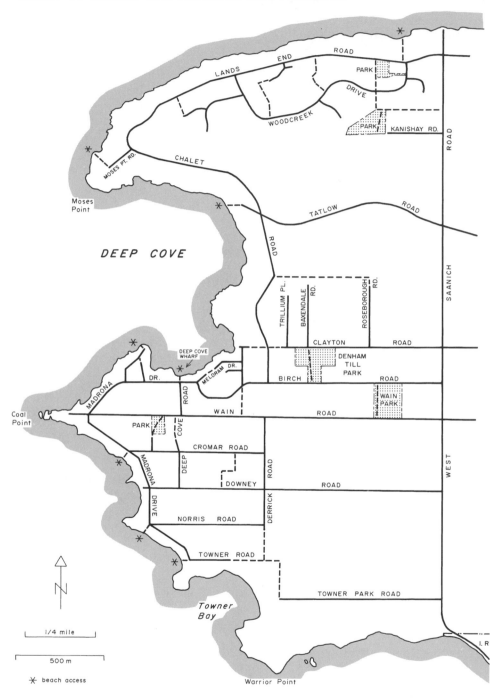

MAP 8: COLES BAY AND ENVIRONS

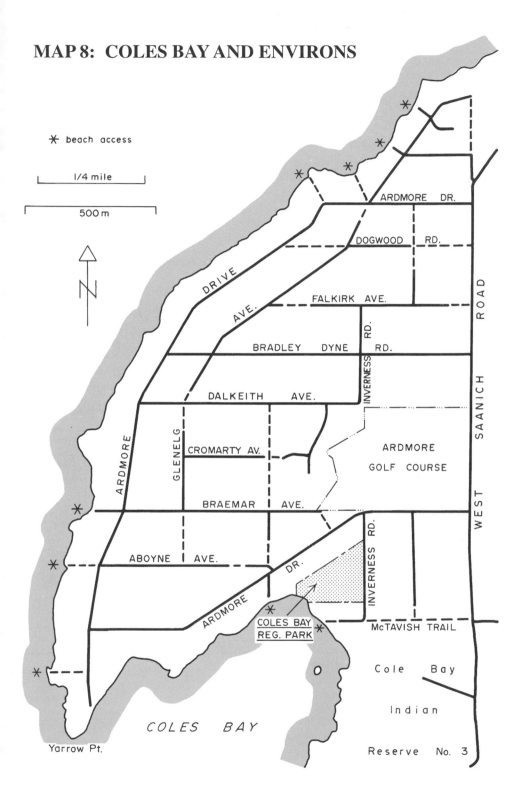

✳ beach access

1/4 mile

500 m

N

ARDMORE DR.

DOGWOOD RD.

DRIVE

AVE.

FALKIRK AVE.

BRADLEY DYNE RD.

INVERNESS RD.

DALKEITH AVE.

ARDMORE

GLENELG

CROMARTY AV.

ARDMORE

GOLF COURSE

BRAEMAR AVE.

ABOYNE AVE.

ARDMORE DR.

INVERNESS RD.

COLES BAY
REG. PARK

McTAVISH TRAIL

SAANICH ROAD

WEST

Cole Bay

Indian

Reserve No. 3

COLES BAY

Yarrow Pt.

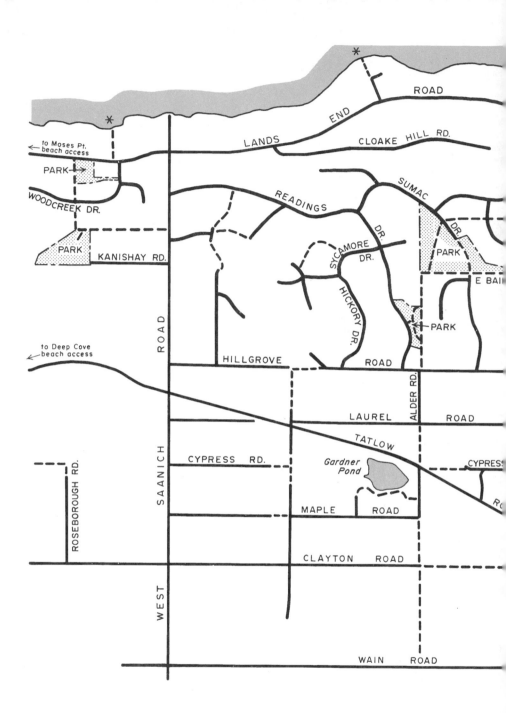

MAP 9: HORTH HILL AND ENVIRONS

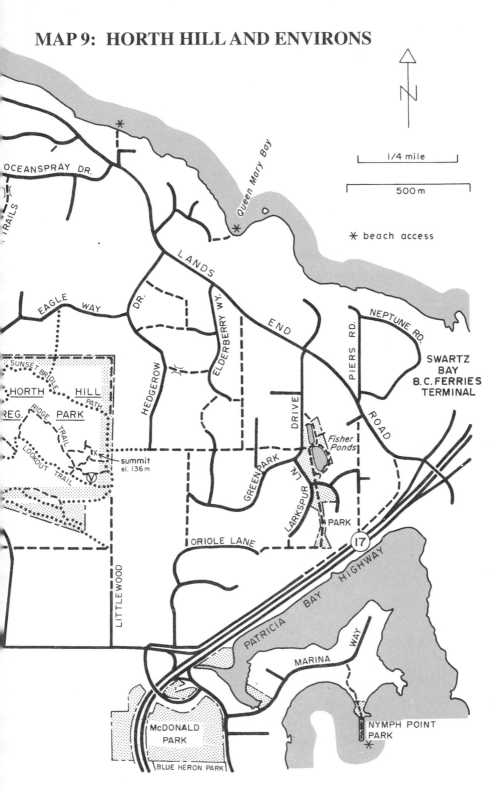

N

1/4 mile

500 m

* beach access

OCEANSPRAY DR.

TRAILS

Queen Mary Bay

LANDS

EAGLE WAY

DR.

END

ELDERBERRY WY.

NEPTUNE RD.

PIERS RD.

SWARTZ
BAY
B.C. FERRIES
TERMINAL

SUNSET BRIDLE

HORTH HILL

REG. PARK

RIDGE TRAIL

HEDGEROW

PATH

LOOKOUT TRAIL

summit
el. 136 m

GREEN PARK

DRIVE

LARKSPUR LN.

Fisher
Ponds

ROAD

PARK

ORIOLE LANE

17

LITTLEWOOD

PATRICIA BAY HIGHWAY

MARINA WAY

NYMPH POINT
PARK

McDONALD
PARK

BLUE HERON PARK

49

HORTH HILL REGIONAL PARK (MAP 9)

From Victoria, travel north on Highway 17 (Pat Bay Highway) toward Swartz Bay. At the Wain Road exit, turn right onto McDonald Park Road, then immediately right again to take the overpass across the highway. Turn left onto Wain Road, then right onto Tatlow Road to the signposted, gated parking lot (open sunrise to sunset) of Horth Hill Regional Park (31 ha) - about 30 km (a 40 minute drive). Additional parking is available at the end of Cypress Road. A grassy area near the parking lot is suitable for picnicking but most of the park is not suitable for wheelchairs. Toilets are not wheelchair accessible. Hiking and horseback riding are both permitted in the park, but cycling is banned. Horth Hill became a regional park in 1966.

From the main parking lot the northern trail through the forest soon divides into the Lookout Trail (the easier of the two) and the Ridge Trail (which is steeper and has loose gravel, so CRD Parks recommend proper footwear and a higher level of mobility). Both lead to fine overviews of the Saanich Peninsula and the surrounding islands, though the summit itself has no viewpoint. As you climb, notice the three forest communities represented: first, the heavily-shaded western red cedar, then the Douglas-fir/swordfern community at middle elevations, and finally the dry, open slopes of the Garry oak landscape near the summit. Horth Hill has wildflowers in season (look for the ladyslipper orchid) and mushrooms in the fall. As you climb the hill, look for exposed weathered outcrops of Comox Formation sandstone. Horth Hill is a cuesta or hogback hill with its smooth slope up the north side and its sharp dropoff on the south. As you explore the hilltops of the Peninsula, look for other hogback hills and evidence of glacial grooves. The deep fjord of the **Saanich Inlet** is testimony to the force of glacial action.

PATRICIA BAY PARK (MAP 6)

Off West Saanich Road, immediately·north of the Patricia Bay Seaplane Base, you'll find this small municipal park overlooking "Pat" Bay. Parking, toilets, and picnic tables are all designed for wheelchair access, and an asphalt loop path provides access to beach level. The nearby kiosk recognizes the contributions of the Provincial Capital Commission and many others toward the development of the park. The Scoter Trail (also known as Embankment Walk) leads northward along the shoreline from the loop path all the way to the Union Bay (Tsecum) Indian Reserve, a distance of almost one kilometre, with additional stair access opposite Munro Road. Note the maze of trails bounded roughly by Mills Road, West Saanich Road, John Road, and Highway 17. Accesses off West Saanich Road include a trail immediately north of house # 10305, and the unopened Sangster Road right-of-way. Union Bay was renamed Patricia Bay after the then Governor General of Canada, the Duke of Connaught, visited in 1912 along with his daughter Patricia.

A foam-to-forest walk from Patricia Bay to John Dean Park is possible (see Map 6) by walking 2 km along the grassy verge of Willingdon Road to Cresswell Road (gravel), and up the Barret Montfort Trail. The return trip would take you from the forested slopes of Mount Newton, through the agricultural plain surrounding the Victoria International Airport, and out to the gravel beach of Pat Bay.

DUNSMUIR LODGE (MAPS 6 and 10)

The Lodge and its grounds are the property of the University of Victoria. Public use is permitted on the Barret Montfort Trail extension between the boundary of John Dean Park and Cresswell Drive, but please be aware that you are on private property and stay on the trail. Horses, dogs and trail bikes are not welcome.

QUARRY PARK (MAP 6)

From Victoria travel north on Highway 17, turn west (left) onto Island View Road at the traffic light, then right onto East Saanich Road. Continue north on East Saanich Road until just beyond the Central Saanich/North Saanich border. The park is on your right and offers a 10-minute loop trail through open forest up to a rocky knoll aglow with wildflowers in spring. Several trails lead out to private lands beyond the park boundaries.

JOHN DEAN PARK (MAPS 6, 10 and 13)

Access is as above. A short distance beyond Quarry Park, the **Gulf View Picnic Site** (maintained by North Saanich Parks & Recreation, and well worth a visit) is on your right. Turn left here from East Saanich Road onto Dean Park Road, which passes through Dean Park Estates before reaching the parking lot. Driving time from Victoria is about 35 minutes - 23 km. A second point of access is off Alec Road. Traveling north from Victoria on West Saanich Road (17A), turn right on Alec Road. After 1.4 km watch for the Merrill Harrop Trail sign on the right.

Dogs must be on a leash. The picnic area is the only area in the park that is wheelchair accessible. Horses are permitted only on the Merrill Harrop Trail, named for a much-respected local horseman who died in 1996. A former jockey, he trained many a horse and rider on the Saanich Peninsula, and authored two books on the subject. His system relied on discipline, patience and kindness, plus frequent rewards (in the form of affectionate pats, not sugar). His oft-repeated advice: "Remember to reward him often, for he works for no wages and knows of no unions."

John Dean was a bachelor and an individualist with a good eye for real estate. He was considered crusty but another side of his nature was revealed after he was persuaded to let the Sidney Boy Scout Troop hold a campout on his property up on Mount Newton. He had feared vandalism, but to his amazement the Scouts - under the leadership of Skipper Freeman King - left the place cleaner than they had found it. From then on John Dean became an ardent supporter of the Boy Scout movement and showed a warm enthusiasm for the young. In 1921, at the age of 70, he donated 32 ha of his property to the province for parkland. This was the first donated Provincial Park in BC. Additions of lands donated by Barret Montfort (64 ha in 1957), Mrs. Ruth Woodward (32 ha in 1958), Sydney Pickles (7.6 ha in 1958), A. Collins (0.56 ha in 1960), and the provincial government (the balance in the late '80s) have increased the park's size to 174 ha. During the 1930s federally funded relief crews constructed what we now call Dean Park Road (originally a fire access road). Bob Boyd was the crew foreman who supervised the construction of trails and of the picnic area sited in a grove of very large trees. The steps, the stone walling and the lily pond which was formerly a swamp are all still there. This area has been described as "the most beautiful example of dry east coast Douglas-fir old-growth forest in the entire Victoria area."

John Dean died in 1943 at the age of 92, having written his own epitaph seven years earlier: "It is a rotten world, artful politicians are its bane . Its saving grace is the artlessness of the young and the wonders of the sky." His grave is in Ross Bay Cemetery beside a large monkey puzzle tree and is worth a visit. (See page 135.)

Pickles Bluff, the lower viewpoint shown on our map, is named after Sydney Pickles, who operated the Marcotte farm (which earlier may have been the first commercial strawberry-growing operation on the Saanich Peninsula) on Mount Newton Cross Road. At that time the municipality of Saanich included seven wards, covering most of the Peninsula. In 1951, Ward No. 6 seceded to become the new municipality of Central Saanich, with Sydney Pickles as its first reeve (mayor). In 1960, the 162-ha farm was sold, and Sydney and Adelaide Pickles moved to Oak Bay, where they designed and built Bryn-y-Mor at 380 Newport Avenue. For Sydney Pickles, it is fitting that Mount Newton should look down on the Victoria International Airport. He served in the Royal Naval Air Service in World War I, and as a pioneer aviator and test pilot, held Britain's commercial pilot's licence No. 9.

To link up with the **Centennial Park** trails and the **Willow Way** circuit (see pages 57 and 60), walk eastwards along Mount Newton X Road from Thomson Road to Saanichton School. Head south on Malcolm Road to connect with Tomlinson Road and the Hovey Road access to Centennial Park.

In 1984, the **Friends of John Dean Park Association** was formed in response to vandalism, garbage dumping and illegal plant removal. The club grew quickly and, in the later '80s, built the major transit trails through the park: from Dunsmuir Lodge via the Montfort, Woodward and Harrop trails to Alec Road and the Slektain trail up the north slope. The Friends are now responsible for trail maintenance, with the goal of counteracting soil erosion, vegetation destruction and soil compaction.

See map for the following notes:

①Park facilities are provided here, including a water pump. Camping and fires are not permitted. Trails north lead to a beautiful pond at the park boundary, with salamanders, frogs and water lilies. A loop around the pond is 15 minutes. Several trails lead back to the parking lot. A circle trip around these trails takes about 15 minutes. If the hike westward up to the viewpoint over the Saanich Inlet is included, add another 45 minutes.

②From the gravel road a trail leads down southward, which becomes the Gail Wickens Horse Trail (very steep at the top). This crosses Thomson Place between the houses numbered 8233 and 8257 (parking here only on shoulder of road) and continues along Thomson Road unopened road right-of-way to Mount Newton Cross Road (parking space here for only one car). It is fairly steep in parts. The return trip takes about 90 minutes. See our Central Saanich section, below, to connect with trails and parks in Central Saanich.

③ A five-minute walk up either the gravel road or the Thunderbird Trail, parallel to the road on the north/left side, will bring you to the federal DOT radar towers. From the viewing platform in the clearing by this site there are good views over the Gulf Islands. Look for wild flowers in season.

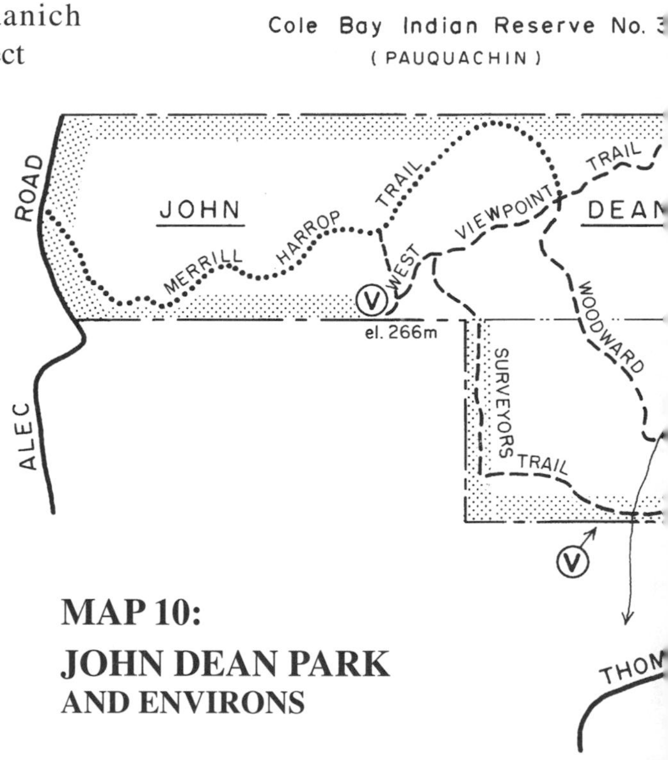

Cole Bay Indian Reserve No. 3
(PAUQUACHIN)

MAP 10:

JOHN DEAN PARK
AND ENVIRONS

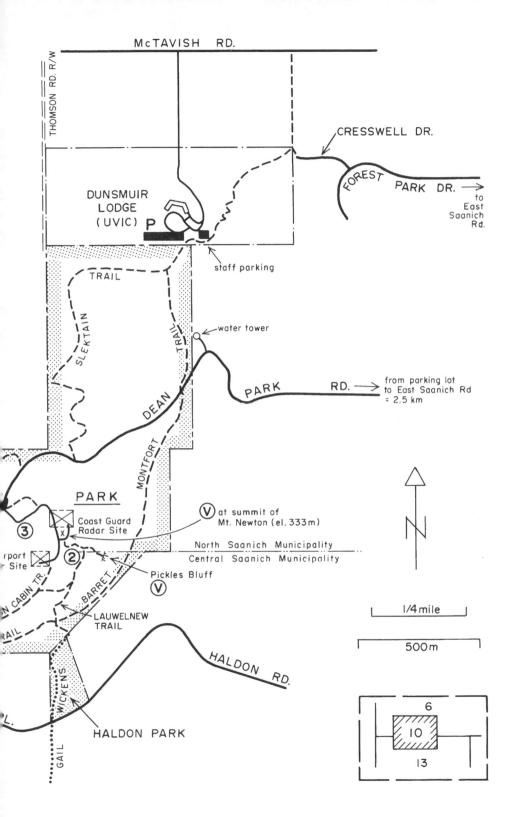

McTAVISH RD.

THOMSON RD. R/W

CRESSWELL DR.

FOREST PARK DR. → to East Saanich Rd.

DUNSMUIR LODGE (UVIC) P

staff parking

TRAIL

SLEKTAIN

DEAN TRAIL

water tower

PARK RD. → from parking lot to East Saanich Rd = 2.5 km

MONTFORT

PARK

Ⓥ at summit of Mt. Newton (el. 333m)

Coast Guard Radar Site

③

②

rport Site

CABIN TR.

BARRET

North Saanich Municipality
Central Saanich Municipality

Pickles Bluff

Ⓥ

LAUWELNEW TRAIL

WICKENS

HALDON RD.

GAIL

P.L.

HALDON PARK

N

1/4 mile

500m

6
10
13

55

Negotiations are on-going between BC Parks and the CRD about a possible park transfer. A brochure detailing the human and natural history of the park is currently available from BC Parks (see page 222); or for further information contact:

Friends of John Dean Park   or: Edo Nyland
P O Box 3000   phone 656-9276
Saanichton, BC   V8M 2C5

A recently-published book, *An Historical First: John Dean Provincial Park*, is available from the author, Jarrett Teague.   Price: $14.00, from PO Box 20093, Sidney, BC V8L 5C9.

⟨5⟩ **CENTRAL SAANICH AREA**   1996 census: 14,611

Just walking the country roads of this rural area can be very pleasant, so don't be surprised to find that we've used some roads to link up the more popular destinations as we expand your hiking horizons. For information on parks and trails in Central Saanich contact:

Central Saanich Municipal Hall, Parks Dept.
1903 Mt. Newton Cross Road, Saanichton, BC   V8M 2A9
phone 652-4444, local 233

JOHN DEAN PARK TO CENTENNIAL PARK (MAP 13)

John Dean Park straddles the boundary between North Saanich and Central Saanich. Descend southward from the park, following the Gail Wickens Trail (very steep at the top) through **Haldon Park**. The Gail Wickens Horse Trail is named for a local horsewoman, a young mother who was killed in a car crash while crossing the Pat Bay highway with her children. Follow the trail to the intersection of Thomson Road and Mount Newton Cross Road. Turn east along the Cross Road, then turn south on Malcolm Road near Saanichton School. You pass through farm land, then woodlands, to reach the Hovey Road and Tomlinson Road accesses to Centennial Park.

CENTENNIAL PARK (MAPS 11 and 13)

Access is as for Willow Way; see Map 13. The Victorienteers (see page 221) have prepared a map of Centennial Park (Scale 1:3000); price: $1.00 to non-members for a photocopy. Our map shows only the main trails.

MAP 11: CENTENNIAL PARK

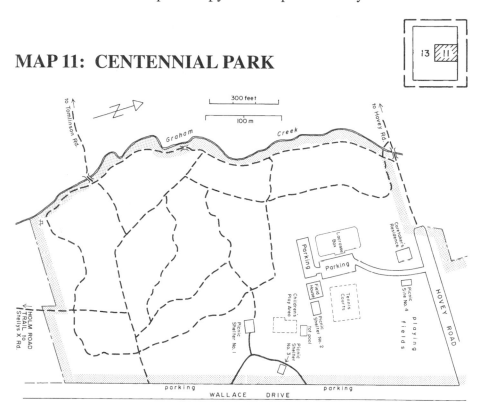

BUTTERFIELD PARK (MAPS 12 and 13)

To approach from the east, travel north from Victoria on Highway 17 to Mount Newton Cross Road. Turn left at the traffic light, pass the Prairie Inn (a historic site and brew pub), the Central Saanich Municipal Hall, and Saanichton School, then turn right onto Thomson Place. Your trip will take you past the Mount Newton Seed Orchard (the barn dates to 1907) and the farm of pioneers Duncan and Helen Lidgate (now a heritage site). Or, to approach from the west, take Highway 17 and 17A (West Saanich Road) to Mount Newton Cross Road and turn right. Mount

Newton Cottage on the corner was once a stopping-place, Pope's Corner, on the old wagon road out the Saanich Peninsula. If it looks familiar, you may have seen it as the backdrop in a recent auto commercial. Continue past the Butterfield Park sign at 1184 Mount Newton Cross Road and turn left onto Thomson Place. Look for the first driveway on your left and park either on the roadside or just inside the gate. Your trip to the park takes you through a lovely pastoral landscape of rolling fields and hedgerows remniscent of an English countryside. Features include the lush farmlands of Woodwynn Farm on West Saanich Road, and picturesque St. Stephen's Church off Mount Newton Cross Road. Believed to be BC's oldest church in continuous use on its original 1862 site, it was identified in 1992 as a municipal heritage site.

From the moment you step out of your vehicle to see wild strawberry plants at your feet, you know you are in for a treat, an opportunity to observe man and mother nature struggle for control of a patch of land. Many of the large native trees would have been here when the pioneer McPhail and Thomson families arrived in the 1800s. Later, the 5.3 ha property was managed by the Butterfield family - Evelyn, John, and their daughter Hilda - as South Hill poultry farm. The residence was built in 1913, from what is most likely a J.C.M. Keith design, in the foursquare or "Edwardian Builder" style. Evelyn and Hilda, along with their Chinese gardener/handyman, Sing, developed the surrounding gardens as a balance between wild and cultivated flowers and plants. The property remained in the possession of this community-minded family for 74 years, until the time of Hilda's death, when it was bequeathed to the Thetis Park Nature Sanctuary Association, to which Evelyn and Hilda had belonged. In 1988 the 5.3 ha property was transferred to Central Saanich as public parkland. For several years the garden was left to grow wild, until 1993, when BC Heritage Trust funding was secured for restoration and stabilization of the buildings and a resident caretaker placed on site. Some attempts have been made to guide the garden gently back to order. In 1996 the project garnered the Hallmark Society's Louis Award for heritage preservation. In *The fair land, Saanich* (Sono Nis, 1982), Betty Bell tells the stories of many of the early Central Saanich (then known as South Saanich) families, including the Butterfields; (Hilda is listed as a contributor). Mrs. Bell gives three possible meanings for the name

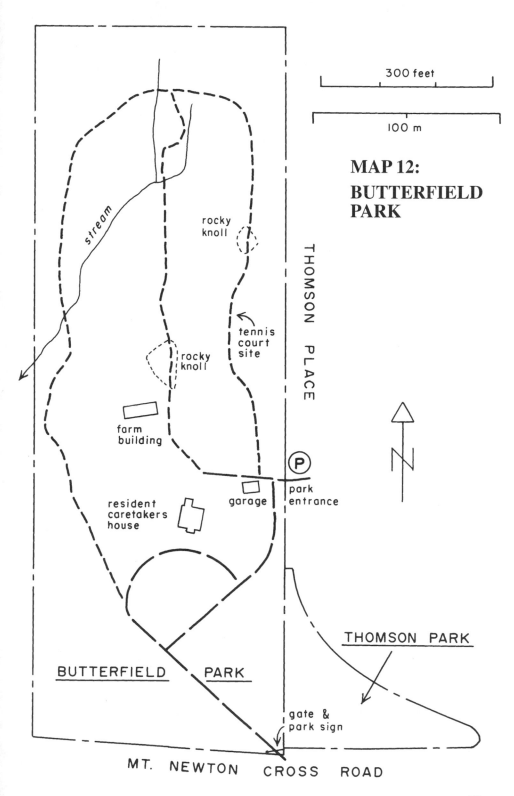

300 feet

100 m

MAP 12:
BUTTERFIELD
PARK

stream

rocky knoll

rocky knoll

tennis court site

THOMSON PLACE

farm building

garage

park entrance

N

resident caretakers house

THOMSON PARK

BUTTERFIELD PARK

gate & park sign

MT. NEWTON CROSS ROAD

59

"Sanetch": "fair land", hence the title of her book; "rising", referring to Mount Newton rising from the receding waters of an ancient flood; or, "always on the lookout", meaning that Thunderbird is watching from his home atop Mount Newton.

As you visit Butterfield Park, remember to tread lightly over and around nature and man's handiwork. Stay on the pathways, and, please, respect the privacy of the resident caretaker.

WILLOW WAY (MAP 13)

Our map shows a pleasant 10-km circle route for cyclists, hikers and horseriders through narrow roads (where care is necessary to avoid cars) and along unopened road rights-of-way beside fences, in the flat or rolling farmlands of Central Saanich. Access from Victoria is by Highway 17, East Saanich Road and Hovey Road to Centennial Park (about 18 km - a half-hour drive) with excellent parking and park facilities. Wheelchair access is limited to the main areas of the park.

① From **Centennial Park,** take the Holm Road trail south, then follow the broad shoulder of Wallace Drive to a footbridge due south of Stelly's Secondary School.

② Follow right-of-way south along west side of ditch switching to east side.

③ Follow Kersey Road (clearly evident at houses) to West Saanich Road.

④ Trail here is rough and grassy. Continue past greenhouses to Greig Avenue.

⑤ Visit **Gore Nature Park**, very pretty and unspoiled. Limited parking here. At this point you can:

⑥ Detour to **Hardy Park** (with picnic tables and a magnificent view) and descend along Sea Drive to the seawall promenade (public beach access, signposted) below the Port Royale development, or continue:

⑦ Via Wallace Drive and West Saanich Road go northeast, then northwest.

⑧ At Stellys Cross Road turn east to Gowdy Road and then on to White Road. The right-of-way runs along the south edge of the orchard, crosses Tomlinson Road and Graham Creek (a tributary of Hagan Creek), then returns to Centennial Park. (A less peaceful route back is via Stellys Cross Rd. and Tomlinson Rd.)

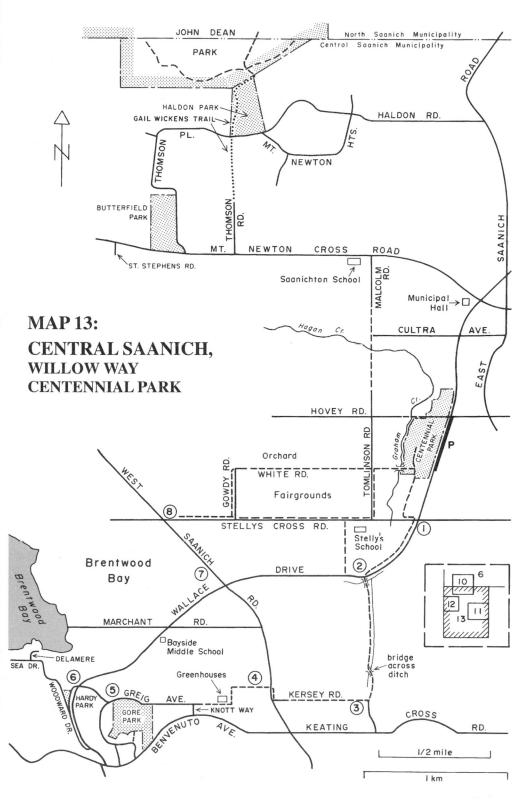

MAP 13:
CENTRAL SAANICH,
WILLOW WAY
CENTENNIAL PARK

Cautions: Be careful of private property, including fences and livestock. Keep off planted fields, especially if on horseback. Keep dogs under control. Please do not smoke, due to fire hazard. No motorcycles please.

BENVENUTO HILL

Roughly bounded by West Saanich Road, Wallace Drive and Benvenuto Avenue, this hilltop Garry oak meadow will soon become a 10-ha park, part of a 57-ha subdivision by Fama Holdings Ltd. We will include map and access information in our next edition.

LOCHSIDE TRAIL
(MAP 14, north section and MAP 23, south section)

The Lochside Trail follows the roadbed of the old CN Railway, roughly parallel to Highway 17, and passing through Central Saanich and Saanich. (See also page 98.) The north section of the right-of-way is almost entirely through open farmland. This makes a very pleasant walk, but note that after heavy rain there can be some muddy sections. A grant from the Provincial Capital Commission in 1996, as part of its Greenways program (see page 217), was used to improve drainage on two kilometres of the trail in the **Martindale Flats** area (see below). From **Lochside Park** in Saanich to Highway 17 at Island View Road the distance is 5.5 km. From here the old right-of-way continues north to the Saanich Historical Artifacts Society grounds (open 8:30-noon every day except Christmas Day; 8:30 am to 4 pm in June, July and August). Admission by donation. Washrooms and trails wheelchair accessible. For more information contact:

> **Saanich Historical Artifacts Society**
> 7321 Lochside Drive
> R R 3 Saanichton, BC   V0S 1M0
> phone 652-5522

Note: The right-of-way does not continue through the Society property; you must make a detour around it and the East Saanich Indian Reserve (Tsawout Village). It is possible that a proper paved detour, suitable for use as a bike path, may be in place in the near future.

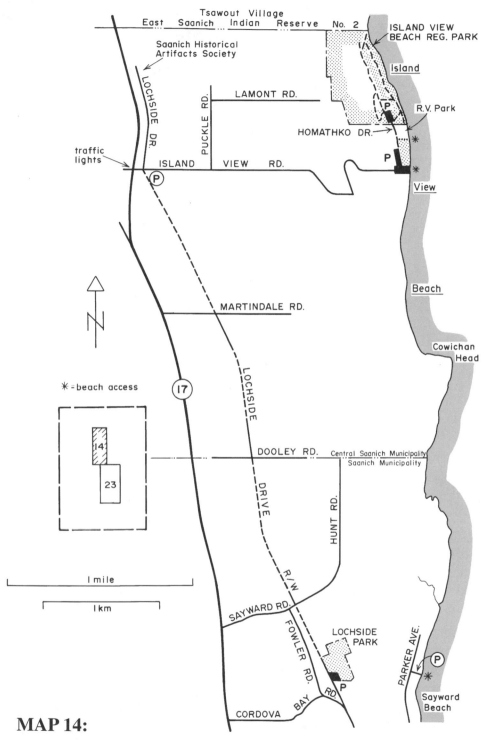

Tsawout Village
East Saanich Indian Reserve No. 2

ISLAND VIEW BEACH REG. PARK

Saanich Historical
Artifacts Society

Island

LOCHSIDE DR.

PUCKLE RD.

LAMONT RD.

R.V. Park

P

HOMATHKO DR.

traffic lights

ISLAND VIEW RD.

P

View

* = beach access

MARTINDALE RD.

LOCHSIDE

N

Beach

Cowichan Head

17

DRIVE

14

23

DOOLEY RD.
Central Saanich Municipality
Saanich Municipality

1 mile

1 km

HUNT RD.

R/W

SAYWARD RD.

FOWLER RD.

LOCHSIDE PARK

PARKER AVE.

P

P

CORDOVA BAY RD.

Sayward Beach

MAP 14:

LOCHSIDE TRAIL (north)
ISLAND VIEW BEACH REGIONAL PARK

ISLAND VIEW BEACH REGIONAL PARK (MAP 14)

From Victoria on Highway 17 travel about 16 km and turn right onto Island View Road at the traffic lights. Another 2.5 km brings you to the large CRD Parks parking lot and to the beach, a good birding area. Your route takes you through what are known as the **Martindale Flats**, an excellent observation area for wintering freshwater ducks, raptors, and the Eurasian Skylark (an introduced species once common on the Saanich Peninsula, but now increasingly rare).

Island View Beach Regional Park, currently 40 ha, benefitted in 1992 from the acquisition of 10.5 ha to the south of the former boundary, and may soon expand again. Access to the park can be made along the beach at all times, or by Homathko Drive. The gate is open sunrise to sunset throughout the year. This is a CRD nature appreciation park (so all dogs must be on leash) with unique sand dunes and a berm. Please treat these natural features with great respect as the ecology is very fragile.

The toilet facilities, located just north of the parking lot, are wheelchair accessible; trail surfaces are crushed gravel. Island View Beach became a regional park in 1966.

From a hiker's point of view this is the best and closest beach to Victoria, with a view across Haro Strait to the San Juan Islands, Sidney Spit and Mount Baker. Note that swimming is not recommended on account of strong currents. On a minus low tide, a 10-km-one-way beach walk is possible from Island View Beach south to Mount Douglas Park with minimal rock scrambling. Note the erosion of the Cowichan Head cliffs. Another very pleasant beach walk takes you north to Cordova Spit, formed as currents carry sand and gravel from the face of Cowichan Head. Please avoid trespass on the East Saanich (Tsawout) Indian Reserve that you pass.

GOWLLAND TOD PROVINCIAL PARK: Wallace Drive / North Access to TOD INLET / PARTRIDGE HILLS (MAP 15)

Access to the Tod Inlet trails within Gowlland Tod Provincial Park is via West Saanich Road (Highway 17A) and Wallace Drive. As you travel Wallace Drive you pass through the Tod Creek watershed and past Heals Rifle Range. Constructed in 1917, and operated by DND, it was the site of the shooting facilities for the 1994 Commonwealth Games. The signposted entry to Gowlland Tod Provincial Park, Tod Inlet access, is opposite **Quarry Lake** with its high security fence. Soon after entering the park you must decide either to take the wider trail past the information kiosk and directly down to the Inlet, or to turn left to take the up-and-down, twist-and-turn path alongside the creek. The latter takes you past drifts of wild Easter lilies (white fawn lilies, Erythronium oregonum) and trilliums (Trillium ovatum) in spring, and will soon connect with the proposed trail (already shown on Park maps, but in need of relocation) through to the **Partridge Hills**.

When you explore around Tod Inlet, you visit the old townsite and cement works of the Vancouver Portland Cement Company (1904-1920s), where about 400 people lived and worked. Just over that high wire fence is Butchart Gardens (you can hear the fountain), created by Jenny Butchart from worked-out limestone quarries. Wallace Drive, from which you approached the park, follows the old railbed of the BC Electric Railway, built to serve Tod Inlet and Deep Cove. Historically, and continuing to the present day, this "place of the Blue Grouse" is significant to the indigenous Tsartlip people. Please remember that it is unlawful to disturb or remove any item, ancient or recent, found within a provincial park.

In our eleventh edition of *Hiking Trails I*, which went to press in November of 1993, we said, "As we go to press, the future of this area is definitely "in the news". Fama Holdings Ltd. of Vancouver owns a 485-ha parcel in this area, and development is pending. If public parkland is created we will include it in our next edition." See below, under **Gowlland Range,** to discover how the story was to unfold. A brochure is available from BC Parks but be aware that park boundaries and trail locations have already changed considerably since the April, 1996, printing date.

MAP 15: GOWLLAND TOD PROVINCIAL PARK: TOD INLET   PARTRIDGE HILLS

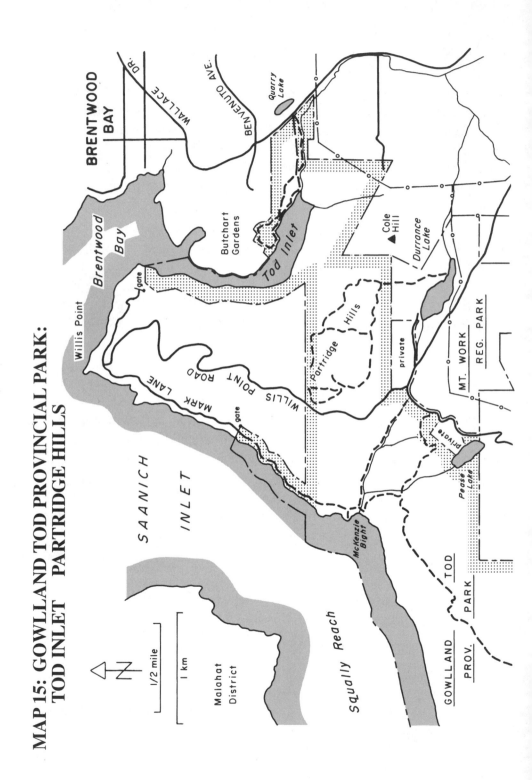

For the history of the limestone quarry at Tod Inlet, turn to Dave Preston's *The Story of Butchart Gardens* (Highline Publishing). Tod Inlet is named after John Tod (some later members of the family spelled their surname Todd), who first came to what is now BC in 1823. He retired to Victoria in 1850 (see our Oak Bay section), where he served on the Council of Government for the colony of Vancouver Island, and later on the legislative council.

HIGHLANDS AREA 1996 Census - Highlands: 1423, Langford Electoral Area: 603

After the positive outcome of its incorporation referendum in September, 1993, Highlands is now the CRDs newest municipality. (Willis Point, a community at the northern edge of the municipality, is outside the Highlands borders and remains unincorporated, as part of the **Langford Electoral Area**, which also includes the area from Langford Municipality to the Malahat, plus the Songhees Indian Reserve. We have lumped Willis Point in with the Highlands.) The new municipality completed its plan for greenways and trails in March, 1997, so we are able to include some new destinations in this, our twelfth edition of *Hiking Trails I*. Of greatest significance to this area is the creation, in 1994, of Gowlland Tod Provincial Park, bringing to a close decades of uncertainty as residents, recreationists, conservationists and developers wrestled over the future of the Highlands. In a "late-breaking news item" as we go to press in October of 1997, Highlands is considering a proposal that would see **Scafe Hill** added to Thetis Lake Regional Park. See Map 16 for the proposed boundaries and Map 31 for trail access. Contact CRD Parks or the Highlands municipal office for current information.

> **District of Highlands**
> 1564 Millstream Road
> Victoria, BC V9E 1G6
> phone 474-1773

Note: When planning an outing in this area, avoid confusing the names of Durrance Lake Road (a dead end road off Wallace Drive, providing access to local residents); Durrance Close (a dead end road off Willis Point Road, leading to Durrance Lake); and Ross-Durrance Road (off Willis Point Road, and your access to the Mount Work parking lot and the Timberman Trail. Beyond **Pease Lake**, Ross-Durrance Road continues south as a very rough, winding, single-lane road with formidable potholes, especially in the winter months. It is posted as for local traffic only. Part way along, at the junction with Hazlitt Creek Road, the road name changes to Millstream Lake Road, which continues south to connect with Munn Road. From Munn Road you can travel east to Prospect Lake Road in Saanich, or west to Millsteam Road, which leads to Langford.)

HAZLITT CREEK PARK (MAP 16)

Access is off Hazlitt Creek Road, which heads west at the junction of Millstream Lake Road and Ross-Durrance Road. Just past Old Mossy Road, look for the locked yellow gate across the fire road. Park well off the road and avoid blocking the gate. The gravel road leads south through forested parkland, coming out at a new subdivision off the end of Millstream Road. After a bit of a climb, look for the signposted trail to your right, which takes you up to a hilltop wildflower meadow. Your descent southward brings you out to the turnaround at the end of the subdivision road. Although this municipal park connects with Lone Tree Hill Regional Park along a dedicated parkland strip, there is no trail connecting it to Lone Tree park and trail. There are, however, roadside trails throughout the Hazlitt Creek Road - Old Mossy Road area.

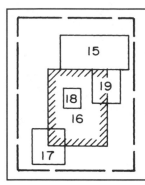 Most of our maps are accompanied by a diagram that shows how the maps interrelate. This diagram, for example, is for Map 16, Gowlland Range, (note the cross-hatching to represent the subject map) on pages 72-73. Map 18 (Lone Tree Hill) is a detail map for a park within Map16. Map 15 (Tod Inlet, Partridge Hills) is to the north; Map 19 (Mount Work) is to the northeast; Map 17 (Goldstream, Mount Finlayson) is to the southwest.

GOWLLAND TOD PROVINCIAL PARK: Middle Access to PARTRIDGE HILLS / McKENZIE BIGHT (MAP 15)

Until the proposed trail in from Tod Inlet (shown already on Park maps but in need of relocation) is complete, your access to the **Partridge Hills** will be along the trail from **Durrance Lake in Mount Work Regional Park** (see pages 81-84). Note that some of the trails shown on the Parks map have been closed. If you are visiting in the wet months, you will encounter places where the old logging roads are flooded into surrounding swampland. Look for flagged detour routes. On the northeast side, look for viewpoints over the Saanich Peninsula. The large building with a green metal roof is Stelly's School (see Map 13).

Formerly part of Mount Work Regional Park, the **McKenzie Bight** trails are signposted and provide short, pleasant hikes with good picnic spots at the Bight, where harbour seals are often observed. Time down - 20 minutes. The **Pease Creek** waterfalls, visible from the newly renamed Cascade Trail on the west side of the creek, can be delightful. A 21-m-wide parkland strip extends northeast from the Bight along a rough road to the end of Mark Lane. Note that the Maidenhair Nature Trail and the former Cascade Trail on the west side of Pease Creek have been closed because they were deemed to be dangerous and impractical to maintain.

The **Timberman Trail**, once part of Mount Work Regional Park, is off Ross-Durrance Road near Pease Lake, and provides a northern access route to the Gowlland Range. Please use the Mount Work parking lot and avoid parking along the narrow road.

GOWLLAND TOD PROVINCIAL PARK: Caleb Pike / South Access to GOWLLAND RANGE (MAP 16)

In our eleventh edition of Hiking Trails I, which went to press in November, 1993, we said, "Nearly 1000 ha in this area are owned by First National Properties of Vancouver. If any new public parkland is created in this area we will include it in our next edition." Here's what happened between 1993 and 1997. In 1994, Victoria hosted the Commonwealth Games, one outcome of which was the creation of the Commonwealth Nature Legacy, which included the largest acquisition of privately owned green space in BC history. The Legacy purchase included (in addition to smaller parcels at Glencoe Cove, Haro Woods and Panama Hill) 703 ha in the Gowlland Range, 60 ha surrounding Mount Finlayson, and 246 ha at Tod Inlet. The total value of this land was $18.7 million, with The Nature Conservancy of Canada contributing $2 million (including $400,000 from Westcoast Energy) toward the Gowlland Range portion; Fama Estates Ltd., $1 million worth of property on Tod Inlet; the CRD, $750,000; and Central Saanich,

MAP 16: GOWLLAND TOD PROVINCIAL PARK: GOWLLAND RANGE

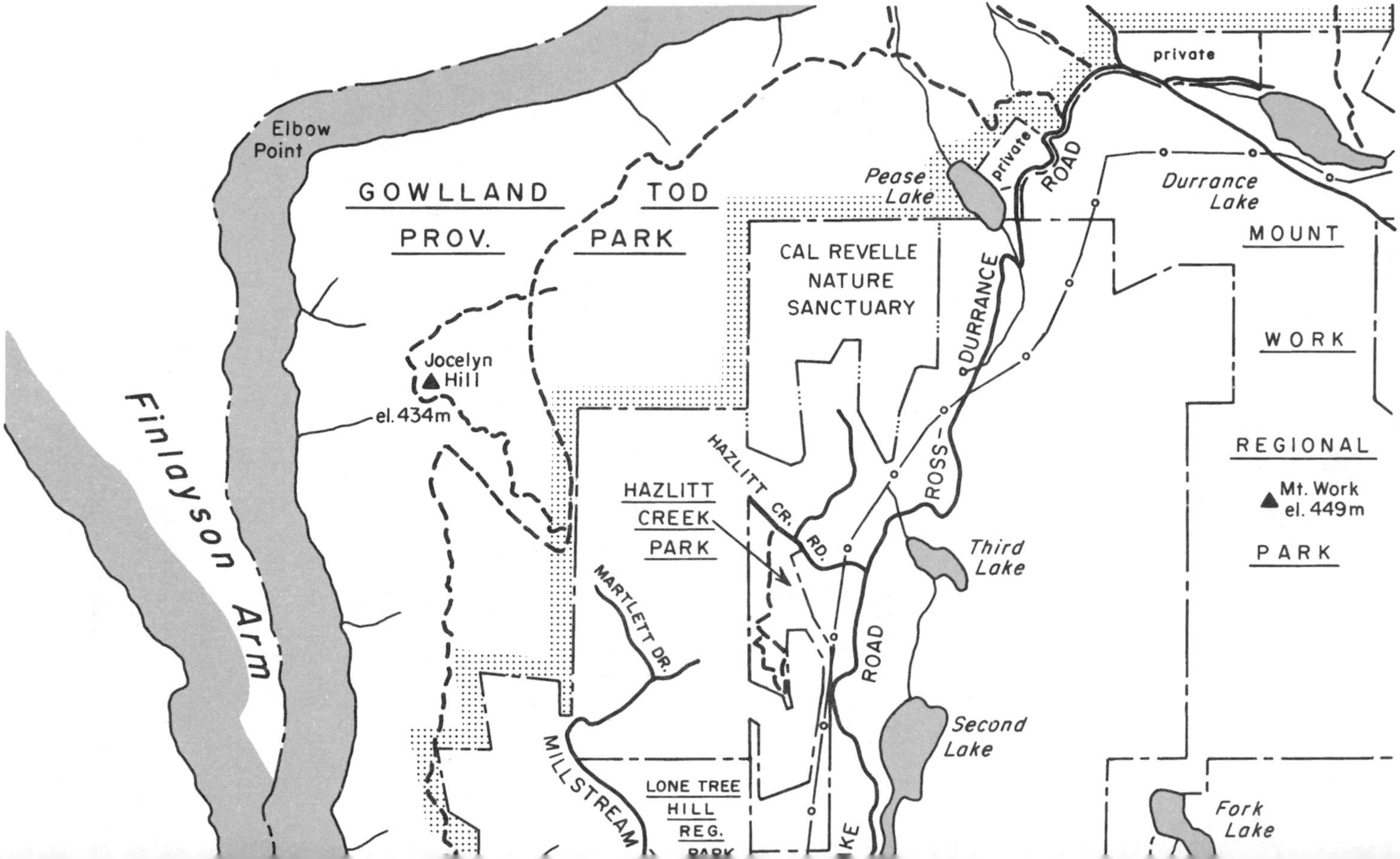

MOUNT

WORK

REGIONAL

▲ Mt. Work
el. 449m

PARK

Fork
Lake

Durrance
Lake

private

ROAD

private

DURRANCE

ROSS

Third
Lake

Second
Lake

ROAD

Pease
Lake

CAL REVELLE
NATURE
SANCTUARY

HAZLITT CR. RD.

HAZLITT
CREEK
PARK

LONE TREE
HILL
REG.
PARK

TOD

PARK

MARTLETT DR.

MILLSTREAM

GOWLLAND

PROV.

Jocelyn
Hill
▲
el. 434m

Elbow
Point

Finlayson Arm

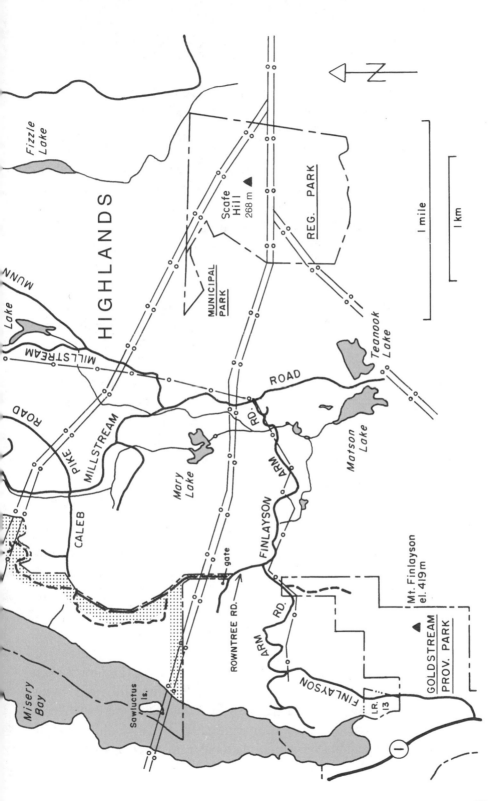

HIGHLANDS

Fizzle
Lake

MUNN
Lake

MILLSTREAM

Scafe
Hill
268 m

MUNICIPAL
PARK

REG.   PARK

1 mile

1 km

Teanook
Lake

ROAD

PIKE   ROAD

CALEB   MILLSTREAM

Mary
Lake

RD.

FINLAYSON   ARM

Matson
Lake

Misery
Bay

Sawluctus
Is.

ROWNTREE RD.

gate

ARM   RD.

FINLAYSON

I.R.
13

Mt. Finlayson
el. 419 m

GOLDSTREAM
PROV. PARK

1

$250,000. The provincial government made up the balance, $14.7 million, from the Crown land acquisition account. Part of the CRD's contribution included title to 64 ha at McKenzie Bight. Thus ended the struggle, begun in 1989 when Derrick Mallard, president of CASE (Citizens to Save the Environment), led a march through the Tod Inlet lands. Highlands residents including Bob McMinn (elected as the first mayor of Highlands municipality), and Nancy McMinn were joined by many other individuals and community and conservation groups, notably the Gowlland Foundation and The Nature Conservancy of Canada. Three levels of government were involved (provincial, regional and municipal), plus private business interests, to reach this positive outcome. Yet to be resolved, however, is the site-specific land claim at Tod Inlet, filed in February, 1994, by the Tsartlip Band of Brentwood Bay. The following year, 1995, saw the donation of 63 ha, worth about $400,000, by Doman Industries Ltd., the first transfer to be made under a new provision of the Municipal Act for protection of parkland. There was also a promise of a 106-ha dedication to the municipality. Finally, in 1996, the park had a name, Gowlland Tod, and a park management plan (preservation first, recreation, second). Park lands also grew by 75 ha with crown land additions to Goldstream Park near Mount Finlayson, to the south end of Gowlland Tod, and near McKenzie Bight, and park lands prospered by $100,000, for trail development, from Forest Renewal BC, a provincial Crown corporation.

Some prime features of the park are as visual greenspace, as natural habitat, and as recreational space. It emcompasses the 430-m-high hills that rise above Saanich Inlet, creating the viewscape from the Malahat Drive. It provides an undisturbed homeland for cougar, black bear, black-tail deer, river otter, mink, red squirrel and other wild animals, and for about one hundred species of birds including raven, bald eagle and Peale's peregrine falcon. It protects stands of Douglas-fir, western red cedar and arbutus. **Finlayson Arm**, below the Gowlland Range, supports sea anemones and the giant cloud sponge. Killer whales and seals may be observed here. The **Saanich Inlet** is significant in being the only deep water fjord on the east coast of Vancouver Island and one of only four "shallow sill" fjords in the world. A very deep basin hemmed in by a shallow outlet, the inlet experiences little tidal flushing, creating a unique marine ecosystem including a bottom layer devoid of oxygen. In 1996 a multi-national team of scientists, including some from the nearby Pacific Geoscience Centre in North Saanich, conducted tests from the drilling ship JOIDES *Resolution*. Among the discoveries were a layer of sludge deposited 11,000 years ago after a massive flood from the Fraser River; a layer of volcanic ash from the eruption 7,640 years ago of Mount Mazama in Oregon; evidence of earthqukes 200 years and 1000 years ago; and indications of recent global and ocean warming. The Steering Committee to Save Saanich Inlet has proposed that the whole of Saanich Inlet be declared a national marine park.

Gowlland Tod Provincial Park is accessible by water for boating and SCUBA diving and by vehicle at **three main access points:** the *Wallace Drive / north access* to **Tod Inlet;** the *McKenzie Bight / middle access* to **McKenzie Bight, the Partridge Hills (from Durrance Lake in Mount Work Regional Park), and Jocelyn Hill (via the Timberman Trail);** and the *Caleb Pike / south access* to **Holmes Peak and Jocelyn Hill.** From the south access you can also reach Mount Finlayson in Goldstream Park (see below). Please note that Martlett Drive, Emma Dixon Road (into the Stonecrest subdivision), and the end of Millsteam Road all lead into private lands, with no access to the park. With the exception of overnight moorage by boaters, this is a day-use-only park, with few facilities and incomplete signage. Our maps show only the main trails as proposed in the park management plan. You may encounter other old roads and trails as you explore, but please keep to the main trails to avoid sensitive, dangerous, or confusing areas. Although you are but a short distance from urban Victoria, you are in a vast wilderness area. Please read our Hints and Cautions and be prepared for a pleasant but safe experience. Equestrians and cyclists can look for the trail being developed from Caleb Pike to Jocelyn Hill specifically for these higher-impact visits. Further information is available from BC Parks (see page 222).

The Gowlland Range is named after John Thomas Gowlland, RN, who was involved in surveying duties on this coast as second master under Captain Richards aboard HMS *Plumper* 1857-1860 and HMS *Hecate* 1861-1863.

GOWLLAND TOD to GOLDSTREAM / MOUNT FINLAYSON (MAPS 16 and 17)

Heading south from the Caleb Pike access, you can either take the road (an easy, steady grade) south to the park boundary, or you can descend behind the information kiosk on the sign-posted Ridge Trail and keep left at the fork. This trail descends to several very rewarding viewpoints, then climbs again to come out on the road, just north of the park boundary. The road runs between private properties, under the powerlines and comes out on Rowntree Road at its intersection with Viart Road. From there you follow Rowntree Road and Finlayson Arm Road to connect with the trail that leads south into Goldstream Park near Mount Finlayson. Upgrading of the Mount Finlayson and connecting trails is planned for the future.

GOLDSTREAM PROVINCIAL PARK and MOUNT FINLAYSON (MAP 17)

Goldstream Provincial Park, situated in neighbouring Langford municipality, is presented here because it lies immediately south of Gowlland Tod Provincial Park, and is readily accessible from it (see above).

Just over 16 km from Victoria, Highway 1 winds its way through Goldstream Park (388 ha) which rises majestically on either hand. There are many parking areas. An excellent BC Parks brochure is available at the Gate House and the Visitor Centre. Randy Stoltmann's "Hiking Guide to the Big Trees of Southwestern British Columbia" describes a walk in Goldstream Park.

The park's diverse terrain (from rain forest to dry ridges of arbutus and pine) attracts groups of all ages. There are many interconnecting forest trails with viewpoints and points of interest which are marked on our map. The Niagara Falls, viewed from the trail below, are a most spectacular sight, particularly in the spring when they are in full spate. The Freeman King Visitor Centre in the Flats provides informative exhibits; in summer, talks are also arranged for visitors at the Meeting Place in the campground. Parking is limited at the campground. Contact BC Parks South Vancouver Island District office at 391-2300 or the Visitor

Centre at 478-9414 for more information on programs. Call 474-1336 to reserve the Group Campsite, accessible from the Parks Headquarters access road, 2930 Trans Canada Highway.

In the late fall crowds gather along the whole stretch of Goldstream River to watch the returning salmon spawn. Please avoid the Upper Goldstream Trail in the Campground area during spawning season. The coho and chinook that spawn in the upper reaches are returning in such low numbers that human intrusion must be avoided. It is critical that pets be kept on leash and under control at all times and that they never enter the water.

The trail from the parking lot to the Visitor Centre, a loop trail along the river, the Visitor Centre itself and the toilets at both the Picnic Area and the Visitor Centre are all wheelchair accessible.

The trails in the park are suitable for hiking year round. Some were constructed by the BC Provincial Parks Branch. The Outdoor Club of Victoria built the Arbutus Ridge, Gold Mine, Prospectors and Riverside Trails, and maintains them with periodic volunteer work parties. An Environment Youth Corp crew, with support from Pacific Coast Savings Credit Union and the Ministry of Environment's Youth Corp program upgraded the Prospectors Trail in 1990. The South Vancouver Island Rangers, a search and rescue group, built the Mount Finlayson Trails. For many years **Mount Finlayson** was private property but open to the public. Finally, in 1994, it was added to Goldstream Park as part of the Commonwealth Nature Legacy. **Take this mountain seriously**: people have lost their lives on Mount Finlayson. The trail is steep and rugged, not suitable for pets or small children. Do not push the limits of daylight. The old trail up the south side of the mountain is still in use, but you are encouraged to descend by the newer trail on the north side, to connect either with the trail north to Gowlland Tod Park, or to circle back along the base of the hill to your starting point. Because planning, construction and signing of these trails is in progress as we go to press, please pay attention to the maps and signs posted in the park, or contact BC Parks for current information. **Skirt Mountain**, south of Mount Finlayson and outside the provincial park, has several mining claims and mine workings, It is not advisable to hike here with pets or small children.

MAP 17: GOLDSTREAM PROVINCIAL PARK, MOUNT FINLAYSON

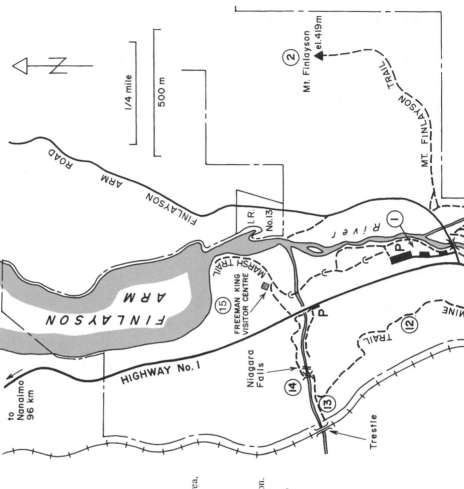

① Main picnic and parking area.

② Mount Finlayson trails are being developed.

③ Prospectors' holes for copper. Good viewpoint.

④ A trail **underpasses** the bridge from this parking area, linking with the Riverside and other trails.

⑤ Campground Meeting Place—for nature talks.

⑥ Goldstream Falls—final barrier for spawning salmon.

⑦ In summer the parking area at campsite #40 is only accessible to campers.

⑧ Hidden Spring Falls.

⑨ Hidden Spring.

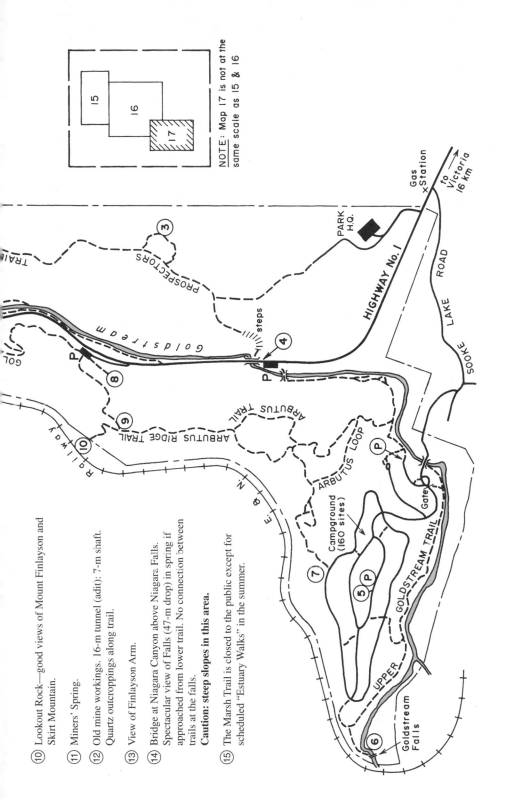

NOTE: Map 17 is not at the same scale as 15 & 16

⑩ Lookout Rock—good views of Mount Finlayson and Skirt Mountain.

⑪ Miners' Spring.

⑫ Old mine workings. 16-m tunnel (adit): 7-m shaft. Quartz outcroppings along trail.

⑬ View of Finlayson Arm.

⑭ Bridge at Niagara Canyon above Niagara Falls. Spectacular view of Falls (47-m drop) in spring if approached from lower trail. No connection between trails at the falls. **Caution: steep slopes in this area.**

⑮ The Marsh Trail is closed to the public except for scheduled "Estuary Walks" in the summer.

LONE TREE HILL REGIONAL PARK (MAPS 16 and 18)

From Highway 1 (Trans-Canada Highway) turn north onto Millstream Road. After 5.5 km take the left fork (signposted to the park) and continue on Millstream Road; it's another 3 km to the park. Not wheelchair accessible.

The steep, rocky trail climbs steadily up to an excellent view of the Malahat, the Gowlland Range, Victoria and the Olympic Mountains. While admiring the views, watch for Bald Eagles, Red-tailed Hawks, and Turkey Vultures. The open slopes invite one to descend over them, but please resist this temptation as the 31-ha park's ecology is very delicate. You will feel as though you are in the middle of nowhere, but actually you are subject to several restrictions: there are no bridle or bike trails and all dogs must be on a leash in this CRD nature appreciation park. Note that there is no trail connection to Hazlitt Creek Park. Lone Tree Hill became a regional park in 1982.

MAP 18: LONE TREE HILL REGIONAL PARK

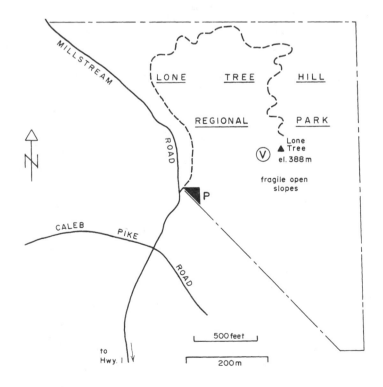

On Lone Tree Hill, time is marked, not in human generations, but by the longer cycles of natural regeneration. Climbing the hill in 1997, you find a young arbutus as the new lone tree marking the summit. Going back one human generation in time, the lone tree before that was a gnarled Douglas-fir that went from being a heritage tree to being a wildlife tree to being a heap of rotting wood. The eponymous lone tree before that was a fir struck by lightning. And the one before that....

MOUNT WORK REGIONAL PARK (MAP 19)

From Victoria, access to the park (now 536 ha) is by Highway 17 - West Saanich Road (17A) - Wallace Drive and Willis Point Road, about 45 minutes by car. Signposted parking lots give access to trails to all areas of the park - note lock-up times: Mount Work (2 gates) and Durrance Lake: open sunrise to 9 pm, April to September, sunrise to sunset, September to April. Mount Work became a regional park in 1970. No camping or fires are allowed in the park, and horses and bicycles are not permitted.

From the parking lot opposite the head of the McKenzie Bight trail to the top of Mount Work allow one hour. It is fairly steep in parts with open hiking areas and beautiful views. At the first lookout take time for views of Central Saanich and the islands in Haro Strait. From the summit overlook there are pleasant views over to Finlayson Arm and the Malahat. This is a good place to look out for Turkey Vultures soaring as they migrate in small flocks. In the Mount Work area hikers are advised to stay on the trails as in foggy weather it is easy to become disoriented.

If you are near the summit of Mount Work and are wondering about that shrub that resembles an arbutus tree, it's hairy manzanita, a close relative.

MAP 19: MOUNT WORK REGIONAL PARK AND ENVIRONS

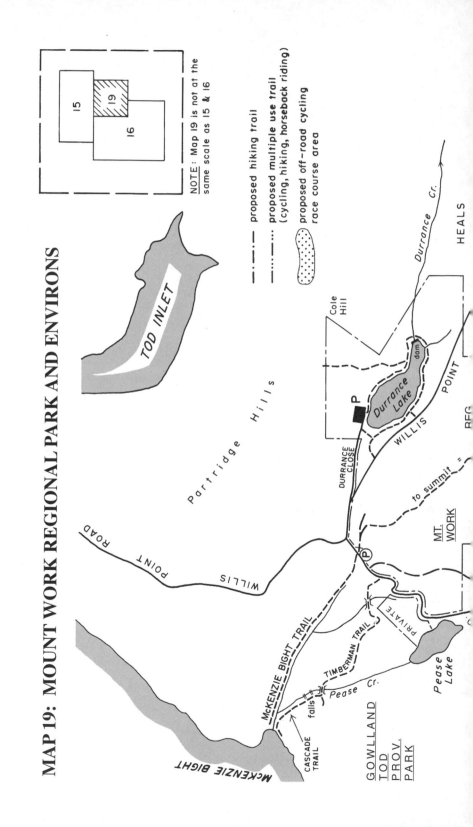

NOTE: Map 19 is not at the same scale as 15 & 16

15   19   16

—·—·— proposed hiking trail

—··—··— proposed multiple use trail
(cycling, hiking, horseback riding)

⋯⋯ proposed off-road cycling
race course area

TOD INLET

Partridge Hills

Cole
Hill

Durrance Cr.

HEALS

dam

Durrance
Lake

P

DURRANCE
CLOSE

WILLIS   POINT

BEG

to summit

MT.
WORK

WILLIS   POINT   ROAD

McKENZIE BIGHT TRAIL

TIMBERMAN TRAIL

PRIVATE

Pease Cr.

falls

Pease
Lake

CASCADE
TRAIL

McKENZIE BIGHT

GOWLLAND
TOD
PROV.
PARK

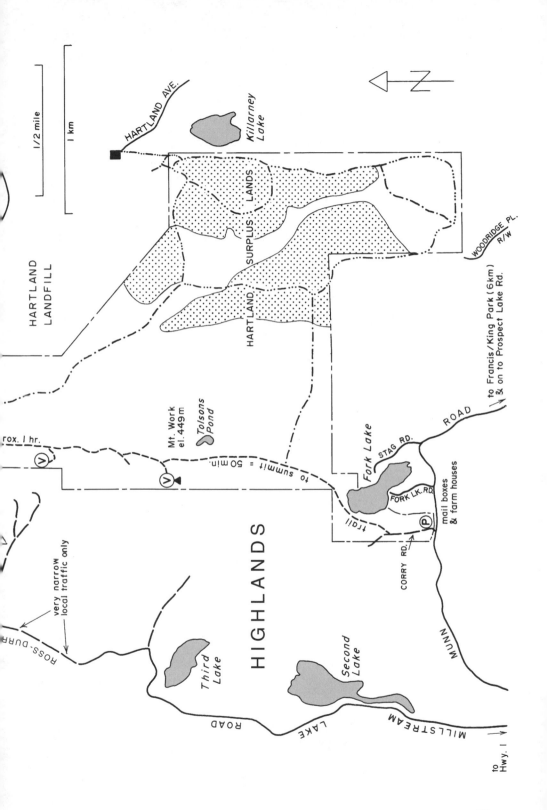

The clusters of pink or white flowers turn into dark berries in the fall. Manzanita appears in our cover photo, left foreground.

Evidence of glacial action is all around you in this area. Mount Work is a monadnock, or residual hill, whose hard rock - Wark gneiss - survived the grinding action, and Finlayson Arm is a glacial fjord. Nearby, as you descend along the McKenzie Bight Trail in Gowlland Tod Provincial Park, look for clay and gravel deposited in layers.

At the south end of the park, the **Corry Road trailhead** is signposted at the small parking lot on Munn Road. This can be accessed by either Prospect Lake Road and Munn Road, about 6 km beyond Francis/King Regional Park on a winding road; or from Highway 1 - Millstream Road - Millstream Lake Road - Munn Road. From the Munn Road parking lot to the top of Mount Work allow 50 minutes - good views along the way. Shortly after leaving the parking lot you will come to a fork in the trail. Keep right here to climb Mount Work; a left turn would lead you along old Corry Road and onto private land.

Durrance Lake is a good place to swim and a pretty trail follows around its shoreline. Dogs are prohibited June 1 to September 15 from the Durrance Lake parking lot to the dam. The toilet at Durrance Lake is wheelchair accessible. Durrance Lake is also your access point to the **Partridge Hills trails in Gowlland Tod Provincial Park** (see page 70).

The former **Hartland Landfill - Surplus Lands** are now part of Mount Work Regional Park, but no development has been done as of 1997, and this area is not yet open to the public. In a recent shifting of local boundaries, the Surplus Lands were transferred to the municipality of Saanich. Over time, recreationists have beaten a path from the end of Woodridge Place through to the Surplus Lands. This unofficial trail deviates from the unopened road right-of-way and trespasses on private land. Similarly, at Eagles Lake, people have been trespassing through private property to connect with the powerlines. **Eagles Lake Park** takes in only 0.8 ha, near the beach. Surrounding lands are private. So are the BC Hydro rights-of-way in the Highlands.

In 1842, James Douglas recorded the name as "Sanetch," his interpretation of the local pronunciation. In interviews with late Saanich elders, Dr. Thom Hess of the University of Victoria was able to determine that the suffix "-nutch" refers to a "behind," and that the peninsula was named for its appearance from across Saanich Inlet. The next time you stop at the Malahat lookout, imagine the Saanich Peninsula as a recumbent giant, sleeping face down, with his behind sticking up. Betty Bell, in *The fair land, Saanich*, offers some other possibilities (see page 58).

As of 1997, Saanich has 129 municipal parks distributed through its 107 square km. We can not describe every one for you, but you can pick up a copy of a colour brochure entitled "Saanich Parks and Recreation - Map & Guide". The 28-page Saanich "Trail Guide", which came out in 1994, is still available and will be updated and expanded when funding permits.

> **Corporation of the District of Saanich**
> Parks and Recreation Department
> 770 Vernon Ave., Victoria, BC   V8X 2W7
> phone 475-5422

We'll cover the major parks and throw in a smattering of the more interesting short hikes, just to get you started. As you travel around Saanich, look for trail markers: posts painted with a figure of a hiker. By connecting these trails with local parks and roadways much longer outings are possible. By permission of private property owners, the editor has led a 12-km jaunt, as follows: leave the south parking lot of Elk/Beaver Lake Park onto Pipeline Road; down a private trail from Goyette Road to West Saanich Road; up Markham and through Quick's Bottom; through Layritz and Glendale properties out to Interurban Road at Viaduct Ave. West; (detour via the Elk Road trail to Quayle Road and the Horticulture Centre for a rest stop); up the Green Mountain trail to Quayle and Mountain Roads; along a private trail to Excelsior and Goward Roads; (here you could could short-cut via Interurban Road/trail); from Goward Road to the back of Prospect Lake Park and School; parallel to West Saanich Road along Interurban Road to Observatory Road; up the steep trail to the Observatory for lunch with a view; by prior permission we cut across to Old West Road and Linnet Lane and took the connecting trail to the west side of Elk Lake; (we had permission also to descend to Old West Road and Doyle Road/Forest Hill Road to the other access trail but decided to cut our route short); finally, back to the south Beaver Lake parking lot.

STRAWBERRY KNOLL (MAP 20)

Access is from the northern, dead end of the 4100-block Holland Avenue. Park off the road just beyond the park sign and climb to the top of Strawberry Knoll for a view over the "First Trestle" flats. The names, First, Second and Third Trestle refer to earlier landmarks from the time when the name "Interurban" referred to the British Columbia Electric Railway line that ran from Victoria out to Tod Inlet (and the cement works near the present-day Butchart Gardens) and Deep Cove (then called Deep Bay). The line only operated from 1913 to 1924, but the railbed remains, partly as road (Interurban Road and Wallace Drive), and partly as a trail roughly parallel to Interurban and West Saanich Roads (see Maps 20 and 15 and page 65, Tod Inlet.) The flooded farmlands here, at Panama Flats to the south, and at Interurban Flats to the north (Third Trestle) have long been favored spots for outdoor skating in winter. (Don't risk accidentally "skating" on this section of Holland Avenue: this narrow, twisting country lane is to be avoided during icy weather.) In a contrast of seasons, this grassy Garry oak meadowland would make an idyllic spot for a summer picnic, but be careful of fire when the grass is dry.

LOGAN PARK (MAP 20)

From Victoria, head north on Interurban Road. A short distance past the Camosun College campus turn left on Viaduct Avenue West. This narrow roller-coaster road leads you up to 6-ha Logan Park. Take along your naturalist's guidebooks for a self-guided tour of the forest and swampy areas. The trail from the back of the park out to Hector Road gives access to country roads for longer rambles.

If you are exploring this area on foot, look for the path that follows the Green Mountain Road right-of-way west to Spring, Quayle and Mountain Roads. It is just north of the Interurban Road/Viaduct Avenue West intersection (just up from the bridge). The trail bridge crosses a tributary stream of the Colquitz River, a stream that was still salmon-bearing in the early '60s. On the opposite side of Interurban Road, the signposted Elk Road right-of-way trail brings you out onto Quayle Road, not far from the entrance to the **Horticulture Centre of the Pacific** (505 Quayle Road, at the corner of Beaver Road.) The Centre is open to the public every day from dawn to dusk. Office hours are 8:30 am - 4 pm, Monday to Friday; phone 479-6162. There is a small admission charge.

From the west end of Viaduct Avenue West you can walk along the road right-of-way to Prospect Lake Road, (near little Mud Lake and Maltby Lake), and from there north to **South Prospect Lake Park** (just past the golf course) for a swim or a picnic. If you turn south instead, you can visit lovely **Trevlac Pond**. This 9-ha naturalist' s delight was purchased as parkland from Gilbert William (Giff) Calvert, who continued to live on the property until he died in 1997. From Viaduct Avenue head south to pass the house and pond at 4373 Prospect Lake Road. Turn in at the wooden barrier by the Saanich Fire Dept. sign and follow the dirt road down to the pond. Here you can either head right, up the hill to a picnic bench overlooking the pond, or you can go straight ahead to circle half way round the pond before returning the way you came. Please respect the privacy of nearby property owners and the area closest to the Calvert residence. As for the nesting Redwing Blackbirds, they'll just ignore you.

GLENDALE LANDS (MAP 20)

The Glendale Lands are bounded approximately by Interurban Road to the west; Quayle Road and the Viaduct Ave. West road right-of-way to the north; and Markham Road, Layritz Park and the Provincial Jail land to the east and south. This large parcel includes the Horticulture Centre of the Pacific, Camosun College's Interurban Campus, and the former Glendale Lodge and Tillicum Lodge facilities. On our map we show

MAP 20: SAANICH (west)

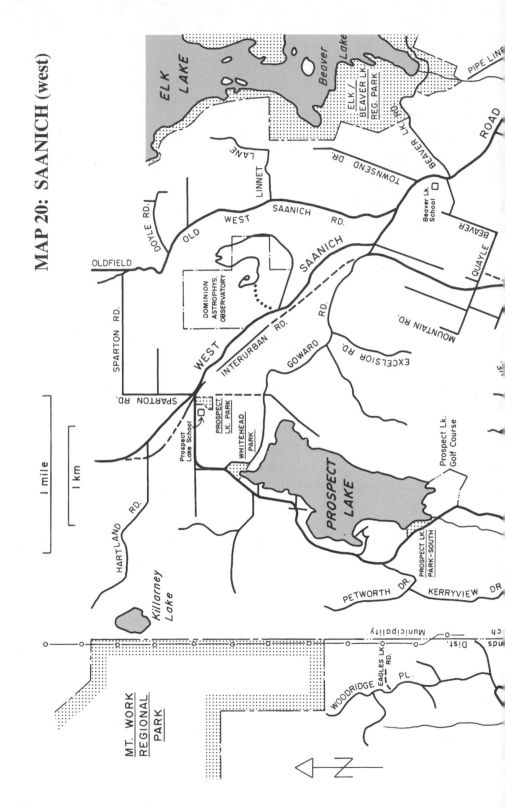

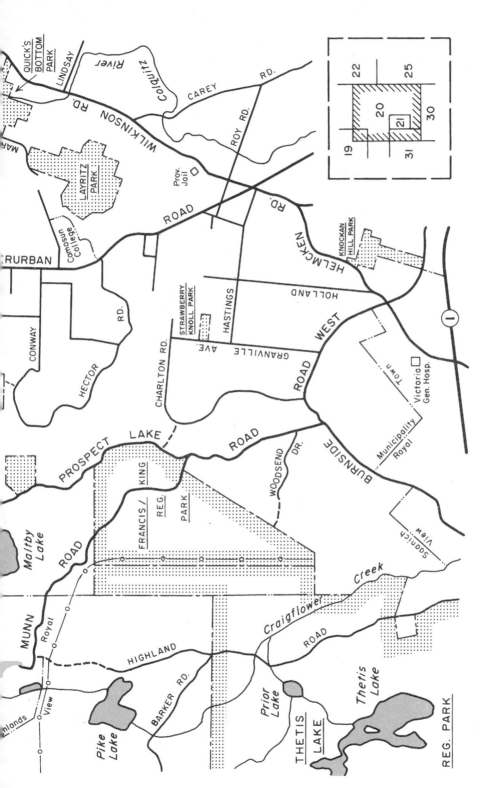

89

only those portions zoned for recreation and open space (11.7 ha of fields and hedgerows), and for natural park (11 ha surrounding the treed knoll), to be added to **Layritz Park**. At present there is a rough road leading from the back of the Camosun College campus up to the tele-communication tower on The Hill, and numerous informal trails. Public access will be formalized later.

FRANCIS / KING REGIONAL PARK (MAPS 20 and 21)

This park is bounded approximately by Prospect Lake Road, to the east, and adjoining Thetis Lake Park, on the west, along the power lines. Access: 1) from Victoria about 7 km NW via Burnside Road West, Prospect Lake Road and Munn Road; 2) follow Prospect Lake Road (caution: narrow and winding) about 6 km generally south from its intersection with West Saanich Road just north of the Dominion Astrophysical Observatory, then right onto Munn Road (see map 20). The gated parking lot is open 8 am - 9 pm, April to October; 8 am - 5 pm, October to April.

Francis Park (43 ha) was donated by the late Thomas S. (Tommy) Francis in 1960 and to this has been added Freeman King Park (20 ha) named in honour of a local naturalist, the late "Skipper" Freeman King, which together with other acquisitions brings the present total to 113 ha.

Within this area can be found a great variety of terrain - rain forest, rocky ledges, woodland meadows and swamp. Trails were cut by members of the Junior Natural History Society under the leadership of Freeman King. Over the years these have been modified and renamed and are well signposted. Most of the trails lead back to the Nature House, where naturalist programs are frequently offered. In 1993, local birders were able to watch a pair of Western Tanagers raising a family in a nearby tree.

An important feature of Francis/King Regional Park is the boardwalk named for Elsie King, wife of Freeman King. This was specially constructed in 1981 so that park visitors using wheelchairs may also enjoy the park. It is complete with its own picnic table and shelter.

Caution: the wooden boardwalk can be slippery when wet. There is a special washroom facility for the disabled behind the Nature House.

This is a Nature Appreciation Park, so all dogs must be on leash. No horses or vehicles (including bicycles) are allowed on the trails, but there is a bridle trail alongside Munn Road. The trail connecting Prospect Lake Road (just north of Oak Meadows Stables) with Charlton Road further extends the possibilities for equestrians and hikers alike. The dedicated access strip from the end of Woodsend Drive goes through swampland, so access here is currently on hold.

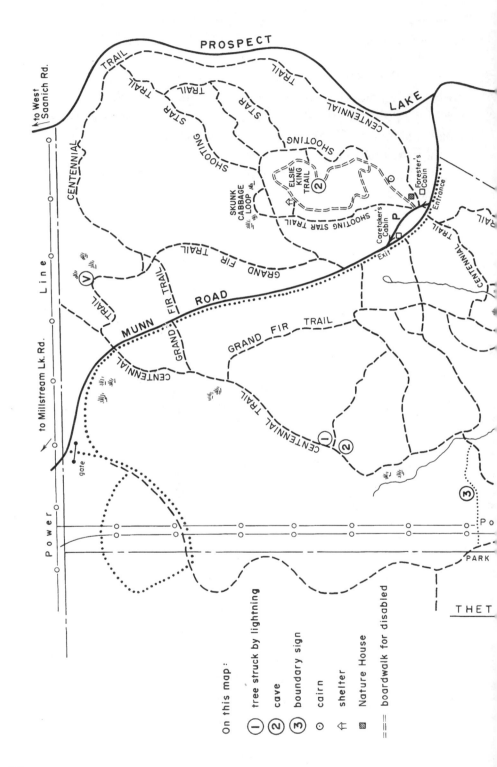

On this map:

1. tree struck by lightning
2. cave
3. boundary sign
⊙ cairn
⛺ shelter
▨ Nature House
=== boardwalk for disabled

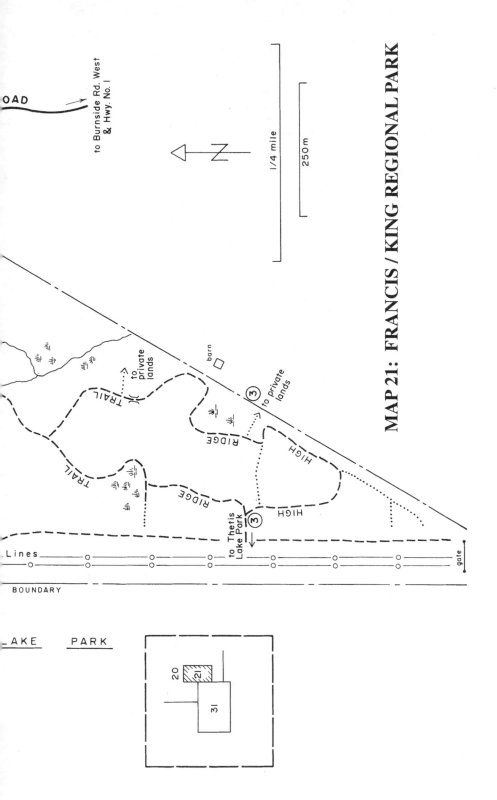

MAP 21: FRANCIS / KING REGIONAL PARK

to Burnside Rd. West
& Hwy. No. 1

OAD

N

1/4 mile

250 m

barn

to private
lands

TRAIL

to private
lands

③

RIDGE

HIGH

TRAIL

RIDGE

to Thetis
Lake Park

③

HIGH

Lines

BOUNDARY

gate

LAKE   PARK

20

21

31

93

BEAR HILL REGIONAL PARK (MAP 22)

To reach Bear Hill, travel north from Victoria on the Pat Bay Highway (#17) for about 14 km; turn left at the traffic light at Sayward Road. Turn left on Hamsterly then immediately right on Brookleigh Road. You now have a choice of access points, with the third being the main access. 1) You can watch for the trail to your right opposite house #541; 2) Continue on past the boat launch and turn right on Bear Hill Road. There is limited parking on the side of the road. Look for the right-of-way beside house #5905; 3) Continue on Brookleigh Road to the T-intersection at Oldfield Road. Turn right on Oldfield, then right on Bear Hill Road. There is room for 3 or 4 vehicles to park near the portal sign, the "front door" to the park.

Trails in the park are steep, rocky and sometimes slippery. They are definitely not wheelchair accessible. There are no facilities in this park, which was first acquired in 1970 and now encompasses 49 ha after further acquisitions in 1993 and 1994.

Bear Hill is a monadnock, a residual hill left behind by the glaciers about 15,000 years ago. Here the ice was perhaps 1,000 metres thick. Now the evidence of its passing is seen in grooves and scratches called striations. On your visit, be sure to climb every knoll and summit in order to catch every one of the views possible to all points on the compass. As you make the 30-minute climb, observe how the forest changes from Douglas-fir to arbutus, then to dry open grass balds and Garry oak meadows. Spring wildflowers include satin flower in March, followed by blue camas, sea-blush and canary violet. The denser woods area is a good place to look for birds such as Varied Thrush and Towhee.

ELK / BEAVER LAKE REGIONAL PARK (north) (MAP 22)

Access as above via Highway 17, Sayward Road and Hamsterly Road to Brookleigh Road. Look for the Hamsterly Beach parking lot as soon as you turn onto Brookleigh. There is a beach access at Hamsterly Beach specially designed for those with disabilities; toilets here are wheelchair accessible.

To get to the new fishing float (wheelchair accessible), continue on Brookleigh Road to Bear Hill Road and turn left. The wheelchair-accessible toilet here is open year-round.

ELK / BEAVER LAKE REGIONAL PARK (south) (MAP 22)

For access to the south end of the park, follow the Pat Bay Highway (#17) north for 12 km. Take the Royal Oak Drive exit, turn left onto Royal Oak Drive to cross the highway, then take the first right turn onto Elk Lake Drive at the traffic light. The park entrance is a half-kilometre beyond. The 7 park gates around the park are open sunrise to sunset.

This 411-ha park receives close to a million visitors a year. It's a multi-use park enjoyed by boaters, cyclists, equestrians, dog-trainers, swimmers and hikers - and Canada Geese! Horse trails are clearly identified with grey horse-and-rider symbols. A walk around Elk/Beaver Lake is about 9 km. Currently, the old V & S line on the west side of the lakes and the trail in from Pipeline Road are the only sections of the park where cycling is permitted. Future plans may include a multiple-use trail circuit; call CRD Parks for an update.

The Colquitz River was dammed in the late 1800s to create Victoria's first water reservoir. Filter beds were constructed in 1896 at the south end of Beaver Lake: Victoria residents were complaining that fish and tadpoles were flowing from household taps. When Victoria changed to Sooke for its water supply in 1914, the filter beds were abandoned. Though they've been filled in for years, many locals can remember playing in the abandoned cement structures as children. Elk/Beaver Lake Park was created in 1923 by the City of Victoria; in 1967 it became a regional park.

On the west side of the lake the trail often follows the bed of the old Victoria and Sidney (V & S) railroad. Opened in 1894, the rail route ran from Victoria through Royal Oak, Keating, Saanichton and on to Sidney. In its peak year, 1913, it carried 123,599 passengers and 45,282 tons of freight. Steam-driven and fired by wood, the V & S was nicknamed the "Cordwood Limited". As you walk the open, flat grade of the old rail line, try to imagine what life was like on that day in April, 1919, when

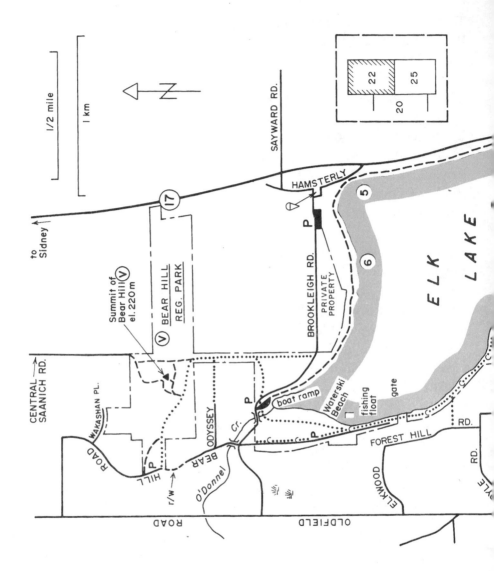

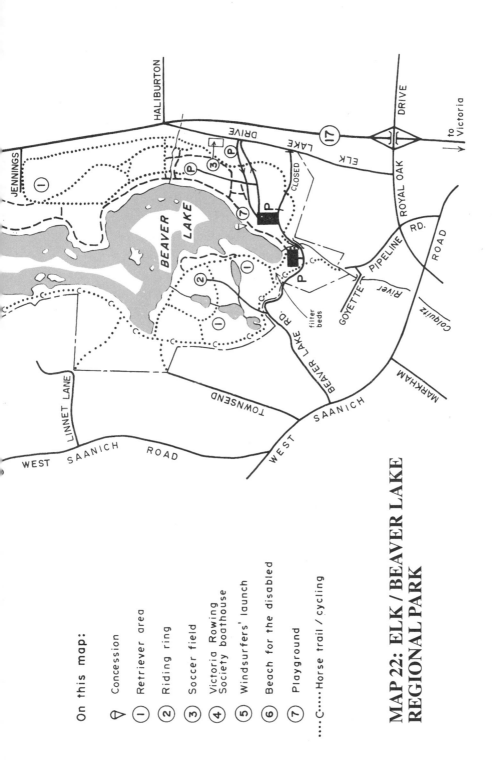

On this map:

▽ Concession
① Retriever area
② Riding ring
③ Soccer field
④ Victoria Rowing Society boathouse
⑤ Windsurfers' launch
⑥ Beach for the disabled
⑦ Playground
····· C····· Horse trail / cycling

MAP 22: ELK / BEAVER LAKE REGIONAL PARK

Old No.1came steaming around the next curve on its last run, with a first class coach, combination baggage-smoker coach and flatcars in tow.

Designated parking areas and wheelchair-accessible toilet buildings are located at Hamsterly beach, the filter beds, at the new fishing float (NW corner of Elk Lake) and near the main parking lot at Beaver Beach.

The walk from Beaver Lake to Eagle Beach is one of the best places near Victoria for spotting cascara trees. On the opposite (west) side of the lake, look for scat evidence of river otters. The lakes are stocked, and hold bass, rainbow and cutthroat trout. There are more freshwater fishing days here than at any other place on Vancouver Island.

The original Saanich name for Elk Lake referred to the weed mats that drifted around the lake. This was thought to be the tangled hair of a monster whom you regarded at your peril.

The Victorienteers (see page 221) have produced a colour map of the Beaver Lake area; price: $5.00 to non-members.

LOCHSIDE TRAIL (MAPS 14, 23 and 26)

The old Canadian National Railway bed can be followed from the Inner Harbour in downtown Victoria (where a portion is now the Galloping Goose Regional Trail and Trans Canada Trail - see pages 149 and 220) to Bazan Bay near Sidney. A good road map is most useful, as north of McKenzie Avenue the right-of-way is mapped and sign-posted as "Lochside Drive"or "Lochside Trail". It is currently partly driveable road and partly usable only by hikers, bikers and horseback riders. It is a mix of pavement through residential areas, and gravel or dirt surface through farm lands, and can be a most pleasant and interesting hike. It will probably eventually be the main trail on the Saanich Peninsula, connecting with the Galloping Goose Trail (see page 112) as part of the Regional Trails System.

At present the Lochside Trail can be picked up in Saanich at McKenzie Avenue and Borden Street. Walk north through the Motor Vehicle

Licencing parking lot to Cedar Hill Cross Road and look for Lochside Drive continuing north. It currently deadends near Blenkinsop Lake so one must detour out to Blenkinsop Road and along to Lohbrunner Road East. Just how the trail will eventually connect around or across Blenkinsop Lake is currently a topic of lively debate. There is a good footpath along this section of Blenkinsop Road, providing access to **Mount Douglas Park** via the sign-posted Mercer Trail. The Lochside Trail is sign-posted at the corner of Lohbrunner Road East and Blenkinsop.

Once on the other side of the lake, from Lohbrunner Road one can proceed south on Lochside through farmland to the lake. Rare and uncommon breeding species of birds to look for include Pied-billed Grebe, Green-backed Heron and Wood Duck. Wintering waterfowl species include Eurasian Widgeon and Ring-necked Duck.

By its very nature, any old railway bed will tend to be flat and straight, so we offer you a variety of opportunities to step off the Lochside Trail as you make your way northward, including a climb to the top of the ridge and a descent to the ocean-front beach. When you leave **Blenkinsop Lake Park** and head north, you soon come to **Donwood Park**, which leads you to a dozen parks and trails in the Broadmead residential development (see below). After crossing Royal Oak Drive, follow paved Lochside Drive a short distance to **McMinn Park** on your right. Here you'll find tennis courts and playground equipment for the children, plus a grassy open area that marks where the McMinn family once had a showhorse training track. A map of the park is included in the Saanich Trail Guide. Just opposite McMinn Park is the entrance to **Grant Park**. This trail will test your leg muscles: it climbs to the top of Cordova Ridge. After leaving McMinn Park and continuing north, on pavement once more, look for **Doris Page Park** on your right. It leads you down to **Cordova Bay Park**, with playground equipment and an excellent beach access. After crossing Claremont Avenue, watch for Doumac Place on you left. It leads you into **Doumac Park**, a lushly wooded ravine. Lochside now comes out onto Cordova Bay Road at Mattick's Farm. Continuing north you will pass **Lochside Park**, with its sports fields, and then cross Sayward Road and Dooley Road (see Map 14). In 1996 Saanich received a $15,000 grant from the Provincial Capital Commission

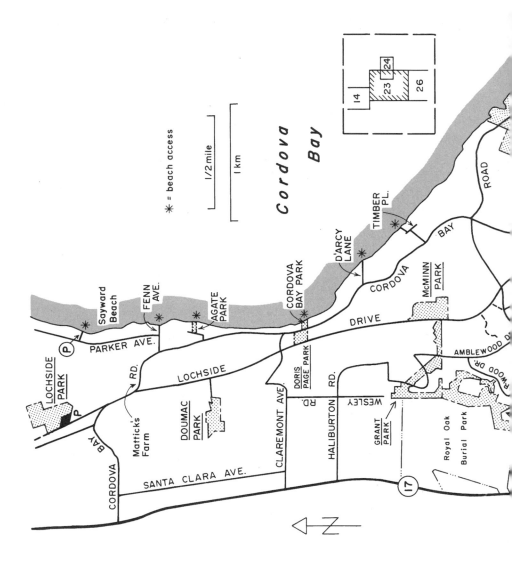

Cordova Bay

* = beach access

1/2 mile

1 km

14 | 23 | 24 | 26

Sayward Beach

FENN AVE.

AGATE PARK

CORDOVA BAY PARK

TIMBER PL.

D'ARCY LANE

CORDOVA BAY

McMINN PARK

DRIVE

PARKER AVE.

P

LOCHSIDE PARK

LOCHSIDE

DORIS PAGE PARK

RD.

AMBLEWOOD DR.

RWOOD DR.

ROAD

RD.

P

Mattick's Farm

DOUMAC PARK

CLAREMONT AVE.

HALIBURTON RD.

WESLEY

GRANT PARK

Royal Oak Burial Park

CORDOVA BAY

SANTA CLARA AVE.

17

N

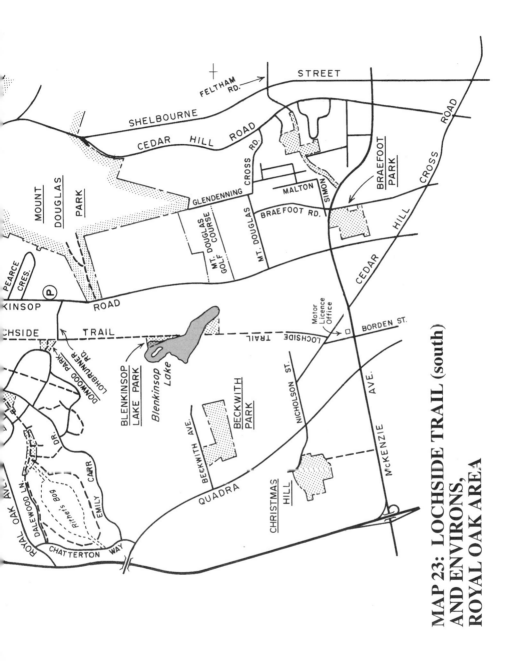

MAP 23: LOCHSIDE TRAIL (south) AND ENVIRONS, ROYAL OAK AREA

to widen and drain the trail from Lochside Park to Dooley Road for use by pedestrians, equestrians and cyclists. From this point on, the terrain is largely farmers' fields as you enter Central Saanich Municipality. North of Island View Road, plan a visit to the **Saanich Historical Artifacts Society** grounds (see pages 62-64) then detour around the East Saanich Indian Reserve by diverting west to follow the Highway 17 right-of-way (visible immediately west of Lochside Drive) to Mount Newton Cross Road, then pick up Lochside Drive again to proceed northwards. At Bazan Bay the old CN track swung west to Patricia Bay. You may continue north on Lochside as it follows the old Victoria and Sidney Railway bed to **Tulista Park** in Sidney (see page 39).

BROADMEAD / ROYAL OAK AREA (MAP 23)

One of the best places to enter the maze of Broadmead parks and trails is near the corner of Dalewood Lane and Chatterton Way. After a 4-km circuit around **Rithet's Bog**, follow the trail out through **Shadywood Park**, then on to **Emily Carr Park**, with play facilities for the children. The 42-ha Rithet's Bog was donated to Saanich in 1994 by the Guinness family of Britain, the brewers of Guinness stout. The gift of land preserves, as a municipal park and an ecological reserve, the last bog remaining of the half-dozen originally found on southern Vancouver Island and the Gulf Islands. The Guinness family developed the British Properties in West Vancouver (they financed the Lion's Gate Bridge in 1938) and, through Broadmead Farms Ltd., the Broadmead subdivision which was started in the 1960s. Much earlier, the land was a Hudson's Bay Company farm, named Dallas Farm, after Hudson's Bay Chief Factor Alexander Grant Dallas. In 1889, Robert Patterson Rithet (the wealthy businessman and one-time mayor of Victoria who built the Ogden Point wharves) purchased 1200 acres and changed the name to Broadmead Farm, after a favorite stallion. In the early days of movie production these hills were the backdrop for several westerns.

Grant Park (see page 103) is another good access point. When you have climbed to the top of the ridge, at the cement buildings, turning north (right) would lead you to the end of Wesley Road or to a short trail down to the end of Seamist Place. Turning south (left) takes you through a wooded area in the shadow of Boulderwood knoll. Ignore the first trail to your right; it takes you out into the developed area of the **Royal Oak Burial Park**. (Saanich has a letter of understanding with the cemetery board to allow public use of the trails where they cross cemetery property.) Also ignore the many little side paths to your left; they lead to private properties. When the path has taken you down almost into the first swampy area, watch for a medium-sized cedar tree with gnarled roots just to the left of the path. Turn left here and climb the bank; the trail straight ahead disappears into the swamp. As you make your way along the path, keep ignoring the left branches, and soon you will come to a second swampy area where, in February, the golden glow of skunk cabbages signals the advent of spring. Continuing on, when you can see that open ground lies beyond the forest, a right turn will bring you out from behind a laurel hedge into one of the older areas of the cemetery; here a left turn will take you on a path that climbs slightly to come out on Deventer Drive (off Falaise Crescent, off Royal Oak Drive). You could retrace your steps at this point, or opt for an alternate, circular route back. There is a path at the dead end of Deventer (east, to your left) that leads you through to Kentwood Terrace and Boulderwood Drive. Climb Boulderwood Drive to its summit and watch for the **Perez Park** tennis courts on your right. Directly opposite, between two houses, the trail marker shows the start of the **Boulderwood Park** loop. Climb the hill and turn right (north) to circle counter-clockwise. You will skirt a residential development at the top of Boulderwood knoll. The views to the east are fantastic, sweeping from Mount Tolmie and "Mount Doug" to the south, along the San Juan Islands to the east (with Mount Baker as a backdrop), and north to James Island with its distinctive high cutbank. Wooden stairs and a metal bridge make your progress easy, but the steepness of the surrounding terrain makes this loop unsuitable for small children and pets. To the north, your view is of wooded **Grant Park**, and here two trails lead down to Bramble Court (no room to park) and Westwood Place (limited parking in the turnaround). You could descend here and return to Grant Park via Amblewood Drive to complete a loop hike. If you decide to continue around to the west side of the knoll, you will again be rewarded with expansive views, this time north to Mount Tuam on Saltspring Island and Little Saanich Mountain (Observatory Hill) above Elk Lake, west to the Malahat and the Sooke Hills, and south to Albert Head and the Olympic Range. Straight ahead, to the west, the double-humped hill with the powerline scars is Scafe Hill, north of Thetis Lake Park; Mount Finlayson is the semi-bald dome beyond. Here you are on a higher terrace above the Grant Park-Royal Oak Burial Park trail described above. Leaving the viewscape behind and descending south through a wooded area, you will cross the access road to the Boulderwood development and return to the trail (opposite Perez Park) that you first climbed. The trail directly opposite, alongside Perez Park, leads you through to Perez Place and the Rithet's Hill reservoir.

With the exception of the newer Boulderwood and Rithet's Bog trails, the parks and trails of the Broadmead area are included in Saanich's 1994 Trail Guide.

BECKWITH PARK (MAP 23)

This park is worth a visit if you happen to be in the high Quadra area. From Victoria head north on Quadra Street. Just before Quadra joins Highway 17 turn right on Beckwith Avenue. The stone house on the corner is Manor House, built in 1908 for the Bull family, who ran a dairy farm in the area. A chip trail follows the perimeter of Beckwith Park and skirts two lovely ponds with Garry oak and lots of birds and other wildlife. A map of the park is included in the 1994 Saanich Trail Guide. Many of the heritage houses in Saanich are described in *Saanich Heritage Structures* by Jennifer Barr.

MOUNT DOUGLAS PARK (MAPS 23 and 24)

Mount Douglas was first known as the "hill of cedars" to the local Songhees people. Later, after these same people harvested lengthy cedar planks from its forests to construct the palisades around Fort Victoria, its title was formalized as "Cedar Hill". Still later, when Capt. G.H. Richards was standardizing the local geographic nomenclature, he called any rise under one thousand feet a hill, and any above, a mountain. He made an exception for Mount Douglas, as he did not wish to "lower" the Governor, and, as he explained, "Douglas Hill does not sound well..." Several of the trails in Mount Doug. Park are named after local pioneer families.

Peter Merriman, John Irvine and Sam Norn purchased Sections 55, 41, and 86, respectively, between April, 1857, and January, 1958. Nearby Cordova Bay was first known by its Saanich name, meaning "white colour", after the snowberry bushes that thrive along its coastline. In 1790, Sub-Lieutenant Quimper of the Spanish naval sloop *Princesa Real* (the seized British *Princess Royal)* gave the name "Puerto de Cordova" (in honour of the forty-sixth viceroy of New Spain) to what is now Esquimalt Harbour. Around 1842 the Hudson's Bay Company transferred the name to this bay. For many years British maps showed it as Cormorant Bay, but in 1905 the Geographic Board of Canada made the name Cordova Bay official.

This parkland was originally set aside in 1858 by Sir James Douglas (the creek and hill are now both named after him) as a Government Reserve, and has been protected as Crown Trust since 1889. In November 1992 it was transferred to Saanich Municipality. In its time it has received some notable visitors, including William Peel (son of Sir Robert Peel). Another, in 1845, was Captain (later Admiral) the Hon. John Gordon (brother of George, the then British Foreign Secretary, later Prime Minister), of HMS *America.* In spite of his sending back rather negative reports on this Cedar Hill area (after Roderick Finlayson took him on a hunting expedition), in addition to the headland, the entire Gordon Head residential area bears his name. The earliest settlers in the area were James Tod (son of the Hudson's Bay Company Chief Trader, John Tod) and his wife, Flora Macaulay. James bought the land in 1852, Flora joined him at "Spring Farm" as a bride in 1857, and their family farmed there for the next half-century. Ursula Jupp's *From Cordwood to Campus in Gordon Head, 1852-1959* chronicles the local history most ably: as Ursula Edwards, and later, Mrs. Jupp, she lived her life in Gordon Head.

The park is 8 km northeast of Victoria at the end of Shelbourne Street. Another 1.5 km up Churchill Drive brings you to the summit parking lot and to several very fine viewpoints. We can credit early Victoria mayor, Bert Todd, with the foresight to construct an "auto road" to the summit as a tourist attraction. Recent parkland purchases have included "Little Mount Doug" and increased the size of the park beyond its original 175 ha.

Excellent parking and picnicking facilities are to be found at:

① from where a trail leads down to the beach. Several trails are signposted from Cordova Bay Road from which you can plan some good hiking. The Irvine Trail leads up to a viewpoint over Cordova Bay.

② No parking is allowed along Cordova Bay Road here. Near the quarry find the Merriman Trail (signed) and follow it to the summit - well defined and easy hiking in the lower section, but somewhat steeper with a little scrambling near the summit.

③ The Norn Trail is well defined and provides easy walking on fairly level ground. It roughly parallels Cordova Bay Road passing through tall timber; other trails lead back to ① or ③.

④ There is very limited parking space for cars along Blenkinsop Road. Between houses #4351 and #4411 find the Mercer Trail (signed) and then pick up the Munson Trail which takes you to the old mine workings. You can then climb up over a rocky ridge with Garry oak and low bush and in spring time will find lovely flowers. Or go north from the mine on the Whittaker Trail and make side trips to excellent views.

⑤ Note the blowdown here caused by a typhoon in the mid-1950s (started in Guam).

⑥ and ⑦. Very limited car parking. The lower section of these trails offers pleasant walking through tall timber. The Summit Trail is steep and in places rocky.

No camping permitted. In the picnic area no horses are permitted at any time; dogs are allowed here from September to April only. Cycling is not permitted on any of the trails.

The **Friends of Mount Douglas** is a society formed to preserve the park in a natural state and to preserve the original park boundaries as set out by Sir James Douglas in 1889. Information is available c/o 4623 Cordova Bay Road, Victoria, BC, V8X 3V6; phone 658-5873. The Victorienteers (see page 221) have produced a coloured map of the park (scale 1:10,000); price: $5.00 to non-members. The Saanich Trail Guide map shows the main trails but does not label them.

ROAD

BLENKINSOP ROAD

PEARCE CRESC.

Little Mt. Dougla

Ⓟ

LOHBRUNNER

MUNSON

④

MERCER

BLENKINSOP ROAD

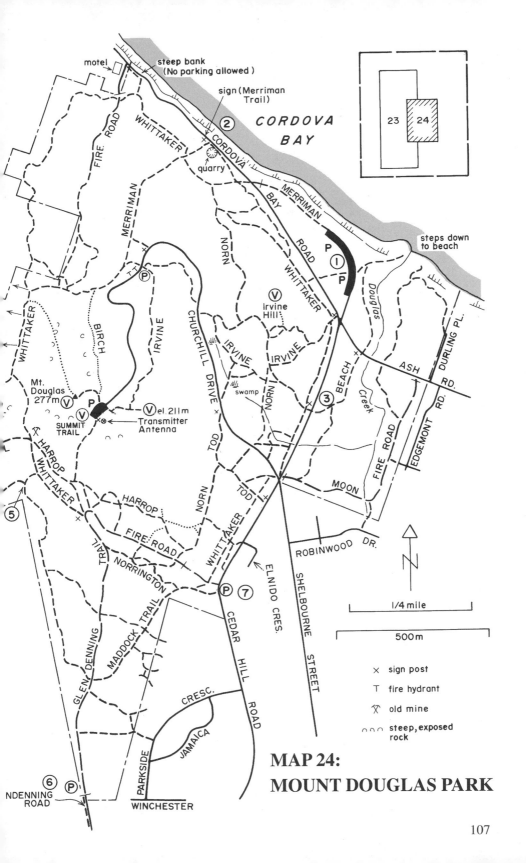

MAP 24:
MOUNT DOUGLAS PARK

COLQUITZ RIVER LINEAR PARK (MAP 25)

Saanich Municipality, with funding from the Provincial Capital Commission, plans to develop a park and trail system from Beaver Lake to Portage Inlet. Part of this has already been developed and elaborately landscaped. The rest will be completed as opportunity arises. It is currently possible to walk from Beaver Lake to Portage Inlet on trails, unopened road rights-of-way and some roads. The name Colquitz appears on a map made in 1855 by J.D. Pemberton, referring to the river and to a farm run by Henry N. Peers and his wife, Elise, née Yale. The river powered the farm's sawmill and gristmill, located near the present-day West Saanich Road. Several etymologies have been suggested, with the most likely being the onomatapoetic word for "baby crying", after the sound of the water tumbling between the riverbanks.

A good place to start your walk is at **Quick's Bottom**, a 15-ha wildlife sanctuary off Markham Street acquired as Saanich parkland in 1969. The Victoria Natural History Society has constructed a bird-watching blind at the southern end of the marsh near the Saanich municipal nursery. Take your time; more than one birder has added to a life list here. The "bottom" land, a depression remaining from the glacial age, is part of the original Quick family farm where William and Esther (née Carmichael) Quick (married 1909 in Cordova Bay) raised their family and tended the first herd of registered Jersey cattle on Vancouver Island. As you leave the park at Wilkinson Road, detour south a short distance to pick up a rough trail off Lindsay Street (hints: one trail begins under a grand fir ("balsam") tree beneath the street light, and another begins over three large, rough boulders.) Be prepared for thistles, blackberries and mud, even in summer. You must also cross a small creek before coming out to the Colquitz River and the trail coming in from **Brydon Park**. It is sometimes possible to cross the Colquitz River here on stepping-stones to join a good trail leading out to Mann Avenue (signposted). Or, use the Casa Linda trail. Once out onto Mann Avenue good trails lead to **Copley Memorial Park** or out to other streets. From Copley Park you can head east through **Moor Park** and along the industrial buffer strip out to Glanford Avenue. You'll be following **Old Joe's Trail**, named for Joseph Edwards, who died at Royal Oak in 1997 at the age of 94. It was Joe's retirement project to keep the trail tidy.

Heading south from Copley Park, cross Carey Road and follow Grange Road to Roy Road. On the other side of Roy Road you are entering the Panama Flats area, so named by an early owner of this flood-prone area, an English man named McDonald who had been one of the engineers for the Panama Canal project. **Panama Hill**, a knoll at the north end of the flats, was acquired as part of the Commonwealth Nature Legacy in 1994. The 12.5 ha parcel to the north and south of Roy Road has since been added to the Colquitz River Linear Park. As of 1997, the stretch of trail from Roy Road south to **Hyacinth Park** has now been completed, making for a "high and dry" traverse of what earlier could be a muddy or impassable section. From Hyacinth Park you can head south to the Tillicum Mall and **Cuthbert Holmes Park** on good trails, most of them wheelchair accessible. This section of the trail parallels Interurban Road, originally the railbed for the BC Electric Railway's line out to Tod Inlet and Deep Cove. There are several access points off Interurban. On the other side of the trail, access is possible on a footbridge from Nora Place (off Rolston Crescent), or from the Pacific Forestry Centre (on Burnside Road). The Saanich Trail Guide includes a map (now out of date) of the Colquitz River Linear Trail.

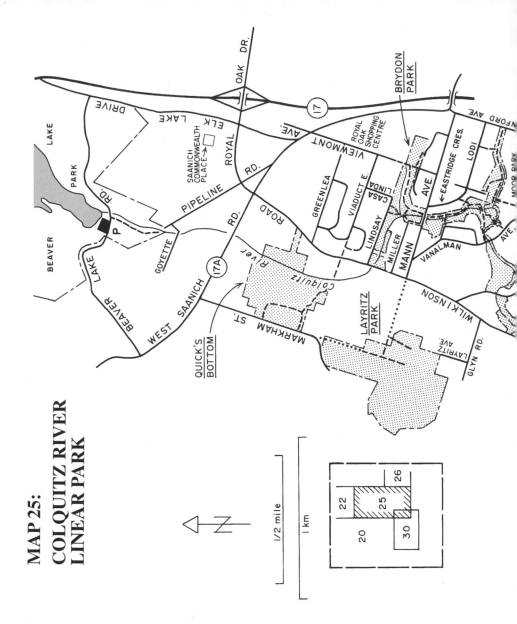

**MAP 25:
COLQUITZ RIVER
LINEAR PARK**

SWAN CREEK (MAPS 25 and 26)

From the **Colquitz River Park** at **Hyacinth Park** you can pick up a trail just off Marigold Road that will take you along Swan Creek all the way to the allotment gardens off Ralph Street. This does involve a short section along heavily travelled McKenzie Avenue, and you arrive to find that the Swan Lake Christmas Hill Nature Sanctuary is just on the other side of busy Douglas Street. The Saanich Trail Guide includes a map of the Swan Creek trails.

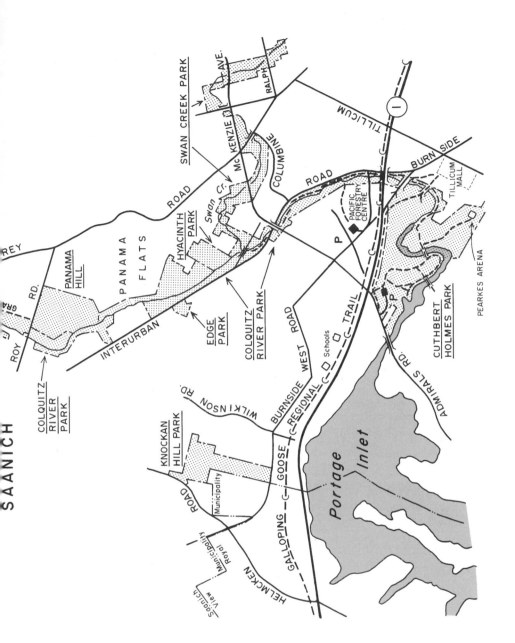

CUTHBERT HOLMES PARK (MAP 25)

Vehicle access is off Admirals Road near Highway 1; pedestrian access is off Dysart Road, from behind the Pearkes Arena, or from the south end of the Colquitz River Linear Park. Asphalt paths and chip trails offer ready access to this forested 27-ha nature park, home to 55 bird species including Great Blue Herons. The Saanich Trail Guide includes a map of Cuthbert Holmes Park and trails.

GALLOPING GOOSE REGIONAL TRAIL, Saanich Spur (MAP 26)

This paved section of the Galloping Goose Trail follows an old CNR line, the Saanich Spur, which was, in 1990, the last local section to be abandoned. It extends from Highway 1 and the Switch Bridge near the Town and Country Shopping Centre, past Swan Lake and out to Quadra Street. On the other side of Quadra, a section adjacent to Borden Mercantile is privately owned (Borden was the last freight customer to use the line, running grain cars from Point Ellice), but from there it continues out to McKenzie Avenue, where it continues northward as the **Lochside Trail** (see page 98). There is limited parking off Saanich Road just north of Lodge Ave. In 1995 the 30-m Brett Trestle and the 140-m Swan Trestle were rebuilt and a 1.15-km section of trail from Darwin Avenue (at the Saanich Municipal Hall) to Quadra Street was paved, with funds provided by The Provincial Capital Commission's Greenways Fund, the Heritage Trust, the provincial Highways ministry, Saanich Municipality and the CRD. Blenkinsop Creek runs roughly parallel to the Saanich Spur, but it often disappears under roads or shopping plazas. The Evening Optimists, in conjunction with the Swan Lake Nature Sanctuary, are working to restore the creek. A highly-detailed one-page map of the Saanich Spur is available from Saanich Parks and Recreation.

GALLOPING GOOSE REGIONAL TRAIL, Victoria - Saanich - View Royal Section (MAPS 28, 26 and 30)

This section of the Galloping Goose Regional Trail follows the old CNR right-of-way for 9.5 km, from Vic West, through Saanich (roughly paralleling the Trans-Canada Highway), and on to Atkins Road in View Royal. The wide paved route allows for cycling, skating and wheelchair use in addition to walking. Map 26 shows the new (1996) Switch Bridge over the Trans-Canada Highway (Highway 1) near the Town and Country Shopping Centre and the connection with the Saanich Spur of the Galloping Goose Trail. When the lines were in active use, this is where rail traffic was "switched" between tracks. The 106-m Switch Bridge, built with $1.1 million in provincial funds, was completed in July of 1996, and opened in a gala ceremony on September 21. Since July, 1993, these Saanich and View Royal sections of the old right-of-way have been leased from the Ministry of Transportation and Highways under a recreational lease which provides for bicycle and pedestrian use while preserving the route for future transportation needs, which may include light rail transit. Near the Switch Bridge there is limited parking at the east end of Crease Ave. By the end of 1997 there will be pedestrian/ cyclist bridges over Interurban and Wilkinson roads, incorporating material salvaged as the old Colwood overpass was dismantled to make way for the new highway into Victoria. A 65-m tunnel for pedestrians and cyclists is now open under Helmcken Road, and the trail will be paved to 400 m west of the Helmcken Interchange. Note the location of the new park-and-ride lot at the southwest corner of the interchange.

If you are travelling along the Galloping Goose from the Town and Country Shopping Centre in Saanich out to Atkins Road in View Royal, a two-block detour will take you past what is believed to be the narrowest house in Canada, at 233 Cadillac Avenue. Only three metres wide, it was built in 1992-93. (Two other very narrow houses are to be found on Centre Road, between Ridge and Fernwood roads, in Victoria's Fernwood area.) Turn right (north) on Harriet Road and then left (west) on Cadillac. A left again on Seaton or Tillicum Road will get you back onto the Galloping Goose. The Galloping Goose Regional Trail is more fully described on page 149.

KNOCKAN HILL PARK (MAP 25)

If, as above, you are travelling along the Galloping Goose Regional Trail between Saanich and View Royal, another interesting side trip can be made by turning up Wilkinson Road to Burnside Road and heading west a short distance to the entrance to Knockan Hill Park. You soon come across a stucco house from the thirties. Known as Stranton Lodge, and designed by Hubert Savage in the English Arts and Crafts Style, it is the former home of Thomas and Maude Hall, sold to Saanich in 1973 as an addition to the original 4 ha of hilltop park. Developed by the Halls, with help from Arthur Lahmer, the surrounding gardens were for many years a showpiece in the Portage Inlet area. The building and grounds have been designated a heritage site, and restoration is being undertaken by the Saanich Heritage Foundation. Past Stranton Lodge ("Hall Cottage") the trail climbs to an open rocky summit affording good views to the north and east. Access is also possible from the end of Mildred Street and off Helmcken Road near the intersection of Holland Avenue. Cycling is prohibited.

"Knockan" may be derived from a Songhees word "nga'k'un'," meaning "coiled up (like a rope)". Possibly it comes from the Gaelic "cnocan", meaning "small hill". The name was established by the time of Walter C. Grant's survey in 1852, and probably was chosen by Robert Anderson, a former HBC employee who owned "Loch End" farm, the property on which the hill is situated. Knockan and Knockanrock are two villages in the very southwest of Sutherland, Scotland. In a personal aside, VITIS member Ron Weir notes, "In 1887 the federal government planned to purchase the Weir farm at Metchosin for an Indian Reserve. Had the deal gone through, it had been great-grandfather's intention to purchase "Loch End", in fact he was living there in January 1888."

The **Friends of Knockan Hill Park Society** was formed in 1990 to preserve the flora and fauna and the natural character of the park. For information or a detailed descriptive brochure contact the society c/o 81 High Street, Victoria, BC V8Z 5C8. The Saanich Trail Guide includes a map of the Knockan Hill trails.

GORGE WATERWAY PARK and GORGE PARK (MAP 29)

Gorge Waterway Park is bounded by Admirals Road, Gorge Road West, Tillicum Road and The Gorge Waters themselves, but there are no bounds to the number of smiles you'll meet from people of all ages as you make your way along the asphalt path. From babies in buggies to seniors with walkers, everyone enjoys the Gorge Waterway. You could combine your walk with a visit to the **Craigflower Farmhouse and School**, two historical sites nearby on Admirals Road. Craigflower Farm, established in 1853, was the largest of four farms managed by the Puget's Sound Agricultural Company (a division of the Hudson's Bay Company) to supply the HBC, the colonists, the Royal Navy and other customers. The name came from Craigflower Farm in England, owned by Andrew Colville, Governor of the HBC from 1852 to 1856. Craigflower School was built in 1854 and welcomed its first pupils in 1855.

The Admirals Road bridge here is a hotspot for herring in season. Less well known is **Gorge Park**, bounded by Tillicum Road, Gorge Road West, the foot of Millgrove and the waters of The Gorge. This stretch of water, known then as Victoria Arm, was first bridged in 1848 by a crude but workable affair consisting of five large logs spanning the narrows on the road from Fort Victoria to the mill at Rowe's Stream (see pages 147-149, View Royal area). Just across the modern version of the Gorge Bridge (via Tillicum Road) is **Kinsmen Gorge Park** in Esquimalt. Under the bridge, you may observe the reversing falls as the tide changes. The waterway was earlier called "Camosack" or "Camosun" and gave its name to the site of the fur-trading post that would later become Victoria. "Camossung" was from the Songhees legend of a little girl who, along with her grandfather, was turned into a stone at the site of the falls. "Camosun" was proposed as the name of what was to be called the Empress Hotel; later it was chosen for Victoria's Camosun College. Over time, the Gorge waters became fouled with garbage, storm-drain runoff and sewer leakage. That trend has been turned around by John Roe and his son Wesley, with support from the Veins of Life Watershed Society. Their goal is to have the Gorge clean enough to swim in again by the year 2000. So far, 90 tonnes of garbage have been pulled out of the water, including 400 shopping carts.

SWAN LAKE and CHRISTMAS HILL (MAP 26)

These two natural areas are managed by the Swan Lake Christmas Hill Nature Sanctuary Society (3873 Swan Lake Road, Victoria, BC, V8X 3W1; phone 479-0211). Access to the main parking lot for the Nature House at Swan Lake, if heading east, is right off McKenzie Avenue, along Rainbow Street, Ralph Street and Swan Lake Road. If heading west, turn left onto Nelthorpe and right onto Sevenoaks to Rainbow. The Nature House (open weekdays 8:30 am-4 pm; weekends 12-4 pm) and the toilets are wheelchair-accessible, and the old parking lot near the Nature House is reserved for handicapped parking. Cycling is not permitted and no dogs are allowed in the Sanctuary.

The Swan Lake portion of the Sanctuary features a 10-ha lake, marshland, fields and thickets, with a wood chip trail encircling the lake. Floating boardwalks, birdblinds and wharves allow visitors to get close to nature and there is a native plant garden. The 10-ha portion on the top of Christmas Hill is reached by way of Nelthorpe Street and a sign-posted trail up from McKenzie Avenue. The Christmas Hill trails have been built to last but the surrounding area with its lichens, mosses, ferns and wildflowers remains fragile; please resist the temptation to wander off the trails. Once out on the rocky hilltop, you have unobstructed views in all directions. With the development of the property at the corner of McKenzie Avenue and Highway 17, a copse of Garry oaks has been dedicated as municipal parkland adjacent to the Nature Sanctuary lands.

Swan Lake is fed by Blenkinsop Lake, via Blenkinsop Creek, and drained by Swan Creek, which flows under Douglas Street and McKenzie Avenue to join Colquitz Creek near Hyacinth Park. Swan Creek and Lake are named after James Gilchrist Swan, an old-time ethnologist. The Saanich Trail Guide has a map of the Swan Lake trails.

BOW / FELTHAM / BRODICK PARKS (MAP 26)

On the east, these contiguous parks are accessed off their namesake streets or off Hopesmore Drive. To the west, access is off Simon Road, and on the south look for a walkway off McKenzie Avenue near the pedestrian overpass. When the decision was made not to push Feltham Road through to McKenzie Avenue, the land was preserved as parkland, a patch of wilderness surrounded by suburban development. **Braefoot Park**, with full park facilities, is just across the road from McKenzie Avenue access, and **Mount Douglas Park** to the north is readily accessible via Malton Avenue and the Glendenning trail. Heading east, if you follow Feltham Road and Torquay Drive (west section), you can enter **Lambrick Park** with its Recreation Centre and outdoor sports facilities. A loop trail encircles the entire park, with exits onto Feltham, Tyndall, Angola, La Fontaine and Torquay (north section). All of these parks and trails are shown in the Saanich Trail Guide. (See also Map 23, page 101.)

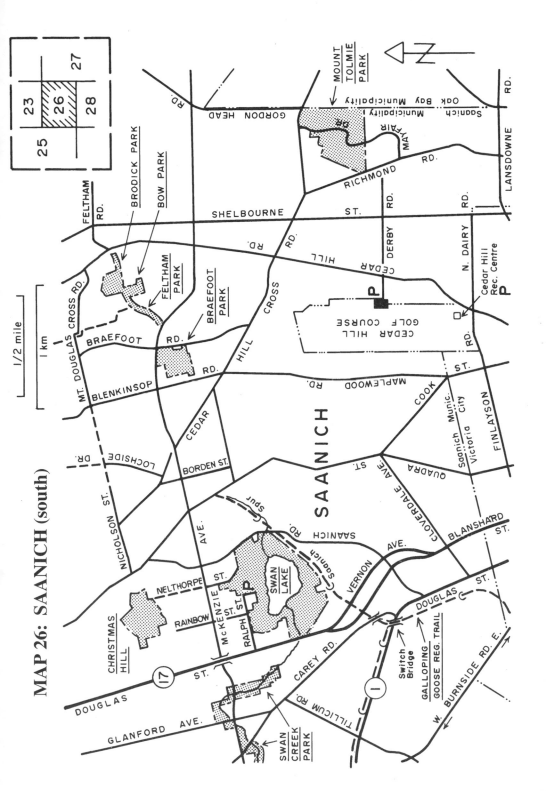

MAP 26: SAANICH (south)

117

CEDAR HILL GOLF COURSE TRAIL (MAP 26)

This walking/jogging trail is roughly in the shape of a figure eight. To begin in the middle, take Cedar Hill Road and Doncaster Drive to Derby Road and the clubhouse parking lot. A circuit of the southern loop or the northern loop would each be a little over 2 km, while once around the circumference would take you 3.5 km. There are a couple of gentle hills on the southern loop; the northern loop takes you past King's Pond with its abundant wildlife, including Red-winged Blackbirds and Virginia Rails. Count yourself lucky if you see or hear a Ring-necked Pheasant; this introduced species was once numerous but they are now increasingly rare. There are numerous benches from which to watch the golfing action. A good street map will show you other access points, including the Cedar Hill Community Recreation Centre. Improvements in 1995 included reclamation of an area stream that feeds into Bowker Creek, which winds its way through the Lansdowne area of Saanich and on through Oak Bay, where the creek banks have been landscaped. The Cedar Hill trails are included in the Saanich Trail Guide.

MOUNT TOLMIE (MAPS 26 and 27)

The University of Victoria grounds are a good setting-off point for hikes through Mount Tolmie Park (18.5 ha). Look on the map for the intersection of Gordon Head Road, Mayfair Drive and Cedar Hill Cross Road for just one place to start. The 360-degree view from the 125- m summit is worth every bit of effort! Cycling is banned from the park trails.

The mountain is named after Dr. William Fraser Tolmie, who arrived in Victoria as a doctor with the HBC. In 1850 he married Jane Work, eldest daughter of Chief Factor John Work and Josette Legace, his wife à la façon du Nord. Later Dr. Tolmie himself became chief factor in Victoria, 1856, and then a member of the Legislative Assembly of BC. Their son, Simon Fraser Tolmie, was "prime minister" (premier) of BC from1928 to 1933. A native perennial plant, Tolmiea menziesii (piggy-back plant or youth-on-age), is named after Dr. Tolmie, who was also a botanical collector, and for Archibald Menzies, the first European botanist on this coast. Dr. Tolmie also published (along with geologist G.M. Dawson) an early guide to the native languages of BC.

The Victorienteers (see page 221) have produced a colour map of the park (scale 1:5000); price: $5.00 to non-members. Saanich's Trail Guide also includes a map of the trails. In 1996, to celebrate "the first 70 years", the Mount Tolmie Conservancy Association (with the Saanich Parks and Recreation Department) produced a Mount Tolmie Park Map and Guide. This excellent brochure is absolutely packed with information on the human and natural history of the park (and Victoria), and includes a black-and-white version of the Orienteers map. It is available from Saanich Parks and Recreation or from the:

Mount Tolmie Conservancy Association
3503 Camcrest Place
Victoria, BC V8P 4V6

UNIVERSITY OF VICTORIA LANDS (MAP 27)

The UVic campus straddles the Saanich/Oak Bay municipal border. Surrounding the campus is a walking/jogging trail known as the "Chip Trip". A circuit will lead you through the University Gardens, which include an outstanding rhododendron collection, and a detour will take you across Cedar Hill Cross Road (take care when crossing!) to the **Henderson Recreation Centre** in Oak Bay (see page 122). A 4.6-ha parcel of land adjacent to the east side of the campus was acquired in 1993 to become an ecological protection area. This forested ravine, an idyllic spot still echoing with legends, is known as **Mystic Vale** and may be reached from Haro Road or the south end of Hobbs Street. As part of the negotiations to acquire Glencoe Cove Park, a three-way land swap involving Saanich, the province and the University of Victoria, a 1.46 ha parcel at the corner of Haro Road and Finnerty Road became part of the Commonwealth Nature Legacy. Known as **Haro Woods**, the property is wooded, with 100-year-old Douglas-fir trees, and will be protected and managed in part by the university.

The Victorienteers (see page 221) have produced a map of the university area (scale 1:7500); price $1.00 to non-members for a photocopy.

GLENCOE COVE PARK

This area, near Ferndale Road and Vantreight, is not shown on any of our maps. Main access to the park is off Gordon Point Drive, off Ferndale Road. A secondary access is at the north end of Shore Way (off Pauls Terrace, off Ferndale Road). Parking here is limited, with room for about 3 cars at the park entrance, and parking restrictions along Shore Way. In 1993, when the Moore family (through Stanrick Group Inc.) proposed development of their 15-ha parcel, a local group, the Friends of Glencoe Cove (phone 477-5177 or 721-0169), was formed in support of developing the property as a waterfront park. Worthwhile features of the area included: aboriginal burial cairns, shell middens, rare plants (including prickly pear), Garry oaks, a cormorant rookery and other animal and bird life plus two small, secluded beaches, a pocket cove, and the potential for a trail system. As of 1995, 2.1 ha have been preserved as municipal parkland under a 99-year lease (to 2094), in augmentation of the 3.31 ha already dedicated as parkland in the subdivision proposal. The balance of the property, including the waterfront above Margaret Bay, has been subdivided into residential lots, with sensitive areas covered by protective covenants. Ferndale Forest, on the east side of Vantreight Drive, is also part of Glencoe Cove Park. Vantreight Park, with playground facilities, is just across the road.

ARBUTUS COVE

Your starting point is the triangular intersection of Gordon Head Road, Arbutus Road and San Juan Avenue. One access point is in the 2200 block of Arbutus Road (observe the parking restrictions) where a signposted trail descends between neighbouring properties. Vehicular access is via Arbutus Cove Lane, off Gordon Head Road. A small parking area and paved paths make this part of the park accessible to wheelchair users. You'll find one picnic table and several benches along the bluff, from which to enjoy the view of the San Juan Islands (USA). Sixty-six steps descend from the bluff to the water. From here you can walk the beach around to Hollydene Park at the foot of Hollydene Place, off Arbutus Road. This loop would make a good little lunch-hour workout.

THE TEN MILE POINT AREA (MAP 27)

Saanich has provided many signposted walkways throughout the area for the convenience and pleasure of the residents. A good street map will point them out to you. As you explore, don't overlook these highlights: at the east end of the Arbutus Road loop look beside house #2809 for a path with rock retaining walls and a metal handrail. It leads to a wooden viewing platform on part of **Phyllis Park.** It's a great place to take a lunch. Nearby, beside house #2801, an emergency road (pedestrians only) leads you to the end of Phyllis Street and the start of a trail that leads down to great views out over the water (though, alas, no easy beach access). Don't overlook **Konukson Park**, on Sea Point Drive. Take your time to observe how the range of plant forms varies as you move from sun to shade and from dry to wet areas. Many native species, and some introduced ones, too, may be found here. Cadboro Point, just south of Ten Mile Point itself, is the actual location of 11-ha **Ten Mile Point Ecological Reserve #66** (see Hints and Cautions, page 15), so please respect the intertidal life in this area. Maynard Cove, named for Joseph Maynard, the earliest farmer in the area, is immediately north of Cadboro Point, at the foot of McAnally Road. Its local name, Smugglers Cove, is a reference to certain illegal activities during Prohibition times. From the intersection of Benson Road and Tudor Avenue, a trail leads to Cadboro View Road and beach access. The beach at Cadboro Bay itself is walkable from the foot of Telegraph Bay Road, through **Cadboro Gyro Park**, and on to the foot of Hibbens Close. All of these parks and trails are shown in the Saanich Trail Guide.

Cadboro Bay is named for the first ship to anchor there, HBC's brigantine *Cadboro*. The bay has given its name, in turn, to a legendary sea monster, Cadborosaurus, affectionately known as "Caddy", who is believed to inhabit the bay and other local waters including Saanich Inlet, reported to be its breeding ground. A retired marine biologist and cryptozoologist, Dr. Edward L. Bousfield, and an oceanographer, Paul H. LeBlond, have together published *Cadborosaurus: Survivor from the Deep*, a collection of scientific reports and data on sightings over the past century. In 1995 the search for Caddy was the subject of a segment on the popular television series *Unsolved Mysteries*.

⟨8⟩ OAK BAY AREA (MAP 27)   1996 census: 17,865

Even in established residential areas you can still find places to get off the pavement. Beginning at the northern border of the municipality at the **University of Victoria** lands (see page 119), the "Chip Trip" jogging path around the campus connects with the winding, woodsy trails of the **Henderson Recreation Centre.** (No dogs allowed.) Please take care in crossing Cedar Hill Cross Road! The University is also a good setting-off point for hikes up **Mount Tolmie** in Saanich (see page 118).

UPLANDS PARK AND SOUTH

The Victorienteers (see page 221) have produced a map of the trails (scale 1:3000); price $1.00 to non-members for a photo-copy. Bicycles are not permitted in Uplands Park; by local bylaw pets must be on leash from April 1 to June 30. The winding trails of the park itself, **Cattle Point**, and the walk south to the **Oak Bay Marina** (at Turkey Head) via **Willows Park** and **Haynes Park** provide great urban opportunities for birdwatching and for observing native flora. Spectacular views are possible from the Esplanade: Mount Baker, the Olympic Peninsula, and even Mount Rainier on a clear day. Mary Tod Islet Park is just offshore in Oak Bay. The islet is named for the second daughter of John Tod of the HBC. The islands further offshore are the Chatham Islands and Discovery Island. The Chathams and the northern half of Discovery are the private property of the Songhees Indian Band. To eliminate fire hazard and the dumping of garbage, the islands are closed to the general public, and are so posted. The southern half of Discovery is Discovery Island Provincial Marine Park. When Captain George Vancouver explored these waters in 1791-95, he was in command of HMS *Discovery*, with the armed tender HMS *Chatham* as consort. (The islands were not so named until the late 1840s.) Cattle Point received its name in the early days when livestock were forced to swim ashore from the supply boats anchored offshore.

By following the **Bowker Creek Walkway** from the back of the Oak Bay Recreation Centre east toward the water, and crossing **Fireman's Park**, you could join this walk along the waterfront. From the Oak Bay Marina, **Windsor Park** is two blocks inland, and the 0.2-ha Oak Bay Native Plant Garden is two blocks south, at the corner of Beach Drive and Margate Avenue.

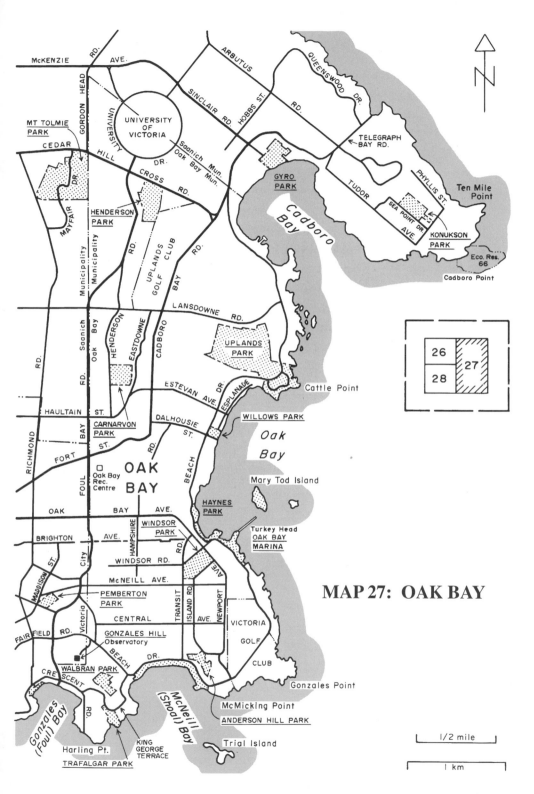

MAP 27: OAK BAY

123

ANDERSON HILL PARK (BLUEBERRY HILL)

Oak Bay's newest park (at only eighteen years) was created from, and is surrounded by, residential property. Even so, it remains a patch of wilderness, carpeted in spring with wild flowers, and a home for nesting birds. (So obey the local bylaw and keep your pet on leash from April 1 to June 30). From the rocky hilltop the views over McNeill (Shoal) Bay and Juan de Fuca Strait are fabulous. Access is off Island Road from Newport Avenue or from Central Avenue. You may descend along a steep trail to Transit Road, emerging between houses #545 and #577. This is just half a block from the park at McNeill (Shoal) Bay. The hilltop was named in 1870 after Alexander Caulfield Anderson, who arrived with the Hudson's Bay Company and stayed on as the first customs collector and postmaster in Victoria for what was then the new crown colony of British Columbia. Dr. O.M. Jones bought this land in 1912 and at one point offered some of it as parkland, but it was not until 1974 that 2.79 ha were purchased, to be dedicated as a park in 1979. Additions came in 1974 and 1992 as the adjacent property of the late Dr. Elkington was developed.

GONZALES HILL REGIONAL PARK

Acquired in 1992, and only 2 ha in size, this is the baby in the CRD Parks system. Have a look at the old Gonzales Observatory, a weather station for 75 years and now a heritage building. To do so, start out at Gonzales (Foul) Bay's sandy beach and climb the stairs at the eastern end of the beach up to Crescent Road. Keep straight ahead on to King George Terrace, then turn left onto Barkley Terrace and climb the stairs to the Observatory, where UVic scientists are gathering data on gasses in the atmosphere. After exploring, descend to Fairfield Road along Denison Road; this brings you close to the Victoria/Oak Bay border, where Fairfield Road becomes Beach Drive. From here you can head back to Gonzales Bay via Foul Bay Road, or go on to McNeill (Shoal) Bay via Beach Drive. Foul Bay was so dubbed because its sandy bottom provided poor anchorage and its southeastern exposure is open to winter storms. In an early example of politically correct language, the name was changed in the twenties to avoid any mistaken olfactory reference. Nearby Gonzalez Point was named by Manuel Quimper in 1790 after Gonzalez Lopez de Haro, his first mate on the *Princesa Real,* so that name was conveniently at hand when a new one was needed for the bay.

WALBRAN PARK

From the Gonzales Observatory, as described above, you can head east from the parking lot along Denison Road to discover Walbran park. Climb the stairs to the top to see the cairn dedicated to Juan de Fuca. Prepare to be "blown away" by the wind and by the view. The cairn inscription will explain why so many place names in this coastal area, from Cordova Spit to Sombrio Point, carry Spanish names. It was 1795 when the Spanish yielded control of these coasts to the British. Walbran Park is named after Captain John T. Walbran, author of *British Columbia Coast Names, 1592-1906,* who was, in his own words, "engaged in the lighthouse, buoy and fishery service of British Columbia".

Across the road, look for remnants of a Second World War observation post. From here, look about to discover an unmarked trail descending to a long (116 steps!) staircase (signposted at bottom) that drops to King George Terrace at Sunny Lane. Once again, you are above McNeill Bay, and there is public beach access, via steps, at the end of Sunny Lane. McNeill Bay is named after Captain William H. McNeill, an American who took command of the Hudson's Bay Company's steamer, *Beaver*, in 1838, and later rose to the post of Chief Factor. He had a homestead on the shore of the bay. (And also lent his name to the community of Port McNeill on northern Vancouver Island.)

SCENIC DRIVE, HARLING POINT

The "Scenic Drive" around the Victoria area waterfront makes a good cycling / walking route to or near many of the destinations we've included for the Victoria, Oak Bay, and Saanich areas. Following the signposted route, making nary a left nor a right turn, you find that the name of the road beneath you changes its name a bewildering number of times. If you start out at the Ogden Point breakwater and follow Dallas Road past Clover Point and Ross Bay, you will round a corner and find yourself on Hollywood Crescent (look for the stone garage behind house number 1734), which skirts Gonzales Bay and becomes Crescent Road. A detour from the Scenic Drive via a right turn just past Gonzales Bay would put you on the other half of Crescent Road, which leads to **Trafalgar Park** (with a beach access) at the intersection of Lorne Terrace and Maquinna Road, and to Harling Point. The point is named after Dr. Fred Harling, a dentist who died of a heart attack in 1934 after attempting to rescue two people from a sinking boat. (His nephew, Art Stott, a 1932 Olympic swimmer, did complete the rescue successfully.) This is the peninsula you look down upon from the **King George Terrace lookout**. The water and mountain elements of Harling Point ensure positive *feng shui* (positioning in harmony with natural and spiritual elements), so it was selected as the location of the **Harling Point Chinese Cemetery**. Established in 1903 (which makes it the oldest Chinese cemetery in Canada), it's managed by the Chinese Consolidated Benevolent Association. The earliest Chinese people to die in Victoria were buried in the Quadra Street Cemetery (now Pioneer Square). Later, when the Ross Bay Cemetery was opened in 1873, Section L was set aside for "aboriginals and Mongolians". Being nearest the sea, this area was subject to erosion during winter storms, with whole sections sometimes swept out to sea, graves and all. When the Chinese community attempted to identify the graves in order to move them to Harling Point, the deceased were found to be listed as "Chinaman # 1, Chinaman #2", etc. Up until the Second World War, the graves at Harling Point would be opened after seven years, and the bones cleaned and sent to China for final burial. The cemetery was closed to new burials in 1950. See page 136 for a history of the Chinese people in Victoria.

When you return to the head of Crescent Road to continue along the Scenic Drive, you'll be on King George Terrace, where there's a lookout stop for admiring the views. The tower just offshore is onTrial Island, which, with its islets, is designated as Ecological Reserve 132, described as "the most outstanding assemblage of rare and endangered plant species in BC." (Macoun's meadowfoam grows in only eight places in Victoria. One of these is on Trial Island, another at Harling Point, and a third at Cattle Point.) Two blocks further you merge right, onto Beach Drive, which bisects the Victoria Golf Club. In 1995 Canada Post printed a series of stamps to commemorate the 100th anniversary of the Royal Candian Golf Association's founding. Look due south, toward Trial Island, to recreate one of the five scenes depicted in the series. Beach Drive then skirts Oak Bay and takes you through the prestigious Uplands residential area before merging with Cadboro Bay Road and continuing on into Saanich municipality at Cadboro Bay. Just before you exit the Uplands through the stone pillars, a triangular plot of land where Midland Road joins Beach Drive has been left as it was when this area, dotted with majestic 1000-yr-old oaks, was selected as a suitable site for Fort Victoria. It has been preserved as an unspoiled patch of Garry oak meadow (see below under Summit Park).

BRIGHTON AVENUE

Start off in Victoria's Fairfield neighbourhood at **Pemberton Park**, corner of Gonzales Avenue and Maddison Street. Head north on Maddison to Brighton and turn right. Follow Brighton, as it repeatedly deadends and starts up again, until you reach Hampshire Road. If you are ready for a tea break, Oak Bay Village is just two blocks north. Continuing along Brighton, you have just four blocks before a path descends to Transit Road and, via St. Denis Street, **Windsor Park**. Ready for a game of cricket?

Stuart Stark's *Oak Bay's Heritage Buildings: More Than Just Bricks and Boards* would make a wonderful guide to the architecture you'll pass by and could send you off on other walks of discovery through our architectural heritage. Updated in 1995, the book is available for $24.95 through the Hallmark Society at 660 Michigan St. (open Wednesdays, 8:30 am-12:30 pm, Thursdays 12 - 3 pm); phone 382-4755. *Only in Oak Bay; Oak Bay Municipality: 1906-1981* was compiled by the municipality to commemorate its seventy-fifth year. Cartoons, photographs and diverse articles together form a collage: Oak Bay past, present, and future. (Read the book for advice on how to keep a cow in the Uplands.)

This completes our sampling of parks and walks in the Oak Bay area. Use of the many back lanes in the older parts of Oak Bay can pleasantly extend many of these walks. You may wish to detour past one of the oldest houses in western Canada, the **John Tod home** (built in 1850, and supposed to be haunted) at 2564 Heron Street. After a long career with the Hudson's Bay Company, John Tod was the first person to retire to Vancouver Island. What a precedent he set! For information on parks and trails in Oak Bay please contact:

Oak Bay Parks and Recreation
1975 Bee St.
Victoria, BC   V8R 5E6
phone 595-7946; fax 370-7127

There are 158 ha of public parkland in the City of Victoria, divided among 104 parks, large and small, but we have limited ourselves to those areas large enough for you to stretch your legs. For a Victoria parks brochure or for further information please contact:

City of Victoria Parks Division Mail: 1 Centennial Square
100 Cook Street   Victoria, BC
phone 361-0600   V8W 1P6

PEMBERTON PARK

This 2-ha neighbourhood park is the setting-off point for the Brighton Avenue walk described on page 127. Fairfield Road and neighbourhood are named after James Douglas' early estate in this area. The Douglas home sat where the Royal BC Museum is now. A scion of the Black Prince cherry tree from the orchard is protected by a black railing near the Douglas Building.

SUMMIT PARK

This 4.6-ha park must have the biggest urban blackberry patch in the Victoria area, demonstrating how an introduced plant (in this case the Himalayan blackberry) can overrun an area, destroying native species. Apart from the blackberries and the Scotch broom (another introduced plant), the park is a good example of the rare Garry oak woodland/grass bald habitat. Occurring only on southern Vancouver Island, on the Gulf Islands, and in a few isolated patches in the Fraser Valley, it may be the most endangered ecosystem in Canada. One threat is from human encroachment, with trees being cut down. A less obvious form of habitat destruction occurs when property owners water, mow and fertilize natural areas. Between human and plant intrusion, many plants that once thrived in the Garry oak woodland are now endangered or extinct. The **Garry Oak Meadow Preservation Society** has been formed in an effort to protect these precious areas. For up-dated information on the Society contact Swan Lake / Christmas Hill Nature Sanctuary (see page 115). The BC Ministry of Environment, Lands and Parks has produced a colour brochure, *Garry Oak Ecosystems*. Manmade features of Summit

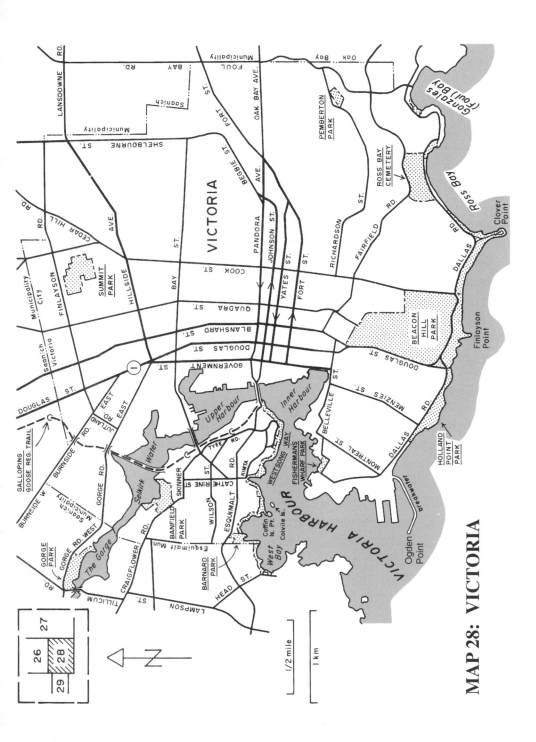

MAP 28: VICTORIA

129

Park include the Greater Victoria Water District reservoir and a microwave tower. Access is from the end of Highview Street, McNair Street, Summit Avenue, Blackwood Street or The Rise.

PEACOCK HILL

Though technically this park is just across the municipal boundary, in Saanich, it is so close to Summit Park that we have included it here. It is similar in nature, too, being a patch of Garry Oak meadow atop one of Victoria's many rocky knolls that afford such glorious views. To find the park from Quadra Street, turn east on Tolmie Avenue, which forms the boundary between Victoria and Saanich. The road will climb and become a dead end atop Peacock Hill. As one looks south from either Summit Park or Peacock Hill, one of the most intriguing buildings is a large red brick edifice, surrounded by Garry oaks, at the southeast corner of Hillside Avenue and Cook Street. Now the Bishop Cridge Centre for the Family, it was opened in 1873 by the Reverend Edward Cridge as the BC Protestant Orphans Home. Over the years, the building was "home" to more than 1600 children.

FERNWOOD

When you look at pictures of Victoria at the turn of the century or earlier, the suburbs you see in the distance are the Fernwood and Spring Ridge areas, now very much a part of urban Victoria. The Fernwood Community Association has produced a brochure, *Fernwood & Spring Ridge Heritage Walking Tour*, which takes you on a 3.5 km jaunt through what was once a pastoral scene with natural springs, later an industrial area for brickworks and gravel pits (souces of the fill under the Empress Hotel). The architecture of the past is featured, including a quintet of 1894 Italianate homes on Yukon Street. For examples of more modern architecture, you can detour a half-block to Centre Road (between Ridge and Fernwood Roads) to view some incredibly narrow homes. Copies of the brochure are available at the Fiddlehead Cafe (under the spire of the Belfry Theatre), at the Tourism Victoria Visitor Info Centre (on Wharf Street), from City Hall or the Victoria Public Library (main branch), or from the Fernwood Community Association office, 1923 Fernwood Road. Phone 384-7441for current office hours. A word of warning: do not park in the Victoria High School parking lots during school hours; your vehicle will be towed away.

BEACON HILL PARK

Victoria's largest park at close to 75 ha, Beacon Hill Park truly has something for everyone: softball, tennis, lawn bowling, soccer and cricket facilities, a putting green, a petting zoo, playgrounds, a bandshell and so much more, all in a setting of lawns, fields, flower gardens and native and exotic trees. The original "beacon" was actually a pair of masts intended as a navigational aid for Victoria harbour. When the masts lined up with a buoy offshore, one was on Brotchie Ledge, earlier known as Buoy Rock, until the barque *Albion,* commanded by Captain William Brotchie, struck it in 1849. (Presumably he had the two poles in neat alignment - see below.)

The Salish name for Beacon Hill was Meeacan, meaning "warmed in the sun" because it looked like a fat man lying on his back to warm his belly in the sunshine. In May each year the hill's south slopes are carpeted in blue camas to create an unforgettable vision. For the Coast Salish, this camas had a more prosaic value as the bulbs were a staple food. For a description of harvesting practices, look to Dr. Nancy J. Turner's *Food Plants of British Columbia.*

A booklet entitled *Beacon Hill Park 1882-1982: A Brief History* is available from the City Parks Division. The Victorienteers (see page 221) have a 5-colour map of the park (scale 1:5000): price: $5.00 for non-members. To contact the Friends of Beacon Hill Park, please phone 592-6659, or join them (and members of the Victoria Natural History Society) in the park for their Camas Day each April.

One block north of Beacon Hill Park (via Quadra Street) is St. Ann's Academy at 835 Humbolt Street. The 2-ha public open space of St. Ann's gardens forms a natural extension of the park. St. Ann's school was founded by Roman Catholic Bishop Modeste Demers and four Sisters of Charity in 1858. Among their pupils were James Douglas' three daughters, along with orphaned youngsters. Later the school was called St. Ann's School for Young Ladies, and a new school opened on View Street in 1860. The original two-room log schoolhouse, built around 1845, was moved to Elliot Street Square, next to the provincial museum and Helmcken House, in 1973. It has the distinction of being the oldest building in Victoria, though not at its original location. The central section of the present Academy building was commissioned as a school building in 1871, and designed by Montreal architect Charles Vereydhen. A cupola and an east wing designed by John Teague were added in 1886. St. Ann's Chapel, Victoria's oldest surviving religious building, was originally built on the north side of Humbolt Street, but it was moved at the time of Vereydhen's construction and later concealed by Teague's addition. In 1910, architect Thomas Hooper oversaw construction of the west wing and remodelling of the chapel. (Hooper also designed St. Joseph's Hospital, across the street.) The formal gardens surrounding the academy were laid out in 1880. The buildings and grounds of St. Ann's Academy were purchased by the provincial government in 1974, but it was not until 1995 that work on the project was begun by the Provincial Capital Commission and the BC Buildings Corporation, at a cost of $15.6 million. A re-opening ceremony was held in July of 1997, but restoration work continues, especially in the chapel and the interpretive centre.

OGDEN POINT TO CLOVER POINT

This is a world class stroll! Start off at the 0.8-km-long **Ogden Point breakwater**, a popular spot for fishing, scuba-diving, bird-watching and just generally getting wind-blown. The Point was named in 1843 for Peter Skene Ogden of the Hudson's Bay Company (so is Ogden, Utah), but the breakwater came much later, in 1913, built from rock quarried at Albert Head. Offshore is **Brotchie Ledge** (scene of numerous marine disasters), with its light and fog bell. The Ogden Point area is being spruced up with brick walkways, planters, and hanging baskets, with the first phase completed in the spring of 1997; after all, it is Victoria's "front door" for 80,000 visitors arriving yearly at the Ogden Point piers. From the breakwater, head east, toward Beacon Hill Park, through 5-ha **Holland Point Park.** The roadside path takes you past the Harrison model yacht pond, named after the mayor of Victoria in the 1950s. The cliffside walk parallels Dallas Road and offers magnificent views of the Olympic Mountains and the Strait of Juan de Fuca. At the foot of Paddon St. there's a bench in a sheltered nook; look for crocuses in February. Offshore is Glimpse Reef. At the foot of Douglas Street you have three choices. You could cross the road to visit the 'Mile 0' monument, marking the western terminus of the Trans-Canada Highway; once across, you might decide to detour two blocks up Douglas Street for a soft ice cream cone at the

Beacon Drive In Restaurant, and then cross Douglas to enter Beacon Hill Park. You could take the stairs down to walk along the beach, or just continue along the cliffside walk. A special pet fountain ahead reminds you that you are in 'doggie heaven': from Douglas Street to Clover Point dogs are permitted to romp free from their leashes. All along your cliffside walk, and particularly at **Horseshoe Bay,** you'll see evidence of the continual erosion of the cliff face, and of the sometimes-controversial attempts to halt that erosion by artificial berms, drains, and the planting of native shrubs including Nootka rose, snowberry, red currant, ocean spray, mock orange, Saskatoon berry and Garry oak.

At the mid-point in your walk, you could stop to rest in the Kiwanis shelter at **Finlayson Point,** named for Roderick Finlayson, Hudson's Bay Chief Factor at Victoria, 1844-1872. Here a plaque advises that this was once the site of an ancient fortified village. Burial mounds, contructed of large granite rocks, may be seen on the southern slope of Beacon Hill, below the flagpole. The plaque also marks the site of a gun battery during the Russo-Turkish war (1878-1892). The powder magazine for the two 64-lb guns was near Goodacre Lake. Remote-controlled model aircraft are permitted here. Continuing eastward you pass a monument to the accomplishments of Marilyn Bell, who swam the Strait of Juan de Fuca in 1956. On the opposite side of Dallas Road, you'll notice what was once the world's tallest totem pole. Later, a taller one (52.7 m) was erected at Alert Bay, off the northeast coast of Vancouver Island. That pole was eclipsed by yet another, in Victoria's Inner Harbour, in 1994. (See Westsong Way, page 139.) At the foot of Cook Street there are public washrooms and a small play area for children. An even better playground is a block further up Cook. If you're visiting in the spring, you'll see the yellow gorse in bloom. *Ulex europaeus*, like the Scotch broom that it resembles, is an introduced species. The BC Forest Service has produced a pamphlet on control of "Gorse, the spiny competitor". As you approach **Clover Point** you are likely to see colourful kites overhead. Those really big kites, with humans attached, are paragliders, akin to hang-gliders. Take special note of the birds in the air and on the waves: Clover Point is one of the best places around Victoria to spot migrating species. The point was named by Sir James Douglas as he landed here from the *Beaver* in 1843. Presumably he saw the reddish-purple flowers of springbank clover (*Trifolium wormskjoldii*), a perennial native species and food source for local indigenous people (other clovers here are introduced species).

Heading east from Clover Point along Dallas Road, you travel a sea-side promenade, which can be spectacular (and sometimes closed) during rough weather. You may wish to detour one block up Memorial Crescent to May St. and from there scramble up one of several steep, rough trails to a rocky outcrop known both as **Moss Rock Park** and **Fairfield Hill.** A more elegant approach is possible from the 1400 block of Fairfield Road, up Masters Road to its dead end. (If you are in a vehicle, obey the parking regulations.) Either route leads you to a fine viewpoint and picnic spot. Two blocks north, via **Porter Park,** you can stroll by a grove of windmill palm trees at 428 Kipling Street on your way up the hill, via Lotbiniere Avenue, to **Government House**, the official residence of our Lieutenant-Governor (the Queen's representative in British Columbia). The landscaped grounds are open to the public during daylight hours. If you happen to be visiting on the Saturday afternoon that falls in the middle of July, you may wish instead to stroll up Moss Street, from Dallas Road to the Art Gallery of Greater Victoria (at 1040 Moss Street near Fort Street). You will find yourself part of the annual Moss Street Paint In, when close to 100 artists create before a crowd of thousands.

If you pass up the detour above, and continue east on Dallas Road, you will soon arrive at **Ross Bay Cemetery,** described below. The beach access for Gonzales (Foul) Bay is just a little farther along via Hollywood Crescent and Crescent Road. Dallas Road was named for Alexander Grant Dallas, chief factor with the Hudson's Bay Company. He married Jane, the second daughter of James Douglas.

ROSS BAY CEMETERY

This 11-ha tombstone cemetery, landscaped with many exotic trees, has been the final resting place of many of Victoria's prominent citizens since 1873. It is a fine example of a typical Victorian cemetery, with its formal landscaping and a variety of interesting headstones. The **Old Cemeteries Society** conducts tours on Sunday afternoons at 2 pm; Tuesday and Thursday at 7 pm, July and August. Meet at Bagga Pasta, 1516 Fairfield Road (Fairfield Plaza). No reservations needed; suggested donation: $5 adults, $3 seniors/students. For information please contact P O Box 40115, Victoria, BC; phone 598-8870. A booklet, "Historic Guide to Ross Bay Cemetery", by John Adams, is available. Similar tours are conducted on summer evenings through Pioneer Square (the old Quadra Street Cemetery) next to Christ Church Cathedral on Quadra Street (see page 138).

INNER HARBOUR, DOWNTOWN, CHINATOWN

Start off at **Fisherman's Wharf Park** on Erie Street. Enjoy a packet of fish and chips from Barb's and a stroll among the moored vessels. Thus fortified, head east toward downtown Victoria. You will immediately need to make a detour, via St. Lawrence Street and Kingston Street, then look for the public access beside the Coast Victoria Harbourside Hotel at 146 Kingston Street. It continues past the two Harbourside condominium developments and leads to **Laurel Point Park** in front of the Laurel Point Inn. Here you have a 240-degree view of the busy harbour. You will exit through **Centennial Park** (don't miss the totem pole) at the corner of Belleville Street and Pendray Street. You will need to make a short detour around the terminal for the Black Ball ferry service to Port Angeles, USA, then you are free to descend to the Lower Causeway. (Or, keep to the Upper Causeway, pass in front of the Empress Hotel and rejoin our route at the Visitors' Centre.) Take time to explore the Inner Harbour docks, (and the buskers, in summer) then follow the promenade right around to tiny **Reeson Regional Park**, with its "Whaling Wall" mural, and the Johnson Street Bridge (the "Blue Bridge"). Note the tiny E & N railway station at the east end of the bridge. When British Columbia joined Confederation in 1871, it was with the promise of a cross-country Canadian Pacific Railway with a western terminus at the Esquimalt naval station. Instead, it was decided in 1878-79 that Port Moody on the mainland's

Burrard Inlet would be the "end of the line". Vancouver Island had to make do with the Esquimalt and Nanaimo Railway, built by Robert Dunsmuir to carry coal from his up-Island collieries to the Esquimalt naval station. Prime Minister Sir John A. Macdonald drove the last spike on August 13, 1886, at Mile 25 at Cliffside, near Shawnigan Lake. E&N Railfreight, a division of CP Rail System, now owns the line (which continues on to Courtenay) and runs the freight service. Via Rail, a federal Crown corporation, runs the daily passenger service.

From the Johnson Street Bridge you can continue your walk by crossing the Blue Bridge to pick up Westsong Way, or you can explore **Old Town** and **Chinatown**. Dating back to 1858, Victoria's Chinatown, though now not so large as some others, is the oldest and most intact in Canada, and has been declared a national historic site. Our first Chinese immigrants arrived in the middle of the last century to work on railroad construction and in the gold fields. At one time there were as many as 3000 inhabitants of Chinatown, making it the largest Chinatown in Canada. Until the establishment of the Chinese consulate in 1909, its government was by the Chinese Consolidated Benevolent Association, which built and ran Chinatown, including its hospital, school and cemetery (see Harling Point, page 125). At that time, the CCBA also controlled immigration and made the local regulations within Chinatown. From the time that Vancouver became the terminus for the CPR line (the line was completed by 1887), and thus Canada's main western port of entry, the number of Chinese began to decline. Later, in 1909, the opium laws were changed, forcing the opium factories and dens to close. Finally, in 1933, a federal ban on Chinese immigration meant that family members back home in China were permanently excluded. Those already here were not allowed to vote and their children were not allowed to participate in the public school system, hence the necessity of the Chinese Public School, which continues to offer classes in Chinese language and culture. The Gate of Harmonious Interest on Fisgard Street is a modern symbol of the rebirth of Chinatown but is also a fitting tribute to the contribution of our Chinese Canadians. On your visit to Chinatown, don't miss Fan Tan Alley, between Fisgard and Johnson streets. Once the site of numerous fan-tan clubs, it's the narrowest street in Canada. *The Forbidden City - within Victoria*, by David Chuenyan Lai (Orca Books), describes Chinatown and its people in detail. Each summer, the Inter-Cultural Association of Greater Victoria (ICA) hosts tours of cultural and historical sites, including Chinatown and the Chinese Cemetery, also the Jewish Cemetery (oldest in western Canada) and Jewish Synagogue Emanuel (Canada's oldest synagogue), the Sikh Temple (our oldest in its original location), and the Hindu Parishad Temple in Saanichton. For information contact Charlayne Thornton-Joe at 744-1985 or ICA at 388-4728. Admission to the tours is $5 per person, with all proceeds going to ICA.

Victoria's downtown area is also well worth exploring on foot. Robin Ward's *Echoes of Empire: Victoria and its Remarkable Buildings* (Harbour Publishing) details the city's architectural heritage. Free walking tours are offered during the summer months by the Vancouver Island Chapter of the Architectural Institute of British Columbia from their office at #203-45 Bastion Square (entrance off Langley Street), Victoria, B.C. V8W 1J1; phone 1-800-667-0753 (Vancouver) or 388-5588 (Victoria) for information. One of the oldest structures in Victoria is **Helmcken House**, located in Elliot Street Square next door to the Royal British Columbia Museum. Built in 1852, it is the former home of Dr. John Sebastian Helmcken and his wife Celilia (daughter of Sir James Douglas). Helmcken House is open to the public; phone 361-0021 for information. Noteworthy as an early Victoria physician, as a member of the first Legislative Assembly of Vancouver Island in 1855, and as a Father of Confederation, Dr. Helmcken was laid to rest in 1920 in Victoria's oldest surviving cemetery, the **Quadra Street Cemetery**. Beside **Christ Church Cathedral**, on Quadra at Rockland Avenue, it is now known as **Pioneer Square**. Its Pritchard Tomb, dating to 1872, has been termed "the most architecturally significant 19th-century monument in B.C." Among the pioneers buried here are David Cameron (first chief justice in the colony of Vancouver Island) and John Work, a chief factor of the Hudson's Bay Company, and, at the time of his death in 1861, a member of the Legislative Council of Vancouver Island. He was born John Wark, in Ireland, but his name was misspelled when he joined the HBC, so John Work he was to remain. The attitudes of the times are reflected in the words of Dr. Helmcken: "He had been entered on the company's books as Work and this was unalterable." The spelling of Wark Point in Victoria harbour has been changed to Work Point, but Wark Street (originally Third Street) does carry the correct spelling of his name.* The first person to die at Fort Victoria, in 1844, was Charles Ross, the HBC chief factor who had supervised the construction of the fort. A burial ground was started just outside the fort (near the present-day intersection of Johnson and Douglas Streets). Around 1858 burials in "the old burying ground" ceased, and the contents of the graves were moved to the Quadra Street Cemetery. On summer evenings during July and August, the Old Cemeteries Society offers Lantern Tours through Pioneer Square. Phone 598-8870 for information. (See also Ross Bay Cemetery, page 135.) Beside Pioneer Square is **Christ Church Cathedral** (Quadra Street at Courtenay Street), which is well worth a visit. If you think you hear echoes, they may be from one of the ten bronze bells. (Toronto, with a 12-bell church, is the only North American city to best us.) Replicas of those at Westminster Abbey, they were cast at the Whitechapel Bell Foundry (as was Big Ben); the largest weighs one-and-a-half tons. Eight of the bells were installed in 1936, the other two in 1983, when Queen Elizabeth and the Duke of Edinburgh attended the installation ceremony. On the other hand, perhaps those echoes you hear are of British imperialism: architect John Charles Malcolm Keith was a native of Scotland who turned to Durham and Lincoln cathedrals for his inspiration; the rose window was designed and made in London; the north aisle windows were made by James Ballantine of Edinburgh; the south aisle windows, by English artist J.E. Nuttgens, were first displayed at the Royal Academy in London; the pulpit was carved from a 500-year-old oak from Sussex; the choir screen came from Westminster Abbey; the bishop's chair, from St. Paul's Cathedral. The Bishop of London was invited to lay the foundation stone, and the Rt. Hon. Winston Churchill laid a stone when he visited in 1929.

---

* A *Times-Colonist* article of September 22, 1997, tells us that Graham, Prior and Blackwood Streets were re-named after three of John Wark's sons-in-law. Originally they had been named Seventh, Eighth, and Ninth Streets. The original First, Second, Fourth, and Sixth Streets are now named Ross, Blanshard, Quadra and Vancouver. Only the name of Fifth Street remains unchanged. John Street and David Street were named after the oldest and youngest of their three boys. Henry Street, where the west end of Hillside Avenue now runs, was named after the middle boy, who died at age 12 in 1856.

WESTSONG WAY

The combined efforts of the City of Victoria, the Municipality of Esquimalt, BC Enterprise Corporation, the Provincial Capital Commission and property developers have resulted in this spectacular 3.5 km waterfront walkway from the Johnson Street Bridge in Victoria to West Bay in Esquimalt. A plaque at the Victoria end identifies this section as **Songhees Way**; a section in the middle, by the Royal Quays condominiums, is identified as **Mariners Way**; and the Esquimalt section has always been known as the **West Bay Walkway**. In October 1990, then-Lieutenant- Governor Lam officially opened the walkway with a combined name of **Westsong Way**. This whole area used to be a heavy-industrial area, with the shore lined with tank farms, Lime Bay home to a shake mill, and Bapco Paint perched on Laurel Point, across the harbour. Starting from the Johnson Street Bridge and heading west make your way to Songhees Point and the site of the world's tallest totem pole (55 m) in front of the Ocean Pointe Resort. Named the Spirit of Lekwammen (an earlier name for Songhees), the pole was erected at the time of the 1994 Commonwealth Games, but, with its steel sleeve, metal guy wires and aviation warning light on top, it became the most controversial of the Games' legacies. In August, 1997, it was taken down and divided into four sections. Two remain at the Inner Harbour, two have been delivered to the Songhees First Nation. To continue your walk, pass the Edith Cavell, Kings Landing and Royal Quays condominium developments and skirt Lime Bay at the foot of Catherine Street (where you will also find Spinnaker's Pub). Next comes Coffin Island Point at the foot of Robert Street. The island just off-shore is Colville Island, named for Andrew Colville, Governor of the Hudson's Bay Company, 1852-56. As you make your way westward, you leave Victoria at **Barnard Park** (part of the former estate of Sir Francis Barnard) and enter Esquimalt. The last section, the **West Bay Walkway**, brings you out to a small parking lot off Head Street, very near to **West Bay Park** (see page 145).

VICTORIA HARBOUR FERRY

You can make your exploration of the Inner Harbour and Westsong Way a loop by taking a ride on one of the little ferries that make stops at the Songhees dock; on the Causeway in front of the Empress; in front of Coast Harbourside; at Fisherman's Wharf Park in front of Barb's Fish and Chips; and at the West Bay Marina at the foot of Head Street. Information is available at the kiosk on the Causeway and at the Tourist Information Bureau. Ferry service is also available to Ocean Pointe (see above); the foot of Fisgard Street in Chinatown (see page 136); historical Point Ellice House (see page 142); Banfield park in Vic West (see page 141); and Gorge Park in Saanich (see page 114). Once a summer-only attraction, they now run year-round (weather permitting) and even do a "boat ballet" in the Inner Harbour each Sunday morning at 9:45 am, from mid-June on to early September. Ferry service may be expanded to the Esquimalt Harbour in 1998.

GALLOPING GOOSE REGIONAL TRAIL, Victoria section

See page 149 for a full description of the Galloping Goose Trail. The 2.5 km section that begins in Victoria at the south end of the Selkirk Trestle (opened September, 1996) passes through **Cecelia Ravine Park.** Here, during the summer of 1997, the underside of the Gorge Road bridge was graced with an imaginative mural by Frank Lewis, who painted the first two murals in Chemainus. This work, an image of a woman and a man reaching out to touch each other, is an initiative of the Burnside-Gorge Community Association, sponsored by the Provincial Capital Commission, the City of Victoria and General Paint. From the ravine, the trail swings north through a light-industrial area out to the Town and Country Shopping Centre in Saanich. This paved, multi-use trail is also signed as the most westerly section of the **Trans Canada Trail** (see page 220). In May of 1995 the old Selkirk railway trestle was the scene of a fire, and for a while it looked as though plans for a link across the Selkirk Water had literally gone up in smoke. Fortunately, the fire turned out to be more spectacular than serious. It did mark, however, the second time this century that Victorians had awaited the completion of the Selkirk crossing. In 1915 railway ties were delivered to Patricia Bay, where work was to start on a branch of the Canadian Northern Pacific Railway (later the CNR) in to Victoria. A temporary terminal was located near Alpha Street until the trestle bridge was completed in 1920 and the railway's terminus in Victoria West finished and put in service. Now, from the southern end of the new Selkirk Trestle, pedestrians can use the trail southward through the Bayside property to access downtown Victoria; cyclists need to check the posted maps for routes to Esquimalt and downtown. The small island at the mouth of Selkirk Water is known as Deadman's Island, though its official name is Halkett Island, so-named (though misspelled) in 1847 after a Captain Hackett. It was an Indian burial ground long ago but all traces of bones and boxes disappeared in a fire in the late 1800s. Selkirk Water, from Point Ellice to Chapman Point, is named after Thomas Douglas, 5th Earl of Selkirk, founder of the Red River settlement in what is now Manitoba.

SELKIRK WATERFRONT

On the northeast side of the Selkirk Water, beside the Selkirk Trestle, Jawl Holdings has cleared the 10-ha former sawmill site (on Gorge Road at the foot of Jutland) for redevelopment that includes industrial, commercial and residential uses. The current plan includes 1.3 ha of parkland divided between a park in the residential section and a waterfront pathway along the entire shoreline of the project. As of 1997, building is well under way, and the first section of boardwalk, nearest the Galloping Goose Trail, is complete.

BANFIELD PARK

Heading south on the Galloping Goose Trail, cross the Selkirk Trestle (water fountains here) into the neighbourhood known as Vic West. Turn right to the foot of Arthur Currie Lane. Only a couple of the homes in this area are true heritage homes; the others are modern imitations, designed to fit in among their elders, including Roslyn House, at 1135 Catherine Street, built in 1890 in the Queen Anne style. A sometimes-muddy trail leads you through to Banfield Park along the Gorge Waterway. The lowermost trail leads around to a public wharf (stopping place for the little harbour ferries) at the foot of Styles Street. Just beyond, benches on a secluded point look across to the buildings and grounds of the Gorge Road Hospital. The upper levels of the park are developed as children's playgounds, tennis courts, and the Vic West Community YMCA building. A Vic West heritage poster with a map and historical photos is available at the Vic West Y for $5.00. Charles Frederick Banfield was King's Printer in Victoria from 1924 to 1946.

BAYSIDE LANDS

On the west side of the Selkirk Water between the Selkirk Trestle and the Point Ellice (Bay Street) Bridge lies the former CN Railway Yard, a 4.7-ha parcel managed by Canada Lands Co. Ltd., a Crown corporation. A current proposal is for redevelopment as Bayside Village, with housing units, a commercial core, and public open space, including a walkway. A crushed gravel trail has been built from the Selkirk Trestle through Bayside lands to the end of Harbour Road (near the Princess Mary Restaurant Vessel). The current Point Ellice Bridge is a sturdy, reliable structure, unlike its predecesor, which collapsed May 26, 1896, under the weight of an overloaded streetcar, creating the worst streetcar disaster in North American history. Just across the bridge, at 2616 Pleasant Street, is **Point Ellice House**, the former home of the pioneer Riley family. Call 380-6506 for information on garden tours, house tours and afternoon tea.

DOCKSIDE LANDS

The City of Victoria owns 11.3 ha, bounded roughly by Esquimalt and Tyee Roads and the Upper Harbour, and stretching from the Johnson Street Bridge to the Point Ellice Bridge. Part of this area is being sold off in several parcels, probably for redevelopment as a business park. Part will remain in public ownership and could include a public corridor to connect the Inner Harbour walkway with the Bayside walkway. Ellice Point was named by officers of the HBC after their Deputy Governor, the Rt. Hon. Edward Ellice. Captain Kellett officially adopted the name in 1846.

ESQUIMALT AREA (MAP 29) 1996 census: 16,151

In 1842, James Douglas wrote "Is-whoy-malth" as his interpretation of the native pronunciation. The word may have referred to a local group, the Whyomilth family, or to the "shoaling waters" of the mud flats where the Mill Stream empties into upper Esquimalt Harbour. Dr. Thom Hess of the University of Victoria interviewed local elders, who informed him that the name refers to the narrowing at the head of the harbour, where the water is "squeezed" between its banks at the site of the present Parson's Bridge. The first recorded ship to visit Esquimalt Harbour was the *Princesa Real* (the confiscated British *Princess Royal*) under Manuel Quimper in 1790. He named the harbour Puerto de Cordova, after the Viceroy of Mexico, which name was later applied to Cordova Bay in Saanich. Esquimalt has always been important for its military presence. HMCS Naden and the Naval and Military Museum are open daily, Monday to Friday, 10 am to 2:30 pm for self-guided walking tours, starting from the museum, where free parking and tour pamphlets are provided. Phone 363-4312 for information.

FLEMING BEACH, BUXTON GREEN, and MACAULAY POINT

Fleming Beach (.8 ha), at the foot of Lampson Street, is home to the Esquimalt Angler's Association and is the gateway to Buxton Green, a perfect picnic area. Adjacent Macaulay Point (4.86 ha) is leased from the Department of National Defence and developed as parkland with great views of Victoria, the Olympic Mountains and Juan de Fuca Strait. "The Bunkers" are the abandoned gun emplacements of the oldest coastal defence battery in BC. The Friends of Fort Macaulay Society has been formed to preserve the historical value of the fort. Wheelchair access is limited.

For several years, the rock cliffs above Fleming Beach have been used for teaching and practicing of rock-climbing skills. Fears over possible lawsuits led Esquimalt council to consider shutting down the climbing wall. In an effort to protect passing pedestrians, the walkway at the base of the cliff was redeveloped, with monetary support provided by the Provincial Capital Commission, the Township of Esquimalt, and the Greater Victoria Climbers Association.

MAP 29: ESQUIMALT

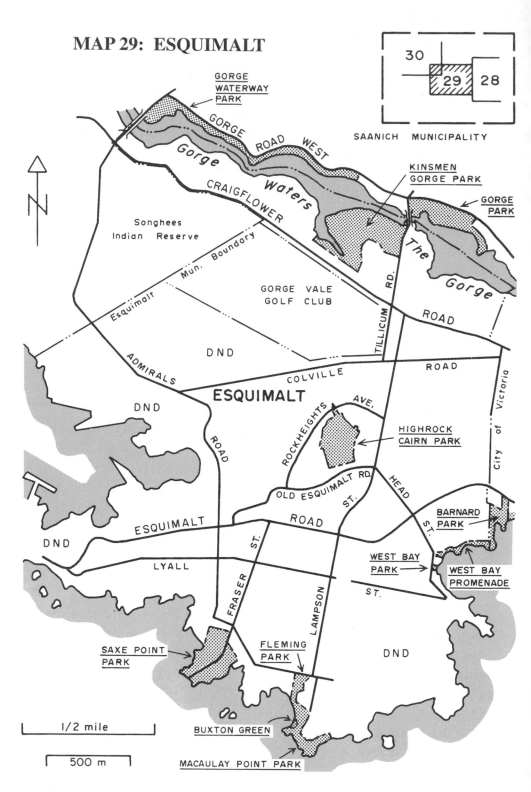

SAANICH MUNICIPALITY

GORGE WATERWAY PARK

GORGE ROAD WEST

Gorge Waters

CRAIGFLOWER

KINSMEN GORGE PARK

GORGE PARK

Songhees Indian Reserve

The Gorge

Mun. Boundary

Esquimalt

GORGE VALE GOLF CLUB

TILLICUM RD.

ROAD

DND

ROAD

ADMIRALS

COLVILLE

ESQUIMALT

City of Victoria

DND

ROCKHEIGHTS AVE.

HIGHROCK CAIRN PARK

ROAD

OLD ESQUIMALT RD.

ST.

HEAD ST.

BARNARD PARK

ESQUIMALT

ROAD

DND

ST.

WEST BAY PARK

WEST BAY PROMENADE

LYALL

FRASER ST.

LAMPSON ST.

ST.

DND

SAXE POINT PARK

FLEMING PARK

1/2 mile

500 m

BUXTON GREEN

MACAULAY POINT PARK

SAXE POINT PARK

The entrance to the 6-ha park is at the foot of Fraser Street. This park offers great variety: extensive herbaceous borders, woodland trails, picnic areas and spectacular views. Limited wheelchair access. The original name given by Lieutenant Commander Wood of HMS *Pandora* in 1847 was Saxe Cape, named in association with the Coburg Peninsula, at Esquimalt Lagoon, and Gotha Point, at the entrance to Esquimalt Harbour. (Queen Victoria's husband was Prince Albert of Saxe-Coburg and Gotha.)

HIGHROCK CAIRN PARK

Much of the 4.75-ha park has been left in a natural state. Climb the hill to the cairn, dedicated on the fiftieth anniversary of the Royal Canadian Navy. The views from the lookout are fantastic. Wheelchair access is difficult.

KINSMEN GORGE PARK

On Tillicum Road, just over the Gorge Bridge from Saanich, lies this 13-ha multi-use park. There's something for everyone: swimming, picnicking, tennis, and paths alongside the Gorge waterway. Earlier this century, the Gorge Regatta was held here each May 24th holiday, featuring boat races, swimming meets and picnics. The roundabout at the entrance to the park is a reminder of the days when this was the turnaround point at the end of the trolley line. Here, too, may be found the skeletal outline of the Takata Japanese Garden, once a popular place to spend an afternoon, but abandoned with the internment of Japanese-Canadians during World War II. The park is wheelchair accessible. (See also Gorge Waterway Park, Saanich section, page 114.)

WEST BAY PARK and WEST BAY WALKWAY

To locate West Bay Park, just look for the nautical blue and white house at 507 Head Street. In the "Steamboat Gothic" style (a mix of Victorian Italianate and French Second Empire) it was built by Captain Victor Jacobsen, a Finnish seaman and shipwright, in 1893. Jacobsen had jumped ship in Victoria in 1881, but he went on to own several of the fifty-odd sealing schooners that called Victoria their home port between excursions to follow the fur seal migrations from Mexico to Alaska and across the Bering Sea. Victoria's sealers prospered from 1884 until 1911, when a pact among Japan, Russia and the United States banned the Canadian fleet. Next door to Captain Jacobsen's distinctive home is West Bay Park, a perfect spot for a picnic before heading off on the Walkway, which starts from a small parking lot on Head Street between Dunsmuir and Gore. This was the first section to be completed of what later was re-named Westsong Way (see page 139). Some sections are not wheelchair accessible. If your olfactory senses are offended, don't worry - it isn't sewage you smell, it's rotting sea cabbage. Wood fibre falls to the bottom of the bay and is not washed out by the tide. Sea cabbage flourishes on the fibre, but eventually rots, creating a stench. The Victoria West Community Association, with help from CFB Esquimalt's Fleet School, did a cleanup of some of the fibre in July of 1997. If you should spot a Purple Martin you can thank the local nest-box program. Contact Darren Copley through the Victoria Natural History Society for details.

For more information on these and other parks in the area, please contact:

Esquimalt Parks and Recreation Commission
1149A Esquimalt Road, Victoria, BC   V9A 3N6
phone 386-6128

⟨11⟩ **VIEW ROYAL AREA (MAP 30)**   1996 Census: 6441

View Royal was named after a 1912 subdivision of land originally purchased by Dr. John Sebastian Helmcken in 1851. Promoters of the subdivision claimed the lots had a "royal view." From the time of early European settlement the development of this area has been influenced by the roads running through it. The Four Mile House and the Six Mile House Hotel were originally stopping places on the road from Fort Victoria to farms located as far west as Sooke. Later, they were to serve the miners travelling to and from gold workings at Leechtown. Look for pending development of the Esquimalt Indian Band lands and municipal lands in the area around the old plywood mill site near Hallowell and Admirals Roads. For information on parks and trails in View Royal contact:

Town of View Royal
45 View Royal Avenue
Victoria, BC   V9B 1A6
phone 479-6800; fax 727-9551

PORTAGE MUNICIPAL PARK

Portage Park, with its woodland trails, beach, and archaeological sites, is just off the Old Island Highway near Four Mile Hill. Entrance to the park is gained through the town hall parking lot. Steep stairs make wheelchair access to the park impossible. The Four Mile Hill is also the site of the Four Mile Roadhouse, now a tearoom, restaurant and pub, and the fourth-oldest house remaining in the Victoria area. Peter Calvert and Elizabeth Montgomery both arrived on the Norman Morison but did not marry until he completed his five years of service with the Hudson's Bay Company in exchange for his free passage. James Cooper, former Company Ship captain, had purchased HBC property beyond Craigflower Farm (as had the fort doctor, John Sebastian Helmcken, and former Company millwright William Richard Parson), and it was from Cooper that Peter Calvert purchased 6 acres upon which he built a four-room farm house in 1858. Due to its proximity to the main road, before long it became a small inn and staging post. World War I and the days of prohibition ended its days as a roadhouse, but not forever. In the late forties it operated as The Lantern Inn, and, since 1979, as the Four Mile Roadhouse once again.

VIEW ROYAL MUNICIPAL PARK

The entrance to View Royal Park is at the corner of Helmcken Road and Pheasant Lane, just where the E & N railway crosses Helmcken. Craigflower Creek skirts one side of the park, offering pleasant picnic spots. (Not so pleasant is the local name for Craigflower Creek: Deadman Creek.) A level chip trail around the perimeter of the park is especially suitable for jogging and there is a playground for children. Wheelchair accessible.

WATERS EDGE WALKWAY/ PARSON'S BRIDGE PARK

From the north end of Parson's Bridge it is possible to descend to a walkway between the Waters Edge residential development and the upper reaches of Esquimalt Harbour. Improvements to the access were made possible by a Provincial Capital Commission grant in 1994. At present it is just a short loop, coming out at Dukrill Road, but it marks the start of what View Royal hopes will become a series of public accesses along its shoreline. Parson's Bridge is named for William Richard Parson, who

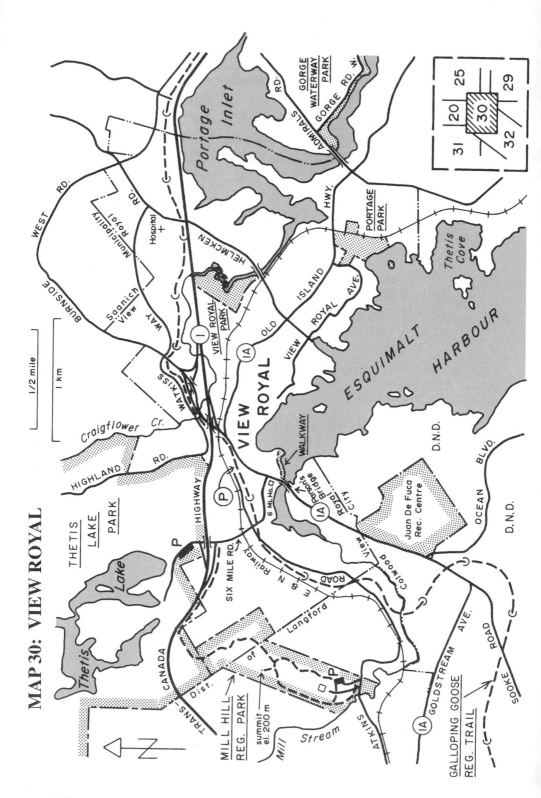

MAP 30: VIEW ROYAL

148

first purchased a liquor license for his Parson's Bridge Hotel in 1856. The inn was well situated, being close to the first sawmill (1848) and to the Mill Stream (earlier known as Rowe's Stream), where ships' water barrels were refilled. The Esquimalt naval station was established nearby in 1864, providing thirsty patrons to join the travellers on their way to and from what is now Colwood, Langford, Metchosin and Sooke.

GALLOPING GOOSE REGIONAL TRAIL (MAPS 25, 26, 28, 30, 31, 32, 33, 35, 36 and 38)

This 60-km section of Canadian National Railway (CNR) right-of-way, from Victoria to the Alberni Canal, was originally part of the Canadian Northern Pacific Railway which had been build across the Prairies. The section from Victoria to Leechtown was started in 1911. The CNR took over the entire Canadian Northern Railway in 1920. The line was used mostly for transporting logs and freight but passenger service ran from Victoria to Sooke (twice daily) starting in 1922, was extended to Youbou in 1925, and ceased in 1931. Passenger service was by a gasoline-powered railbus known as the "Galloping Goose". This type of coach was used throughout Canada and was commemorated on a postage stamp in the 1980s. One person handled all the duties of engineer, conductor and baggage handler. Although use of the line declined around the 1930s, the Victoria-Deerholme section was used up until the 1970s: munitions were transported to Rocky Point, and poles were carried from Leechtown to a poleyard at Milne's Landing. This service ended in 1979 and by 1982 the rails had been removed. In 1987 an agreement was reached between the Province of BC and the CRD to lease this section of the abandoned CNR right-of-way for regional park use for 21 years (until 2008). Over the last 25 years, many groups have had a part in preserving the corridor; it now forms part of the Regional Trail System (see page 217), the Vancouver Island Recreational Corridor and the Trans Canada Trail (see page 220). The currently-developed portion out almost to Leechtown is just the first section of a planned trail from Victoria all the way to Youbou via Shawnigan Lake and Lake Cowichan. Currently the rail right-of-way travels alongside Sooke Lake, Victoria's water source. One recommendation of the 1996 Perry Commission on the Greater Victoria Water District was that land would be acquired to reroute the Galloping Goose Trail well away from Sooke Lake.

The Galloping Goose Trail offers pleasant urban walks and, although never far from a highway, it removes one from the hurly-burly, with surprising glimpses of animal life, hedgerow flowers in season and some beautiful lookout points. Many trails lead off from the right-of-way but please resist the temptation to stray onto private lands. Once out to Metchosin the trail leads you to or through several public parks.

No motorized vehicles are permitted, but hikers, horse riders and cyclists share the trail. Courtesy between user groups is encouraged, with cycling clubs giving the right-of-way to hikers, and with hikers giving way to equestrians. Safety dictates that all users should keep right, except to pass; courtesy dictates users should alert others when approaching from behind. Dogs should be kept on a lead and under control at all times. Dog owners must pick up their dog's droppings.

The more urban sections are now paved but many of the unpaved sections, too, including the section near the Luxton Fairgrounds, are suitable for wheelchair use; however, the only wheelchair-accessible toilets are at Roche Cove Regional Park. Both the Luxton and Roche Cove accesses have good parking. Other parking lots are located at the dead end of Atkins Road where it used to join the Old Island Highway, and at the intersection of Sooke Road and Aldeane Ave.

The most remote section of the Galloping Goose runs from Charters Creek almost to Leechtown. Formerly, the Sooke River Railway Preservation Society operated a railway service along part of this section, and many were saddened to see this service end. For a time, the trestles over Tod and Charters Creeks were deemed unsafe for public use, but with their reopening in 1995, the trail was again complete. Note that the developed portion of the Galloping Goose Trail ends just short of Leechtown itself. Leechtown has more than once been the scene of human disappointment. The Leech River (and thus Leechtown) were named after Peter John Leech, who arrived with the Royal Engineers in 1858, and stayed on to be part of the Vancouver Island Exploration Expedition in 1864, at which time gold was discovered here. By 1865, the boom was pretty much over, with the Victoria merchants and outfitters profitting more than most of the miners. Now, over a century later, expectant hikers approach Leechtown with thoughts of finding a "ghost town" with crumbling buildings and discarded articles strewn about. They are disappointed to discover that there's nothing there. Even the ghosts have evaporated.

Contact CRD Parks (see page 222) for updated information on this and other sections of the Galloping Goose Regional Trail.

THETIS LAKE REGIONAL PARK (MAP 31)

To reach Thetis Lake Regional Park (635 ha), travel about 8 km west of Victoria on Highway 1 (Trans-Canada). Take the Colwood exit onto Highway 1A then turn right at the traffic light onto Six Mile Road. Continue straight ahead to the parking area.

Gates open sunrise - 9 pm, April to September; sunrise - sunset, September to April. From late May to late August, paid parking at the main lot generates funds for the maintenance of the park. Elsewhere, there is limited parking only. The park is spectacular for its many wild flowers in spring, outcrops of moss-covered bedrock, arbutus, Garry oak and Douglas-fir. Park facilities include a swimming area, change room and toilets. Power boats and camping are prohibited. Cycling is permitted only on fire roads at least 3 m wide and on trails specifically designated with bicycle and rider symbols.

For a short one-hour hike, follow the trail just east of Lower Lake to the bridge at the junction of the lakes, then the fire road back to the parking area. Allow two hours to hike around both lakes. The high trail east of Lower Lake leads up onto Seymour Hill to a cairn and good viewpoint.

The area west of the lakes has numerous unmarked trails. Access is possible via Bellamy Road; off Phelps Avenue; via Millstream Road at Lost Lake Road; and via Highland Road at Barker Road (where parking space is very limited indeed). Going northwest from the Upper Lake an excellent hike can be made to Scafe Hill, with good views from both its summits. From here, with pre-arranged transportation, one can hike out to Millstream Road. As we go to press in October, 1997, a zoning bylaw amendment is being considered in adjacent Highlands municipality that could see **Scafe Hill** become a Regional Park. (See also page 68 and Map 16.)

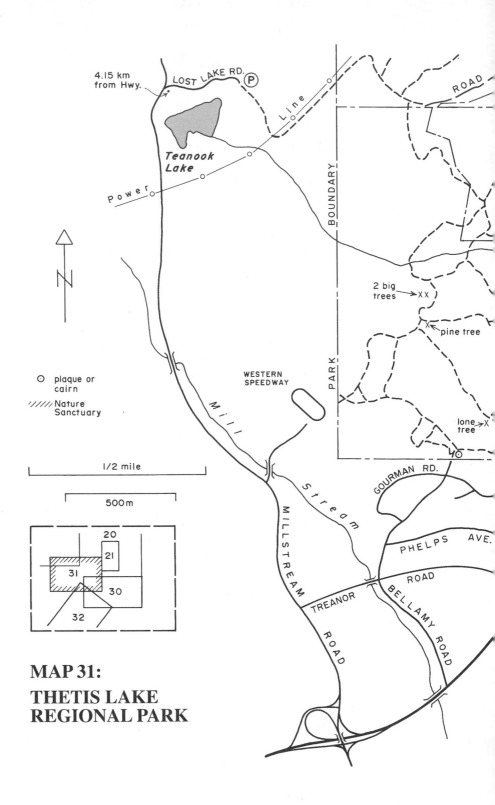

4.15 km from Hwy.

LOST LAKE RD. Ⓟ

Line

Teanook Lake

Power

BOUNDARY

ROAD

2 big trees ⟶ X X

X ⟵ pine tree

PARK

WESTERN SPEEDWAY

lone ⟶ X tree

⊙ plaque or cairn

///// Nature Sanctuary

Mill

1/2 mile

500m

Stream

GOURMAN RD.

MILLSTREAM

20

21

31

30

32

PHELPS AVE.

ROAD

BELLAMY ROAD

TREANOR

ROAD

MAP 31:
THETIS LAKE REGIONAL PARK

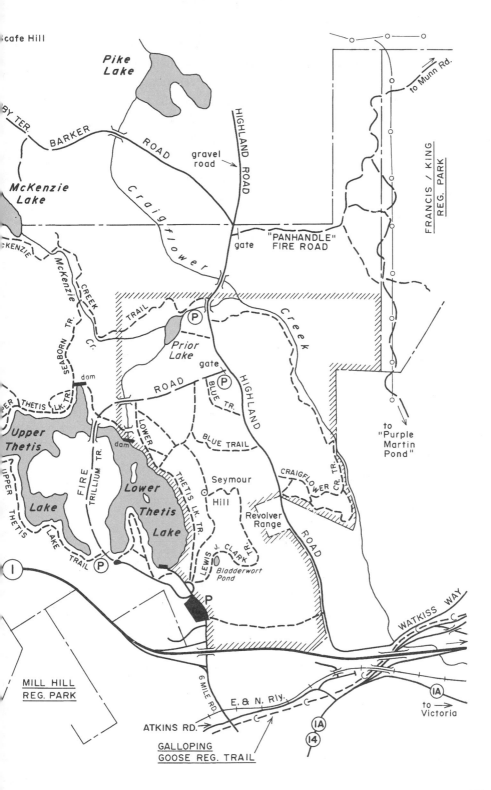

cafe Hill

Pike Lake

McKenzie Lake

BY TER.

BARKER

ROAD

HIGHLAND ROAD

gravel road

Craigflower

gate

"PANHANDLE" FIRE ROAD

to Munn Rd.

FRANCIS / KING REG. PARK

KENZIE

McKenzie

CREEK

Cr.

TRAIL

SEABORN TR.

THETIS LK. TR.

dam

Prior Lake

P

gate

ROAD

BLUE TR.

HIGHLAND

Creek

P

UPPER THETIS LK. TR.

Upper Thetis Lake

FIRE

TRILLIUM TR.

LOWER

dam

BLUE TRAIL

Lower Thetis Lake

THETIS LK. TR.

Seymour Hill

Revolver Range

CRAIGFLOWER CR. TR.

ROAD

to "Purple Martin Pond"

UPPER THETIS LAKE TRAIL

LEWIS J. CLARK TR.

Bladderwort Pond

P

1

LAKE TRAIL

P

P

WATKISS WAY

MILL HILL REG. PARK

6 MILE RD.

E. & N. Rly.

GALLOPING GOOSE REG. TRAIL

ATKINS RD.

1A

1A

14

1A

to → Victoria

153

Thetis Lake Park was transferred from the City of Victoria to CRD Parks in 1993. The **Thetis Park Nature Sanctuary Association** has produced a booklet "Natural History of Thetis Lake Park near Victoria, British Columbia", available from the Field-Naturalist store, 1126 Blanshard Street, Victoria. For membership information, call 727-7675. The TPNSA was formed in 1957 to protect Thetis Lake and its environs from the encroaching post-war housing boom. A map of the trails, along with a guide to wild flowers, is located at the Jessie Woollett Memorial (named for a founding member), near the main entrance to the park. Ron Seaborn, for whom a trail is named, is credited with earlier mapping of the trails in the park. Another trail is named for Lewis J. Clark, a founding member and naturalist who wrote a series of field guides to wild flowers in the Pacific Northwest. The Victorienteers (see page 221) have produced a coloured contour map of the park. Price: $5.00 to non-members.

Note:

- Trails lead east to **Francis / King Park** via the "Panhandle" fire road and south to **Mill Hill Park** via the Six Mile Road underpass (the Thetis Interchange). The **Galloping Goose Regional Trail** is accessed via Highland Road and Watkiss Way to the east, or Six Mile Road to the west.

- No fires permitted. The moss gets very dry in summer and is easily ignited.

- Please take out your garbage.

- Don't pick flowers or mushrooms.

⟨12⟩ LANGFORD and COLWOOD AREAS (MAP 32)
1996 census - Langford: 17,484; Colwood: 13,848

In this book the District of Langford is combined with the City of Colwood because CRD Parks' Galloping Goose Trail snakes back and forth between the two. Colwood, Constance Cove, Craigflower and Viewfield were the names of the four farms established near Victoria by the Puget's Sound Agricultural Company (a division of the Hudson's Bay Company) between 1851 and 1853. Colwood Farm, at the head of Esquimalt Harbour (also known as Esquimalt Farm or Mill Farm) was managed by Captain Edward Edwards Langford, who arrived here with his family aboard the *Tory* in 1851. The municipality of Langford incorporated in December of 1992, and passed a $1.5 million trails initiative in 1996, so we can look forward to new hiking opportunities in that growing community, starting with the Goldie Park Trail across Mill Stream between Goldie and Treanor Avenues. To the west of Langford Lake, Goldstream Meadows Ltd. is proposing to develop a 55-ha property known as the Nixon gravel pit and roughly bounded by Highway 1, Langford Lake, Lakehurst Drive and the E&N Railway line. About a third of the property has been proposed as a lakefront park and as an ecological reserve around a glacial kettle known as Turner's Bog. Alexander and Amy Turner purchased the land in 1947. They farmed half and let out a gravel operation on the other half, which was bought out by the Nixons in 1975. Another proposed large project is the Olympic View development, shown on our Map 32 as the part of the Olympic View Golf Course lands that straddle the Langford/Colwood border and lie between Latoria Road and Metchosin municipality. The development proposal is for about 760 dwelling units, a village, school site, parks and trails.

For information on local municipal parks please contact:

District of Langford
2805 Carlow Road
Victoria, BC   V9B 5V9
phone 474-0068

City of Colwood
3300 Wishart Road
Victoria, BC   V9C 1R1
phone 478-5590

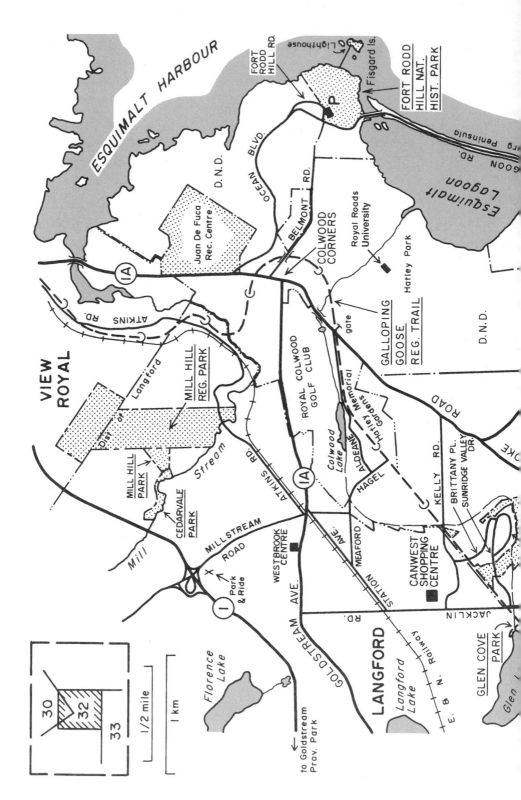

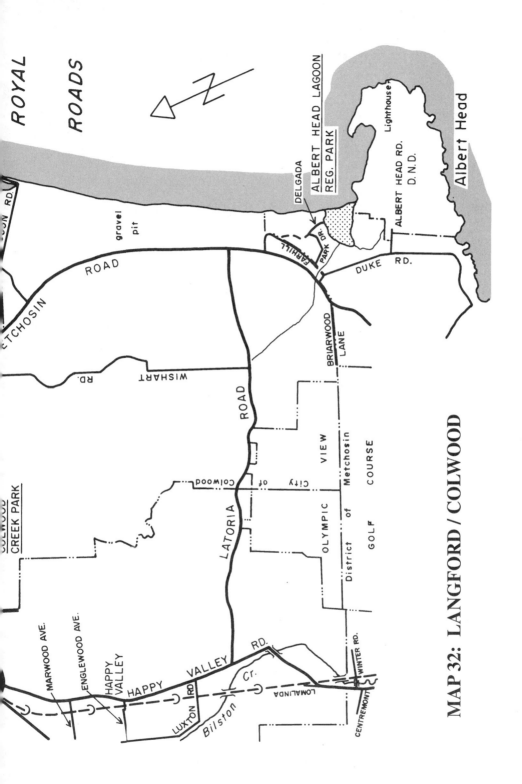

MAP 32: LANGFORD / COLWOOD

GOLDSTREAM PROVINCIAL PARK and MOUNT FINLAYSON (MAP 17)

The park lies within Langford Municipality, but it is immediately south of, and easily reached from, Gowlland Tod Provincial Park in the Highlands, so we have placed it in section 6, Highlands area (see page 76).

MILL HILL REGIONAL PARK (MAPS 30, 31 and 32)

From Victoria take Highway #1 (Trans-Canada Highway) for 12 km to the Millstream interchange (exit 14) and head south on Millstream Road. Just before the Langford shopping district and railway tracks turn left again on to Atkins*. Continue over the Mill Stream bridge; then, immediately after the turnoff to CRD Parks Headquarters, turn left to the large parking lot. The gate is open 8 am - 8 pm, April to October; 8 am - 5 pm, October to April. Picnic tables and toilets are near the parking lot. Trails are not wheelchair accessible. There are no bridle or bike trails. In this Nature Appreciation Park, all dogs must be on leash.

Evidence of shell middens can be found near the base of the Summit Trail. Before European contact, the Songhees people camped at the mouth of the Mill Stream. Later, the Mill Stream (also referred to as Rowe's Stream) supplied the power for the first sawmill on Vancouver Island, which was located at Esquimalt Harbour near Parson's Bridge. It was in operation as early as 1848.

Acquired in 1981, Mill Hill Regional Park (53 ha) is a good place for early spring flowers, and in the shaded areas you will find the calypso orchid. For a field checklist of the 109 wildflower, 24 shrub, 3 fern and 16 tree species found in the park, contact CRD Parks (see page 222). Time up to the viewpoint on the Calypso Trail is about 20 minutes. From the 200-m summit, the site of an old lookout tower, there are magnificent

---

*Atkins is known both as Atkins Road and as Atkins Avenue, depending on which street sign, which map or which municipality you consult.

views in all directions. Now that highway construction in this area is complete, it is possible to descend the north side of the hill to connect with Thetis Lake Park and with the Galloping Goose Trail via Six Mile Road.

GALLOPING GOOSE REGIONAL TRAIL: Colwood highway interchange to Colwood Corners (MAP 32)

For a general description of the Galloping Goose Trail, see page 149. There is a roomy parking lot on Atkins Road where it deadends close to Highway 1A (Old Island Highway). Take the Colwood underpass from the Trans-Canada Highway (#1), turn right at the traffic light onto Six Mile Road and right again onto Atkins. The pedestrian/cycling bridge over Six Mile Road, opened in June of 1997, was built from recycled materials from the old Colwood overpass. As of 1997, paving of the Galloping Goose is complete as far as Atkins. The highlight of this 3-km section is the Mill Stream, crossed by a sturdy bridge near the falls, which are especially lovely on cold, bright days in winter.

JUAN DE FUCA RECREATION CENTRE (MAP 32)

1767 Island Highway, Victoria, BC   V9B 1J1; phone 478-8384

In addition to the pool and ice arena buildings visible from the highway, the Centre has golf, baseball, tennis, soccer and more. It was also home to the velodrome and lawn bowling facilities for the 1994 Commonwealth Games. Currently the new Juan de Fuca branch of the Victoria Public Library is under construction. For joggers and hikers there is a chip trail around the perimeter of the 40-ha grounds and a loop path around the high ground near the highway. A favorite but unofficial use of the grounds is for tobogganing when Victoria gets a snowfall, which it did in December, 1996, the "Blizzard of the Century". (The 64.5 cm that fell Dec. 29 was the third-highest one-day total ever recorded for a major Canadian city.) Also, as of January, 1997, on a one-year trial, the Rec. Centre is home to the first official disc golf course on Vancouver Island. Disc golf is played like ball golf, except that you toss a frisbee toward a marked target instead of hitting a ball.

The Victorienteers (see page 221) have produced a colour contour map (scale 1:6000), price $5.00 to non-members.

FORT RODD HILL and FISGARD LIGHTHOUSE NATIONAL HISTORIC SITES (MAP 32)

603 Fort Rodd Hill Road, Victoria, BC   V9C 2W8

Open daily 10:00 am-5:30 pm (limited services Nov. - Feb.) Before planning a visit, phone 478-5849 for a recorded message about times and admission fees. Access is via Highway 1A and Ocean Boulevard.

When Lt.-Commander James Wood of HM surveying vessel *Pandora* surveyed Esquimalt Harbour, its geographic features were named after the captain and officers of HM frigate *Fisgard* (stationed there 1844-47), including Duntze Head, after Captain (later Admiral) John A. Duntze; Rodd Point, after John Rashleigh Rodd, first lieutenant (later Admiral); Cole Island after Edmund Picoti Cole, master (later Commander); Inskip Island after Robert Mills Inskip, naval instructor (later chaplain); and Fisgard Island after the ship itself.

In 1860, at the recommendation of Sir James Douglas, the first governor of the Crown Colony of British Columbia, Fisgard Rocks and Race Rocks (off East Sooke, now Ecological Reserve 97) became the sites of the first two permanent lighthouses on Canada's Pacific coast. The Fisgard house and light tower were built of plastered brick and fitted with lightworks from England and a circular cast iron staircase from San Francisco. Along with the lightworks, the first keeper, George Davies, arrived in August, 1860 with his wife, three children, and an assistant, William Roberts. For 68 years a succession of keepers kept the oil lamp burning nightly from sunset to sunrise, which involved trimming the wick every four hours. Problems for the early keepers included having plaster falling from the walls, allowing rain to enter, and having the lantern shattered by the noise of the nearby Fort Rodd guns during firing practice. By 1928 the light was automated, to be watched only during World War II, when the light needed to be put out during blackouts. The present causeway to the lighthouse was not built until 1951 (until then, the crossing was by boat, a sometimes-precarious venture) and electricity was not installed until 1958. Now the lighthouse is preserved as a national historic site.

Since 1962 Fort Rodd Hill also has been protected under the National Parks Act. Most of the structures are original; those that are reconstructions are painted a distinctive brown-green color to distinguish them from the original. Use of Esquimalt Harbour by patrolling warships of the British Royal Navy began in 1848. When British Columbia joined Canada in 1871, Esquimalt remained a station of the Royal Navy's Pacific Squadron. This was in the days of steam, so Esquimalt became one of the Royal Navy's 12 coaling stations located strategically around the globe. Temporary defences around Victoria and Esquimalt in 1878 were followed by more permanent installations starting in 1893. Fort Rodd's three batteries (Upper, Lower, and Belmont), were constructed between 1895 and 1900. By 1906, the British troops had been withdrawn (since then Canada's coastal defences have been under the Canadian Armed Forces), and by 1956 the weaponry was obsolete. The guns were fired for the last time and the defence station was closed. During peak times, the Rodd Hill Friends Society operates a concession from the Historic Canteen next to the Lower Battery. For several years, band concerts have been given each Sunday at 2 pm (July and August only) by the band of the 5th (British Columbia) Field Regiment, Royal Canadian Artillery. As Victoria's oldest military unit, "The Fifth" provided militia artillerymen from 1878 to 1956 to man the guns of the Victoria and Esquimalt defences, including those at Fort Rodd Hill. On October 19, 1997, The Fifth Regiment fired a 100-gun salute to mark 100 years since the gunners of the Royal Marine Artillery set off the first salvo on October 22, 1897.

Fort Rodd Hill and the Fisgard Lighthouse are great places to explore and have a picnic. Be prepared, though, to share the grassy slopes with the resident deer.

ESQUIMALT LAGOON (MAP 32)

Just a short distance farther along Ocean Boulevard brings you to the Esquimalt Lagoon. As you walk the 3-km length of the Coburg Peninsula, on one side you have the open ocean and on the other the sheltered waters of the Esquimalt Lagoon, a Waterfowl Sanctuary; both offer great opportunities for bird-watching, especially at times of migration. Inland, across the lagoon, one can see the buildings and grounds of Royal Roads University (see below). (See also Saxe Point Park, page 145.)

GALLOPING GOOSE REGIONAL TRAIL
Colwood Corners to Hatley Park (MAP 32)

There is no pedestrian crosswalk at Sooke Road and Aldeane, so this section is probably best enjoyed as an extension of a visit to Royal Roads University, described next.

ROYAL ROADS UNIVERSITY, HATLEY PARK (MAP 32)

Hatley Castle, in historic 263-ha Hatley Park estate, was designed by Victoria architect Samuel McClure and completed in 1908 for James Dunsmuir, premier of BC from 1900 to 1902 and lieutenant-governor of the province from 1906 to 1909. James was the son of Robert Dunsmuir, the Scottish coal baron who built Craigdarroch Castle, and was himself a very wealthy man, having sold his Wellington Colliery Company Limited coal mines near Ladysmith, plus assets in San Francisco, for $11 million in 1910. Built of sandstone from Valdez and Saturna Islands, Hatley Castle took two-and-a-half years and four million dollars to build. On the main floor were pantries, kitchen, morning room, dining room, drawing room, library, den, reception room and billiards room. On the second and third floors were 22 bedrooms and 9 bathrooms; the fourth floor had a ballroom. The gardens, planted in 1910, were designed by Brett & Hall landscape architects of Boston, and required 100 workers. Because the estate was self-supporting, there were kennels, horse stables, a dairy, a laundry, a slaughterhouse and smokehouse, a refrigeration plant and even its own Chinese village. Boilers to heat the greenhouse and conservatory burned 100 tons of coal (no problem for a coal baron), and 200 cords of wood a year. The Dunsmuir's son, named James after his father, but known as Boy, was a great horseman; he died when the Lusitania was sunk in 1915. The elder James Dunsmuir died in 1920, and his wife, Laura, in 1937. In 1940 the castle and grounds were purchased by the federal government for $75,000. Not included in that sale were the 20 acres of waterfront and Cavendish House, or Dolaura, belonging to Dola, the youngest of the Dunsmuir daughters. Raised in Hatley Castle, she married Cmdr. Henry Cavendish (who was related to the Duke of Devonshire) but after they divorced she worked in London for the Molyneux fashion house. Dola returned to Victoria to care for her three nieces after her sister, Kathleen, was killed in an air raid in 1941. The house she built was named Dolaura, after her father's steam yacht. Actress Tallulah Bankhead would visit there. After Dola died in 1966, the house was used by Parks Canada as an administration building, among other uses, but it was vacant as of 1987, fell into disrepair, and was demolished in July, 1996. For many years, Hatley Park and Castle were occupied by Royal Roads Military College, a degree-granting university for Canadian officers. As of 1995, the buildings plus 56.7 ha of the grounds have been leased to the provincial government as the campus for the new Royal Roads University, which first offered courses in the fall of 1996. The campus plus the remaining 202.4 ha of national defence property (mostly old-growth forest, though selectively logged over the years) has been declared a national historic site as of 1997. Since 1996 an annual Paint-in and Picnic has been organized each May by the Friends of Hatley Park. The campus grounds, which are open to the public, are extensive, attractive and varied, with grand architecture, ponds and streams, Italian and Japanese gardens, rose and bog gardens, tennis courts - and resident peacocks. Future plans for the DND grounds are undetermined, and access is currently limited.

For further information please contact: Royal Roads University, 391-2511. The Victorienteers (see page 221) have produced a colour map (scale 1:10,000); price $5.00 to non-members.

Long the home of the Straits Salish and Songhees people, this area was explored by the Spaniard, Lieutenant Don Manual Quimper, in 1790. He named the bay outside the lagoon Valdez y Bazan. Later, when Britain controlled these shores, it was renamed by Captain Henry Kellett of HM Surveying Vessel *Herald*, as Royal Bay. This was in honour of Queen Victoria and Prince Albert, as the area was situated between the city of Victoria and Albert Head, but even then it was commonly called Royal Roads, which name has stuck. (The term road, or roadstead, refers to a place less enclosed than a harbour, but where ships may safely anchor.)

While you are at Royal Roads University, include a visit to **Colwood Creek**. Head down the main access road, and, just before a road branches off to the left, look for an unmarked trail on your left. It descends into the shady valley where you can follow the creek for some distance until your way is blocked and you must turn to retrace your steps. This idyllic spot is worth a visit. For a second view of the creek, continue down the road to the sign for the Glen Gardens and trail. A steep descent through the recently-developed gardens brings you down to creek level, where you can follow a woodsy trail out to Esquimalt Lagoon. You can circle back by way of the Castle gardens.

GALLOPING GOOSE REGIONAL TRAIL
Hatley Park to Happy Valley (MAP 32)

Two parks in the vicinity of Glen Lake afford opportunities to step off the Galloping Goose to explore or take a lunch break. The first is **Colwood Creek Park**. Turn onto Brittany Drive where it crosses the trail near the Canwest Shopping Centre and follow Brittany around to its intersection with Sunridge Valley Drive. Enter the park and take the bridge across Colwood Creek to the main, open area of the park. You'll find picnic tables and playground equipment for the children. After crossing the creek again, pick up the trail on the other side of Sunridge Valley Drive. You'll regain the Galloping Goose Trail just behind Belmont School. Another small park is **Glen Cove Park** at the foot of Glen Lake, a second opportunity to step off the Galloping Goose for a break. After entering Metchosin Municipality near Winter Road you will cross Bilston Creek, which, with its tributaries, flows into Witty's Lagoon, which is named after John Witty, an early landowner. The Bilston Watershed Habitat Protection Association was formed with the aim of protection and restoration of these local streams. Work on an inter-municipal Bilston Creek Watershed Management Plan began in 1994 through the Bilston Intergovernmental Consortium. Around 1860 some former slaves immigrated to Happy Valley, hence its up-beat name.

MOUNT WELLS REGIONAL PARK RESERVE

Acquired in 1996, this 88-ha park reserve is located in Langford, off Humpback Road, near the Humpback Reservoir. It is to the east of, and adjacent to, the southern portion of the new Sooke Hills Wilderness Park. As park reserve, this area is not yet open to the public, but when it is, you will discover a hill with wildflowers and Garry oak meadows and views of the Sooke Hills, Colwood, and Langford. In the meantime, contact CRD Parks for current information.

The original inhabitants of this area called it "Smets-shosin", meaning "place of stinking fish" after a time when a dead whale was washed up on shore. In 1842 James Douglas recorded it as "Metcho-sin", and it has come to us as Metchosin.

The District of Metchosin has so far managed to retain its rural charm for the pleasure of residents and visitors alike. Some of the prettiest stretches of the Galloping Goose Regional Trail (see page 149) are to be found in Metchosin, and most of our other hikes in this area could be combined with a section of the Galloping Goose to stretch your legs a bit further. One good parking area for access to the Goose is on Rocky Point Road, about 4 km past the intersection of Kangaroo and Rocky Point Roads, from which point several loop hikes are possible. Be aware that many of the public trails in Metchosin lead to bridle trails on private property. If you don't know if the land is public or private, ask; always behave as though you are a guest. After exploring the trails, you may wish to explore the history of the area. The old Metchosin school, the first public school opened after BC joined Confederation, turned 125 this year. Located on Happy Valley Road across from the Municipal Hall, it has been turned into a small museum by the Metchosin School Museum Society, which was founded in 1971. The project won the 1997 President's Award from the Hallmark Society. Open Saturdays and Sundays, 1:30-4:30 pm from mid-April to mid-October and also by special arrangement.The Society is also developing the Metchosin Agricultural Equipment Museum across the road, currently open only by special arrangement. Call 478-3451 (Ron Bradley) or 478-6848 (Daisy Bligh). In 1983, to honour the pioneers of Metchosin's first half-century, the Society published *Footprints - Pioneer Families of the Metchosin District, Southern Vancouver Island, 1851-1900. Footprints* is now out of print, but available at all branches of the Victoria Public Library. If you are visiting Metchosin in the spring, be sure to stop at St. Mary's Church (consecrated in 1873), where the Easter lilies surround the church building with a vision of white blooms.

Bus service to Metchosin has recently been expanded to include limited Sunday service. Some Western Communities buses are now equipped with bike racks to carry two bikes each. Phone BC Transit at 382-6161 for details.

For more information on trails and parks in Metchosin please contact:

District of Metchosin
4450 Happy Valley Road, Victoria, BC   V9C 3Z3
phone 474-3167

ALBERT HEAD LAGOON REGIONAL PARK (MAPS 32 and 33)

To reach Albert Head Lagoon from Victoria, take Highways 1A (Old Island Highway) and 14 (Sooke Road). Turn left onto Metchosin Road, travel 4 km and turn left onto Farhill Road just before reaching the far end of the gravel pit. Turn right at the first junction and proceed to the end of the road: Farhill becomes Park Drive becomes Delgada Road. Resist any temptation to try to drive off the road or your vehicle will become bogged down in sand and gravel. Gate open 7 am to sunset. Parking is limited and there are no facilities at this park. This is a nature sanctuary and a CRD nature appreciation park. Dogs are not permitted at the lagoon or on the shore around the lagoon, but are allowed on the ocean beach year-round. In 1846, Captain Kellett named Albert Head after HRH Prince Albert, husband to Queen Victoria, because of its proximity to the town of Victoria.

Just north of the parking lot is the site of the first steam-powered sawmill on Vancouver Island, constructed for the Vancouver's Island Steam Sawmill Company in 1853. The sawmill suffered many financial and mechanical difficulties before burning to the ground in 1859. The earlier inhabitants of this site, the Stsangal band, had fared no better: considered a lower class people, they were raided for slaves by other bands.

Only 7 ha in size, the park encircles a picture-perfect lagoon which is almost closed off by its gravel berm. Take along your favourite field guides; see how many plants you can find along the berm, and how many birds you can identify around the lagoon. (Keep an eye out for mute swans and migrating waterfowl.) A short walk north along the cobble beach is possible.

MAP 33: METCHOSIN

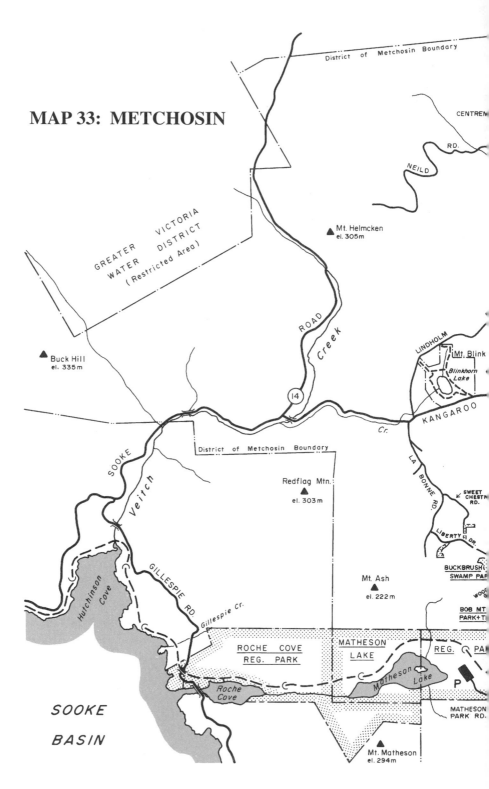

District of Metchosin Boundary

CENTREM

RD.

NEILD

GREATER VICTORIA
WATER DISTRICT
(Restricted Area)

Mt. Helmcken
el. 305 m

ROAD

Creek

LINDHOLM

Mt. Blink

Blinkhorn
Lake

Buck Hill
el. 335 m

14

KANGAROO

Cr.

SOOKE

District of Metchosin Boundary

LA BONNE RD.

SWEET
CHESTN
RD.

Veitch

Redflag Mtn.
el. 303 m

LIBERTY DR.

BUCKBRUSH
SWAMP PAR

GILLESPIE RD.

Mt. Ash

WOOD

Hutchinson
Cove

Gillespie Cr.

el. 222 m

BOB MT
PARK + T

ROCHE COVE
REG. PARK

MATHESON
LAKE

REG.

PA

Roche
Cove

Matheson

Lake

P

SOOKE

Matheson Lake

BASIN

MATHESON
PARK RD.

Mt. Matheson
el. 294 m

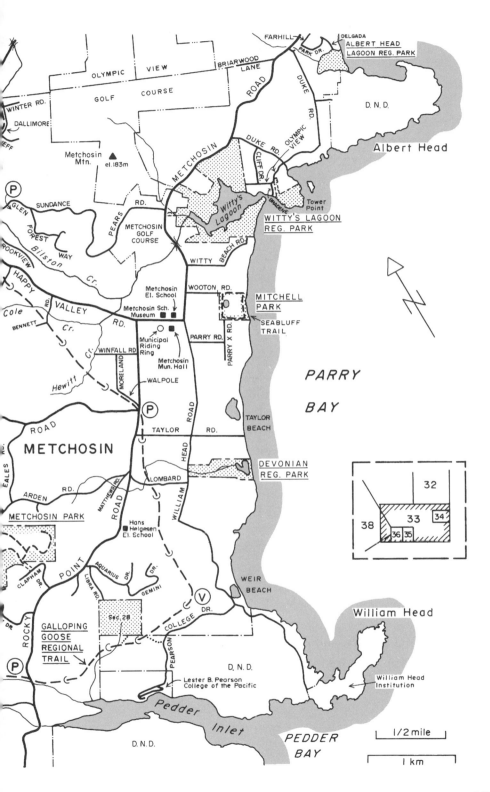

169

WITTY'S LAGOON REGIONAL PARK (MAPS 33 and 34)

Access from Victoria is via Highways 1, 1A and 14, then turn onto Metchosin Road. Follow this for about 6 km to Pears Road and the Metchosin Golf and Country Club (open to the public). Opposite, on the left, is the main entrance to the park, where you will find ample parking, toilet facilities and, since 1993, a temporary CRD Nature House. Allow about 40 minutes' driving time from Victoria. Other more limited parking areas are shown on the map, principally at Olympic View Drive and at the end of Witty Beach Road.

This was the site of the village of the Ka-Ky-Aakan band in the 1850s when the first settlers arrived. Metchosin was purchased from this band by the Hudson's Bay Company by agreement (the Douglas Treaties) dated May 1, 1850, by which the band received the equivalent in blankets of £43/6/8. The agreement, signed with an X by Quoite-To-Kay- num and Tly-a-Hum, described the area as "the whole of the lands situated and lying between Point Albert [Albert Head] and the inlet of Whoyung [Pedder Bay] from the sea to the mountains behind". The village was abandoned in the early 1860s when the few surviving members, most of mixed Clallum blood but practiced in Songhees ways and traditions, moved to Esquimalt to join the main Songhees tribe whose jurisdiction extended from William Head to Sayward Beach and the D'Arcy Islands.

The park (56 ha) was originally created in 1969 and became a CRD park in 1986. The old Nature House, never designed as such, was closed in January, 1992, and development of a management plan for the park was begun. Some of the issues the plan addressed were handling of introduced species, wildlife trees (see note below) and archaeological sites. Witty's is a CRD nature appreciation park: here you will find an interesting combination of forest, grassland, salt marsh, beach, lagoon and rocky shore, with many birds and plants in these various habitats. This is one place where you may find cyclamen growing wild. Sitting Lady Falls, on Bilston Creek, can be spectacular in winter and spring after heavy rain.

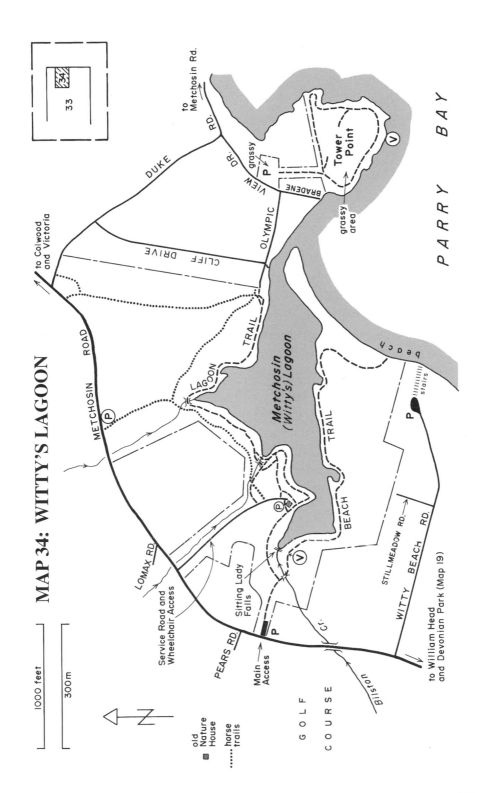

MAP 34: WITTY'S LAGOON

1000 feet

300m

N

old Nature House

horse trails

to Colwood and Victoria

METCHOSIN ROAD

DUKE

VIEW DR.

CLIFF DRIVE

OLYMPIC

to Metchosin Rd.

grassy

P

BRADENE

Tower Point

V

grassy area

LAGOON TRAIL

Metchosin (Witty's) Lagoon

beach

stairs

P

BEACH TRAIL

TRAIL

V

LOMAX RD.

Service Road and Wheelchair Access

Sitting Lady Falls

PEARS RD.

Main Access

P

Cr.

Bilston

GOLF COURSE

STILLMEADOW RD.

WITTY BEACH RD.

to William Head and Devonian Park (Map 19)

PARRY BAY

33 34

171

Tides permitting, a hike along the beach from here to Taylor Road or Devonian Park is possible. Horses should stay on the designated horse trails or roads; bikes are prohibited throughout the park. Dogs must be kept under control at all times. For information on access to the wheelchair-accessible picnic area, washrooms and trails, please contact CRD Parks, 478-3344. A CRD Parks brochure (partially funded by The Field-Naturalist store), "Birds of Witty's Lagoon", lists all of the birds (with their scientific names) that have been spotted in the park. Witty's Lagoon is named after John Witty, a neighbouring landowner from 1867 on.

Tower Point, though not adjoining, is a part of Witty's Lagoon Regional Park. From its Rocky Bluff Trail you have a front-row view of harbour seals on the rocks just off shore. The pocket beaches on the west side of the point are excellent places to study pillow basalt, formed about 55 million years ago when molten rock (magma) was cooled by ocean waters. There is limited wheelchair accessiblity to the picnic area, with a water tap and picnic tables. The trails (uneven, not paved) and the toilets (there's a step up) are not accessible. Access is off Olympic View Drive, off Duke Road. Gate open 8 am to sunset, but in winter the grass parking area is closed so you must park on the road.

Note: **Wildlife trees** are old, dead or decaying trees used by wildlife for nesting, food, shelter, denning, roosting and perching. For more information about wildlife trees or a pamphlet, "Hanging Wildlife Tree Sign", please contact:

Wildlife Tree Coordinator
c/o Integrated Management Branch
Ministry of Environment, Lands and Parks
780 Blanshard St., Victoria, BC   V8V 1X4

MITCHELL PARK / SEABLUFF TRAIL (MAP 33)

One of the newer hikes in Metchosin is the Seabluff Trail, donated by Geoff and B.H. Mitchell, long-time Metchosin residents. It is a short hike around open fields, along sea view bluffs (50 m high, looking south to the Olympics), and through woods, skirting a small irrigation pond. Please do not disturb the sheep; dogs MUST be on a leash at all times; leave gates closed. Please note that only the perimeter trail is park. The open space in the centre is part of an operating farm. Please do not hike over this area.

Access is by Metchosin and Wootton Roads or by William Head, Parry and Parry Cross Roads. Parry Bay and William Head were named by Captain Kellett of HMS *Herald* after his friend, the noted Arctic explorer Rear Admiral Sir William Edward Parry.

BLINKHORN LAKE (MAP 33)

Blinkhorn Lake is a pleasant spot to visit, with a woodsy trail encircling the picturesque lake. (Turn left at the red gate.) Access is off Kangaroo Road. It is Greater Victoria Water District property but is not closed to the public. Blinkhorn Lake and Mountain are named for Thomas Blinkhorn, who, with his wife, Anne, arrived in 1851 as independent settlers to manage the Metchosin farm of Captain James Cooper. Thomas Blinkhorn served as a magistrate from 1853 to his death in 1856. Years earlier, as a stockman in Australia, Blinkhorn had rescued Captain Sir John Franklin, lost in the bush.

DEVONIAN REGIONAL PARK (MAP 33)

Access from Victoria is by Highways 1, 1A and 14, then by Metchosin Road and William Head Road, about 40 minutes' drive from Victoria. About 500 m beyond Taylor Road you will find Devonian Park (13 ha) with an ample parking lot and a picnic area. Gate open sunrise to sunset.

In 1857, John McGregor purchased a parcel of land (Section 5, Metchosin District), from the government of the Colony of Vancouver Island, which included the present-day park, and here he established his home which he named "Oakwood". The McGregor's two youngest daughters, Agnes and Jean Katherine (Kate), were both born there. The eldest daughter, Mary, who had been born in Scotland in 1845, was married at "Oakwood" on March 12, 1861, to John Van Houten of the Sandwich Islands (Hawaii).

On November 12, 1862, Hans Lars Helgesen married Lillian Colquhoun in Victoria; on January 13, 1863, they purchased "Oakwood" and renamed it "Sherwood". Here seven children were born to the Helgesens. Two of the sons died at an early age and were buried on the farm. Their remains were later exhumed and reburied in the new St. Mary's church cemetery which opened in 1873. Many descendants of the Helgesen family still live in the Metchosin area.

In 1980, through the generosity of the Devonian Foundation and the provincial government, the CRD acquired 11.3 ha comprising Devonian Regional Park. The CRD purchased an additional 2.2 ha in 1983 to provide for the Helgesen bridle trail along the park boundary.

Sherwood Pond used to be one of the many lagoons found along the Metchosin coast. Its barrier spit eventually closed off the lagoon, leaving it, and the population of cutthroat trout, landlocked. Usually trout fry leave for the ocean in their second or third year, and return to spawn in their fourth. This population has adapted to fresh water for life. The cobble barrier is porous enough to allow some passage of water, so the level of the pond can vary by as much as two metres. Year round the pond is a delight for birdwatchers.

Allow about 25 minutes to reach the beach from the parking lot. Tides permitting, a 3-km one-way walk is possible from nearby Taylor Beach (a shelving, pebble beach) to Witty's Lagoon. Note that there is also beach access at Taylor Road. The steep trails and the toilet facilities are not wheelchair accessible, but the picnic area could be. This is a CRD nature appreciation park so all dogs must be on a leash or under control.

METCHOSIN WILDERNESS PARK (MAP 33)

Metchosin has been granted a 10-year Licence of Occupation (expiring in 2000) for the trails over the Crown land of Section 25. Known also as Clapham Park and Hundred Acre Park, it is located northwest of Rocky Point Road between Arden Road and Clapham Drive. Its trails are shared by hikers and horseback riders, leading to several viewpoints. Its deep woods and small creeks offer an excellent shady hike for a hot day.

From the Clapham Drive access follow the main trail, keeping right to the viewpoint. Or, bearing left from the access, cross the sturdy wooden bridge. The trail ahead used to lead you out of the park and onto private lands. Now, with the development of those lands along Liberty Drive, it leads you from the viewpoint down through the prosaically-named **Connector Park** to Liberty Drive. You come out opposite **Buckbrush Swamp Park**, which is sign-posted and has its own trail around the swamp. Turning right after the bridge takes one to the Arden Road access. From the Arden access at Brian Hunter Place, take the first left (and cross a bridge) and later a second bridge to a "T", left to the viewpoint or right to Clapham Drive. Our map shows two projections from the even rectangle of Section 25. These make up **Metchosin** (municipal) **Park**.

BOB MOUNTAIN PARK (MAPS 33 and 35)

Though small in size (1.3 ha), this park is immensely useful in providing a trail link between the Metchosin Wilderness Park area, Matheson Lake Regional Park, and the Galloping Goose Trail. See Map 33 for the sign-posted start of the trail on Liberty Drive near Woodley Ghyll Drive. The trail meanders a fair bit, but the park itself is just a narrow corridor, so please do not wander off on other old roads and trails onto private property. The trail's final loop takes you up into Matheson Lake Regional Park near the summit of Mount Ball with its several viewpoints. If you continue straight ahead, on what appears to be the same trail, you will find yourself on the Mount Ball Trail, heading west and downward toward Wildwood Creek and Wayne's Rock. You will probably miss the intersection where the Mount Ball Trail drops down to the Galloping Goose Regional Trail near the eastern border of Matheson Lake Park (closest to Rocky Point Road).

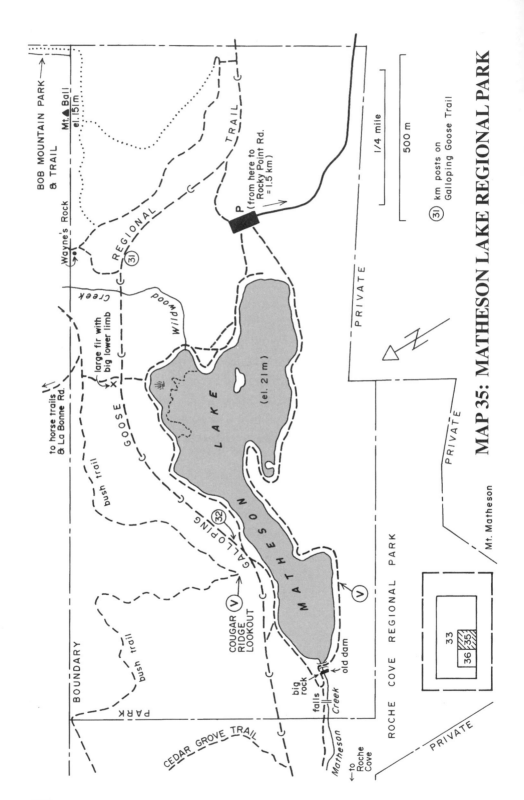

MAP 35: MATHESON LAKE REGIONAL PARK

BOB MOUNTAIN PARK & TRAIL

Mt. Ball el. 151 m

Wayne's Rock

REGIONAL

TRAIL

(31)

Creek

Wildwood

large fir with
big lower limb

X

to horse trails
& La Bonne Rd.

bush trail

GOOSE

GALLOPING

(32)

LAKE

MATHESON

(el. 21 m)

COUGAR
RIDGE
LOOKOUT

V

V

V

BOUNDARY

PARK

bush trail

CEDAR GROVE TRAIL

big
rock

falls

old dam

Matheson Creek

to
Roche
Cove

ROCHE COVE REGIONAL PARK

P (from here to
Rocky Point Rd.
= 1.5 km)

PRIVATE

PRIVATE

Mt. Matheson

N

PRIVATE

1/4 mile

500 m

(31) km posts on
Galloping Goose Trail

33

36 35

MATHESON LAKE REGIONAL PARK (MAPS 33, 35 and 36)

Access from Victoria is via Highway 14 - Metchosin Road - Happy Valley Road - and Rocky Point Road (29 km). Just before the road forks (left to Rocky Point; right, to East Sooke) turn right onto Matheson Lake Park Road (signposted) and about 1.5 km brings you to the parking lot. Gate open sunrise - 9 pm, April to September; sunrise to sunset, September to April. For many years a provincial park, Matheson Lake Park (162 ha) was transferred to the Capital Regional District in 1993.

In addition to hiking, there is swimming and some fishing. There is no boat launch, but electric-motor-propelled vessels (cartop size only) are permitted. The southeast corner of the lake is the best place to launch canoes.

The Galloping Goose Regional Trail links the park to Roche Cove (4.5 km one way). Trails circle Matheson Lake, and from the Galloping Goose at Wildwood Creek a trail leads up to Wayne's Rock (about 10 minutes' walk). Wildwood Creek has three fords and in the area just north of our map several horse trails have been developed. Just beyond Wayne's Rock a trail leads west over the creek and in 15 minutes brings you again to the Galloping Goose Trail.

Trails lead up to **Mount Ball** from whose summit the view is northward to Mount Redflag. Another good viewpoint, towards Victoria and the sea, is a little lower down, near the Bob Mountain Trail (see above). If you are hiking the Mount Ball Trail eastward from the Wildwood Creek and Wayne's Rock end, watch carefully for the trail that veers right near the summit to descend and join the Galloping Goose Trail where it heads out of Matheson Lake Park toward Rocky Point Road. If you miss the intersection you will find yourself heading out of Matheson Lake Park along the Bob Mountain Trail and out to Liberty Road.

The trail along the creek from Matheson Lake to Roche Cove was the oldtimers' portage trail in the 1850s and '60s, part of the Lake Pass and Barde Knockie Trail route from Sooke to Bilston Farm (and from there on to Victoria).

No camping; no fires; no cycling (except on the Galloping Goose Regional Trail). Pets must be on a leash or under control in this CRD nature appreciation park.

LESTER B. PEARSON COLLEGE OF THE PACIFIC (MAP 33)

Named for Lester Bowles Pearson, former prime minister of Canada and recipient of the Nobel Peace Prize, the College is one of nine United World Colleges. Students attend from around the globe, and follow the International Baccalaueate Program. The classrooms, dormitories and other buildings are off-limits to the public, but the trails are shared for the enjoyment of all. The campus borders Pedder Bay, named by Captain Kellett after a friend in the navy. Earlier, Manuel Quimper had named it Rada de Eliza, after Lt. Francisco Eliza, who gave the orders to explore southward in the *Princesa Real* (*Princess Royal*).

Pearson College to Section 28:
As you approach the College along Pearson College Drive, there's room for several vehicles on the side of the road, just before the first College sign. After a short walk around a bend in the road, past the Wallace Haughan Drive sign, look for an inconspicuous trail sign on the right. A five-minute-walk brings you out to the Galloping Goose Trail, with the 28 km marker in sight. Head west on the Galloping Goose for about five minutes, looking for a similarly difficult-to-spot sign on the right. The trail climbs up to Section 28, Crown Land leased to Metchosin as parkland. Keeping to the left on the trail will bring you out to the end of Libra Road; heading uphill and to the right brings you out to a bend on Gemini Road. The route takes you through several different forest types: cedar, Douglas-fir, and arbutus. Reference to our Map 33 will suggest several possible loop hikes that include Section 28.

Deep Woods Trail:
Near the second sign welcoming you to Pearson College, look for the signposted trailhead on the right. If there are several vehicles in your party, you will need to continue to the parking lot at the end of the road, and hike back up to start the walk. The trail climbs gently and leads you in a wide loop that approximately follows the perimeter of the College

property. Budding entomologists will love the huge anthills; nowhere else could they be so large and so numerous. When you have followed two sides of the rough rectangle, the trail drops to the left. At this point, you can take a five-minute detour out to the Galloping Goose Trail, where the turnoff is marked by a pile of rocks. Continuing downhill instead brings you out through an outdoor exercise and rope practice area onto the old pipeline trail that skirts Pedder Bay. A left turn will take you back to the College Parking lot. Time for the circuit: under an hour (double if the kids love ants).

⟨14⟩ EAST SOOKE AREA (CONTENTS MAP)

East Sooke is an unincorporated area within the Capital Regional District. It contains two of the large CRD parks, Roche Cove and East Sooke Regional parks:

ROCHE COVE REGIONAL PARK (MAPS 33, 35 and 36)

Access to Roche Cove Regional Park (159 ha) is by Highway 14. Just past 17 Mile House turn left onto Gillespie Road and 3 km will bring you to the ample parking lot with wheelchair-accessible toilet facilities. It is about a 45-minute drive from Victoria. The Cove itself is accessible to shallow-draught vessels.

Cross the road and go on foot past the barrier to the walk-in picnic area. The road ahead leads to the coast past the caretaker's residence on your left. Boundary markers indicate the limits of the park and the Grouse Nest private property beyond. A walk northward is possible on the Galloping Goose Regional Trail.

Returning to the barrier, a trail immediately to your left leads to Kellett Point, three beaches, lovely grassy slopes and beautiful views of the Sooke Basin and Olympic Mountains. It is an excellent picnic area. Be sure to listen for and spot the Belted Kingfishers in the area. River otters live here too; look for their scat.

Recross the road into the greater part of Roche Cove Park where you can continue on the Galloping Goose or follow the Matheson Creek Trail into Matheson Lake Park; or explore other trails recently created from older roads. An especially good viewpoint northeast of Roche Cove is shown on our map.

Roche Cove Regional Park was purchased by the CRD in June of 1985. Forty hectares of former Crown Lands designated for park purposes on the north slope of Mt. Matheson were added in 1990. A private parcel west of Kellett Point was purchased in 1996, bringing the park's size up to 159 ha. The cove (and Roche Harbour, San Juan Island, USA) are

180

MAP 36: ROCHE COVE REGIONAL PARK

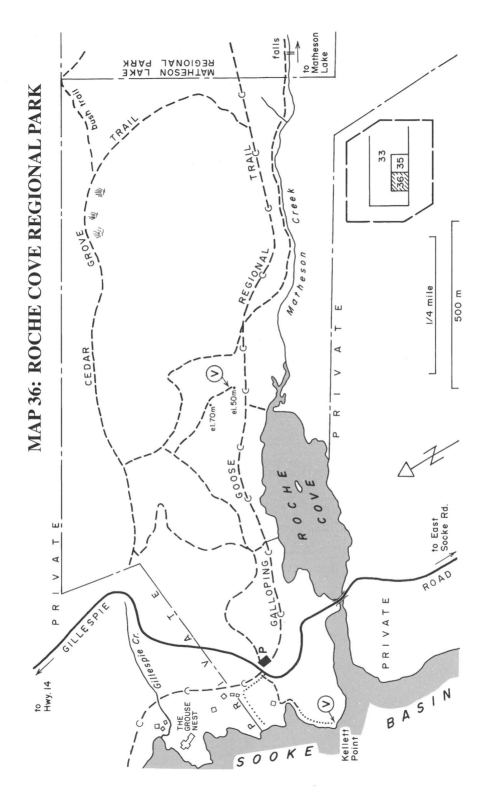

named after Richard Roche (later Captain), RN, who served as midshipman under Captain Henry Kellett (for whom Kellett Point is named) aboard the *Herald*. When Captain Kellett was appointed to this survey in 1845, he had first to take the *Herald* to the Arctic in search of Sir John Franklin before undertaking the survey of Victoria and Esquimalt harbours and Sooke inlet, in 1846, in company with the smaller surveying vessel *Pandora*. Roche also served as mate, again with Captain Kellett, on the Arctic exploring ship *Resolute*, 1852-54. The *Resolute* had to be abandoned in the ice in 1854, but she drifted free and was picked up by an American whaling boat and taken to New Bedford. She was presented back to Queen Victoria and Great Britain by the US government in 1856, and remained on the navy list until 1879. Vice Admiral Sir Henry Kellett, KCB, published an account of the search for Franklin aboard the *Resolute*.

EAST SOOKE REGIONAL PARK (MAP 37)

Access from Victoria is via Highways 1 and 14 and thence either by Gillespie Road and East Sooke Road; or via Metchosin, Rocky Point and East Sooke roads. The distance to Aylard Farm is about 34 km, an hour's drive from Victoria. This park was acquired as a regional park in 1966.

There are six access points to the 1424-ha park, but note there are only three parking lots with facilities - at **Aylard Farm** (gate open sunrise to sunset), **Anderson Cove** and **Pike Road**. Families will find hiking from the Aylard Farm end the most rewarding, as there are regular parks facilities, green meadows and good access to sandy beaches, also lookouts at Creyke Point and Beechey Head. This is a popular spot each fall as throngs turn out for the annual "Hawk Watch" from the **Beechey Head** viewpoint, commonly referred to as Hawk Lookout or simply The Lookout. Sightings of Turkey Vultures migrating over the Strait of Juan de Fuca or Georgia Strait may be reported by mail to: Olympic Vulture Study c/o Diann MacRae, 22622 - 53 Ave. SE, Bothell, Washington, USA 98021 or by e-mail to: tvulture@SCN.ORG. **Babbington Hill**, another excellent viewpoint, can also be reached from Aylard Farm. The Aylard Farm area and toilets are the only part of the park suitable for wheelchair use.

There is limited parking at the access on East Sooke Road. Another access to the same area of the park is off **Parkheights Drive**. Drive to Leda Road and park at the intersection but don't block the narrow extension of Parkheights as it is a fire road and also leads past a private home. Walk the extension of Parkheights for about 350 m to the park entrance which has a locked chain barrier.

The **Mount Maguire** area may be accessed by taking **Copper Mine Road** for about 1 km to Valentine Road. Park on the roadside but don't block either road. Walk up Copper Mine Road about 30 m to Gordon Road with a "no exit" sign on the right. Follow Gordon Road about 200 m to the park entrance, which is gated.

Iron Mine Bay at the west end of the park has a good pebble beach and some fine views. The bay's name, and that of Copper Mine Road, are reminders of mining enterprises between 1863 and 1971. See CRD Parks' brochure, *Mining in East Sooke Regional Park,* for details. There is still evidence of old logging roads throughout the peninsula, but in the main our map shows only the officially signposted trails. Stick to these marked trails: more than one hiker has unintentionally spent the night in East Sooke Regional Park. You will find sign boards showing "points of interest". Please do not damage or remove any of these signs.

This semi-wilderness park, within easy reach of Victoria, is good for year-round hiking offering extensive trails for day hikers. There are many interconnecting trails, all well-cut and signposted. Distances can be deceptive because of the rough terrain so we give here some approximate hiking times. It is wise to start your hike early in the day and not overestimate your capabilities. Always allow more than enough time to return to your vehicle before dark. For the more energetic hikers the **Coast Trail** is the best of all. Its scenery is magnificent with good views of the Olympic Peninsula. The coast itself, with deep bays, cliffs and chasms, has an atmosphere of remoteness and adventure.

In spring and summer, flower enthusiasts may find the following: fringe cup, orange honeysuckle, stonecrop, monkey flower, hardhack, harvest brodiaea, white campion, western buttercup, red columbine, small-flower

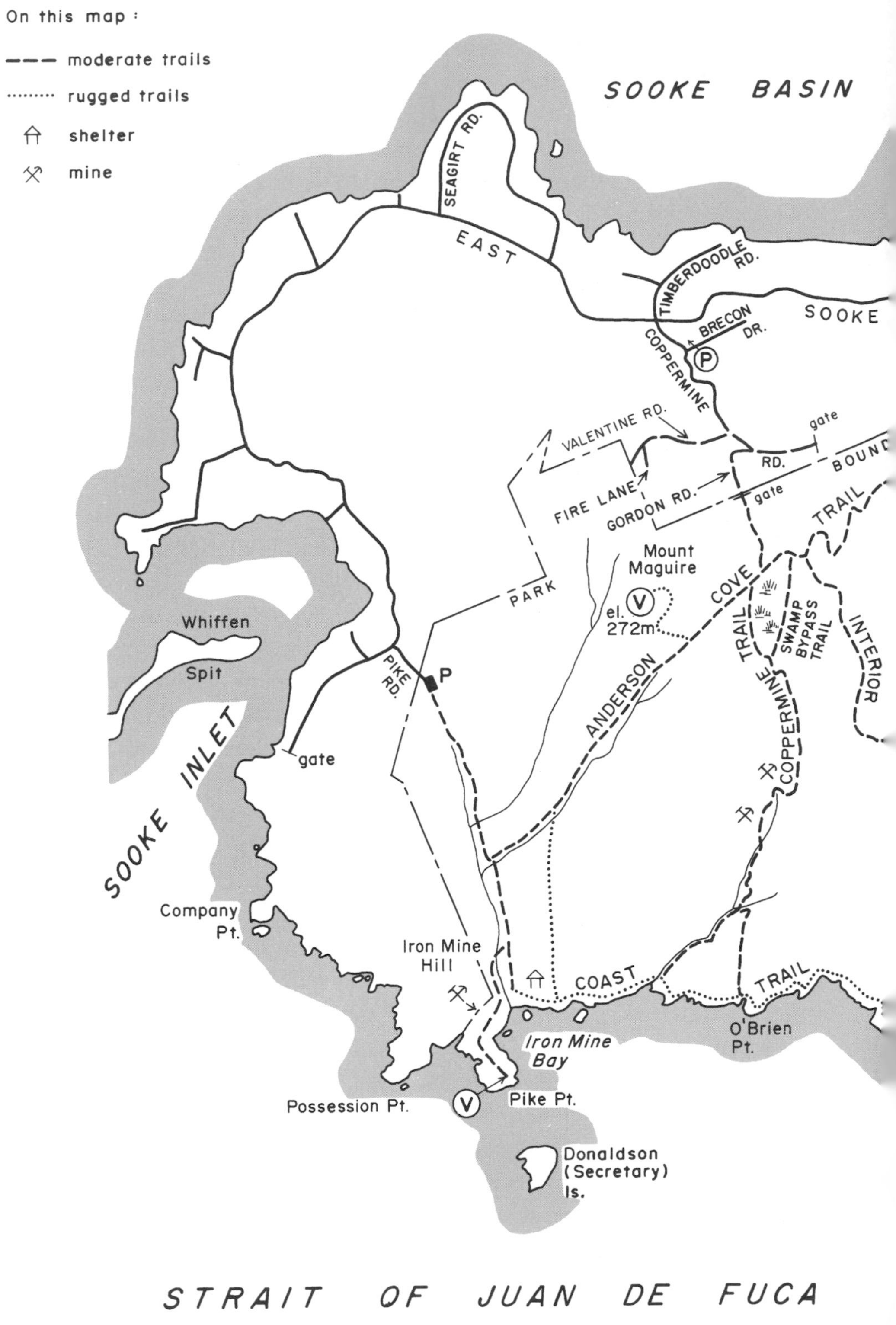

On this map:

– – – moderate trails

.... rugged trails

⌂ shelter

⚒ mine

SOOKE BASIN

SEAGIRT RD.

EAST

TIMBERDOODLE RD.

BRECON DR.

SOOKE

COPPERMINE

Ⓟ

VALENTINE RD.

FIRE LANE

GORDON RD.

RD.

gate

gate

BOUND

TRAIL

INTERIOR

Mount
Maguire

el. Ⓥ
272m

COVE

PARK

ANDERSON

TRAIL

SWAMP
BYPASS
TRAIL

COPPERMINE

Whiffen

Spit

PIKE RD.

P

gate

SOOKE INLET

Company
Pt.

Iron Mine
Hill

⌂

COAST

TRAIL

O'Brien
Pt.

⚒

Iron Mine
Bay

Possession Pt.

Ⓥ

Pike Pt.

Donaldson
(Secretary)
Is.

STRAIT OF JUAN DE FUCA

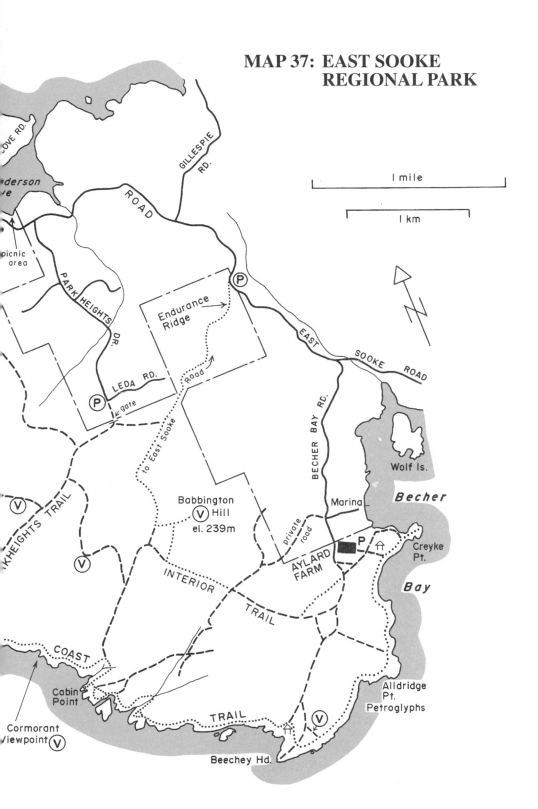

MAP 37: EAST SOOKE REGIONAL PARK

1 mile

1 km

COVE RD.

GILLESPIE RD.

nderson ve

picnic area

ROAD

PARK HEIGHTS DR.

Endurance Ridge

P

LEDA RD.

P

gate

Road

to East Sooke

EAST SOOKE ROAD

BECHER BAY RD.

Wolf Is.

Becher

(V)

KHEIGHTS TRAIL

Babbington (V) Hill el. 239m

INTERIOR

(V)

TRAIL

private road

Marina

P

AYLARD FARM

Creyke Pt.

Bay

(V)

COAST

Cabin Point

Cormorant Viewpoint (V)

TRAIL

Alldridge Pt. Petroglyphs

(V)

Beechey Hd.

185

alumroot, white clover, Queen Anne's lace, Indian paintbrush, seaside woolly sunflower, hedge nettle, clustered white rose, red elderberry, mullein, sea blush, Columbia tiger lily, nodding onion and white triteleia. When hiking in the swampy areas observe the skunk cabbage. In the spring, bears enjoy the centres of skunk cabbages and dandelions. The cougar scratches his territory out like a domestic cat and near the turnoff to **Cabin Point** there are some alder trees with cougar marks. On the Parkheights Trail there is quite a raccoon settlement. From the top of Mount Maguire you may see hawks, eagles and pigeons. There is fishing off Beechey Head and at Pike Point. Families of otter living on the rocky beach at Aylard Farm or at Alldridge Point may be seen feeding in the early morning or late evening. You may also see them up and down the Coast Trail. From here seals will be seen frequently and in the summer there can be magnificent viewing of whales. You may see deer at the Aylard Farm end and grouse on the Interior Trail from Babbington Hill onwards.

Alldridge Point, with its petroglyphs, was designated a Provincial Heritage Site in 1927. Note the correct spellings of Alldridge Point, named after Lt. (later Captain) George Manly Alldridge, an officer in the surveying branch; **Creyke Point**, named after Richard Boynton Creyke (later Captain), a surveying officer; **Becher Bay**, named after Commander (later Rear Admiral) Alexander Bridport Becher, RN, a surveying officer; and **Beechey Head**, named after Captain (later Rear Admiral) Frederick William Beechey, RN, an Arctic navigator who was President of the Royal Geographical Society at the time of his death in 1856. All were named by Captain Kellett in 1846.

Notes:

- Do not hike alone. Allow time to get out before nightfall.
- The Aylard Farm parking lot is closed at night.
- Don't rely on creeks for water; always carry your own.
- Carry a map. A CRD Parks brochure is available.
- No camping and no fires are permitted.
- Carry out your own litter.
- The waterfront area near Anderson Cove is a pleasant picnic site.

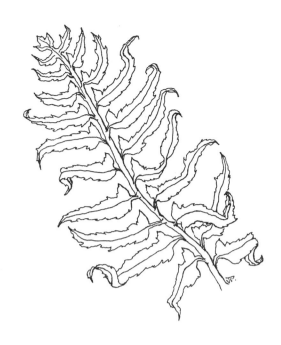

Approximate hiking times in East Sooke Park: **Hours**

Aylard Farm to Pike Road parking lot	6½
Aylard Farm to Beechey Head, via coast	1
Beechey Head to Cabin Point	1½
Cabin Point to Iron Mine Bay	3
Iron Mine Bay to Pike Road parking lot	½
Pike Road parking lot to Anderson Cove, via Anderson Cove Trail	2
Pike Road parking lot to shelter at Iron Mine Bay	½
Pike Road parking lot to Mount Maguire	1
Coppermine Trail to Interior Trail, from coast	1
Parkheights Trail to Interior Trail, from coast	½
Anderson Cove to Babbington Hill	2
Interior Trail, from Anderson Cove Trail to Parkheights Trail	1¼
Aylard Farm to Babbington Hill	1¼
East Sooke Road to Babbington Hill	1¼

The Victorienteers (see page 221) have produced a map of the Aylard Farm area; price: $1.00 to non-members for a photo-copy.

Sooke is a large unincorporated area within the Capital Regional District. It was, for a short time, home to Vancouver Island's first independent settler, Captain Walter Colquhoun Grant, who arrived in Victoria from Scotland in 1849 as official surveyor for the Hudson's Bay Company. In 1851 he planted about a dozen seeds of Scottish broom (Cytisus scoparius), which he had received from the British consul during a visit to the Sandwich Islands (Hawaii). He left the colony in 1853 and, after rejoining the army, died in India in 1861. Meanwhile, his home and land were sold to the Muir family, who spared the three surviving broom bushes because they reminded Mrs. Muir of her Scottish homeland. Broom has spread throughout Vancouver Island and it is getting established on the mainland. Though a thing of beauty when its yellow blooms gild the hillside in May and June, the plant is too successful in its new habitat. A nitrogen-fixing legume, it builds soil conditions that encourage the spread of orchard grass, another introduced species. Together, the two choke out native species. Where it grows native in the British Isles and Europe, broom is kept under control by natural parasites, insect pests and local conditions. Here, it has no enemies and flourishes in its adopted environment. The BC Forest Service has produced a pamphlet, *Broom: putting it in its place.*

Many of the place names around Sooke are named after local people, thus Milne's Landing and Edward Milne Community School; Charters Creek and Hill; Muir, Veitch, Tugwell and Kirby Creeks; Glinz Lake; Helgesen Road (the sign is misspelled) and Hans Helgesen Elementary School; and Sheilds Lake (so often misspelled). Their stories are told in *101 Historical Buildings of the Sooke Region*, published in 1985 by the Sooke Region Historical Society. The region's name comes from that of the T'sou-ke people, a Salish group whose territory extended to Point No Point. The first Europeans to explore Sooke inlet were Sub-Lt. Manuel Quimper and his crew, who claimed the port for Spain in 1790, naming it "Puerta de Revillagigedo", after the Viceroy of New Spain or Mexico. They buried a bottle containing details of the claim, and erected a large cross. At first the name was spelled Soke or Soake, later Sooke, after

Captain Kellett visited in 1847 and named features after members of the Royal Navy, thus Goodridge Peninsula, Cooper Cove, Whiffin Spit, Trollope Point and Mount Shepherd (Mount Manuel Quimper). Sheilds Lake has also been called Smokehouse Lake (by hunters smoking venison nearby) and Lake of the Seven Hills (from the surrounding terrain). Grassy Lake was named for the reeds along its shoreline, and Crabapple Lake for the trees that used to grow around it. All three lakes were watering stops for the pack animals during the Leechtown gold rush. The Alpine Club had a cabin at Sheilds Lake in the 20s (later used as a forest detention camp in the 70s), and junior forest wardens took shelter in a cabin at Crabapple Lake.

The YM-YWCA has developed some good bush trails around **Camp Thunderbird**, all signposted. You may hike there from mid-October to mid-April, but must obtain permission before doing so; phone 386-7511. The Victorienteers (see page 221) have produced a coloured map, scale 1:10,000; price: $5.00 to non-members.

An interesting section of the Galloping Goose Regional Trail (see page 149) starts at **Veitch Creek (Hutchinson Cove)**, via Manzer Road just past Glinz Lake Road. Distance from Victoria is about 30 km. The old right-of-way along here seems almost to hang out over the water and it must have been a memorable train ride in bygone days. From Veitch Creek to Sooke Potholes Park is 10 km one way, about a 3-hour hike. Ample parking is also available off Sooke River Road, about 500 m past Meota Drive.

Sooke Potholes Provincial Park is a delightful spot for swimming and picnicking and the area round about on both sides of the river is well worth exploring. **Note:** While the designated park area itself is safe for family use, do not include small children and pets in your party if you strike off into the surrounding country. **Exercise extreme caution**, especially when traversing slippery rock surfaces. People have lost their lives in the Sooke River.

From the Galloping Goose Trail, beyond Sooke Potholes Park, you can see the skeletal beginnings of Deer Trails, a 1980s attempt by developer Albert Yuen to create a huge riverside convention centre.

MAP 38: SOOKE AREA

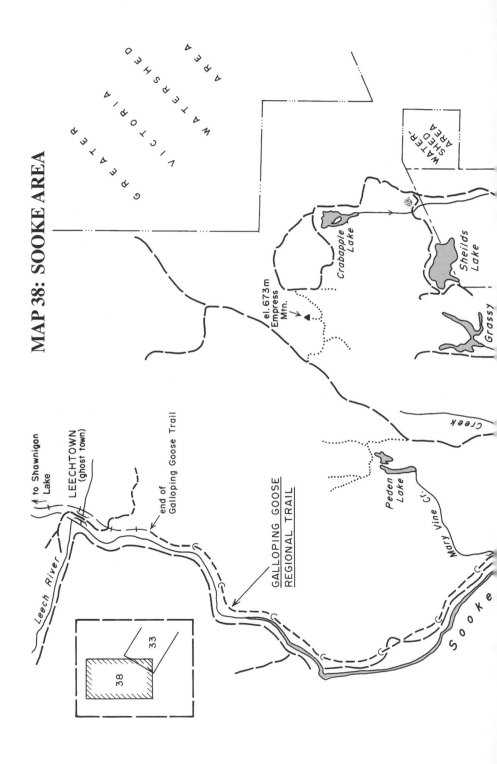

GREATER VICTORIA WATERSHED AREA

WATER-SHED AREA

Crabapple Lake

Sheilds Lake

Grassy

el. 673m Empress Mtn.

Creek

to Shawnigan Lake

LEECHTOWN (ghost town)

end of Galloping Goose Trail

Leech River

Peden Lake

Mary Vine Creek

GALLOPING GOOSE REGIONAL TRAIL

Sooke

33

38

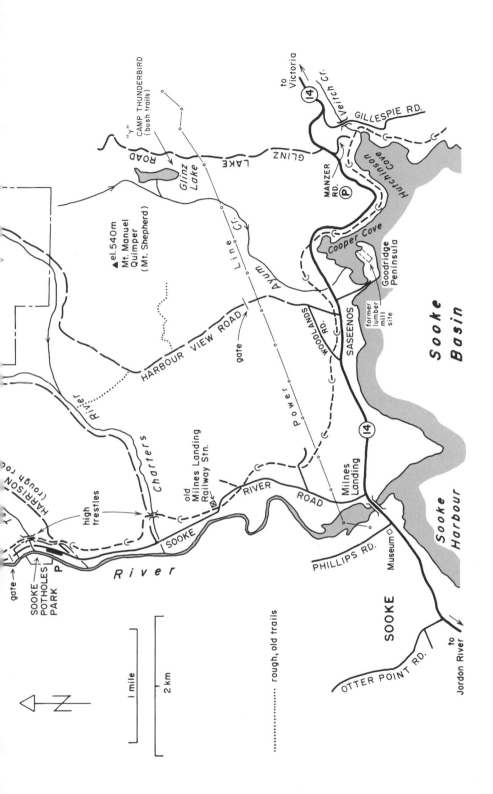

Harrison Trail (a rough old road) leads up towards the top of Empress Mountain from the Sooke Potholes and the view from the top (673 m) can be grand. The trail is named for the late Claude Harrison, a former Victoria mayor, who lobbied for the creation of Sooke Mountain Provincial Park, and who used to hold Guy Fawkes Day bonfires, visible from Victoria, atop Empress Mountain.

Sooke Mountain Provincial Park has been used as a wilderness recreational area since its creation in 1928. Access (currently ungated) is from the end of Harbourview Road and along a rough road accessible only to four-by-four vehicles, cyclists and pedestrians. For a full description of the area refer to *More Island Adventures, volume 2* by Richard K. Blier (Orca Books Publishers). For up-dated information contact BC Parks Public Information Officer (Victoria) 387-4609.

Whiffen Spit:
This is a great spot for observing shore birds and migrant flocks. From Sooke village travel 1.8 km west on the West Coast Road toward Jordan River. Turn left and take Whiffen Spit Road all the way to the beach. The spit is named after John George Whiffin, a clerk aboard the Royal Navy vessel "Herald" in 1846, and is near where Sooke pioneers, the Muir brothers, operated the area's first successful steam sawmill in 1855. Their earlier mill, built in 1852, had been water powered, but when the steam boat *Major Tompkins* was wrecked at Macaulay Point on February 10, 1855, the Muirs purchased the boilers at auction to use in their mill. For information on Whiffin Spit and other Sooke parks contact:

Sooke Parks and Recreation
2168 Phillip Road, Sooke   Mail: Box 421, Sooke, BC
phone 642-6311   V0S 1N0

Ayum and Charters watersheds:
Several local conservation groups, including the Western Canada Wilderness Committee, are lobbying to have Crown lands in the Ayum and Charters Creeks area designated as park land both for ecological preservation and as recreation corridors within a **Sea-to-Sea Greenbelt Proposal**. The Habitat Acquisition Trust (an offshoot of the Victoria

Natural History Society) along with the Society for the Protection of Ayum Creek have made an offer to purchase 5 ha at the mouth of Ayum Creek from Munns Lumber. Enhancing the salmon run and providing nesting sites for Purple Martins are but two of the goals for habitat restoration in the area. If the property can be acquired, it will become a regional park.

SOOKE HILLS WILDERNESS REGIONAL PARK / GVWD NON-CATCHMENT LANDS (see CONTENTS MAP)

As an outcome of the Perry Commission on the Greater Victoria Water District, legislation was introduced in April of 1997 to create a huge new park on Victoria's doorstep. Approximately 4,400 ha encompassing the Waugh, Niagara, Humpback and Veitch watersheds (which do not drain into Victoria's water supply) will be managed as a wilderness park by Capital Regional District Parks. Until a management plan is in place, this whole area, so highly valued for its beauty, its ecological importance and as a buffer for the water catchment lands, will be out of bounds to the public. Recreational uses will no doubt be incorporated into the management plan, but the protection of the ecological values and the security of the adjacent water supply area are the first priorities. One recreational proposal is for a "sea-to-sea" hiking corridor to link Saanich Inlet with the Sooke Basin. In the meantime, please contact CRD Parks for up-to-date information on the area.

⟨16⟩ SOOKE to PORT RENFREW (see CONTENTS MAP, MAPS 38 and 39)

Sooke village, at the intersection of Highway 14 (West Coast Road) and Otter Point Road, is shown at the bottom left corner of Map 38. A word of caution: do not leave valuables in your vehicle when visiting any of the accesses described below. Set your odometer to 0 and mark your westward progress as follows:

Note: The numbered access roads below are designated for emergency access and evacuation. They are not intended to be public access roads.

0	Traffic light at Sooke village centre
6.8	Otter Point Resort, the site of barracks during WW II
10.4	Gordon's Beach. Look for the Sheringham Point Lighthouse in the distance.
12.2	Tugwell Creek bridge
13.5	Muir Creek bridge
18.7	Sheringham Point Road (to lighthouse) in the community of Shirley
21.7	French Beach
25.1	Point No Point teahouse and restaurant (public phone)
28.2	Sandcut Creek bridge
28.7	Sandcut Creek trail
31.6	Jordan River and Western Forest Products Ltd. office
32.5	Jordan River bridge, Shakies Drive-In (public phone), Breakers Cafe (public phone)
35.9	Uglow Creek bridge
36.7	China Beach
43.6	Clinch Creek bridge
53.6	Loss Creek bridge
55.5	access road 7: gated
56.2	access road 8: gated
56.8	access road 9: very rough, steep, gravel; 2.2 km down to Sombrio Beach trailhead of Juan de Fuca Park
60.9	Minute Creek
66.4	access road 10: rough, narrow; 3.8 km to Parkinson Creek trailhead
72.4	Port Renfrew Recreation Centre; right on Deering Road to Cowichan Lake; straight ahead to Cerantes Road and Botanical Beach.

FRENCH BEACH PROVINCIAL PARK

About an hour's drive from Victoria (21.7 km west of Sooke Village), or 8.2 km west of the Muir Creek Bridge, look for the sign-posted road to the ample parking lot. Park facilities include 69 campsites, a phone at the intersection, and a Sani-station across the road. Easy trails, a beautiful sandy beach, and accessible toilets make the day use area wheelchair accessible. For a brochure showing the campsites and trails (including one from the picnic site on the west side of Frenchome Creek), contact BC Parks. The beach is named for James George French, who settled in this area around 1890, and was a pioneer conservationist.

SANDCUT CREEK TRAIL (in WFP Ltd. TFL 25)

From Victoria, 65 km, or from Point No Point Resort 3.6 km to the parking area. Not signposted; no facilities. A pretty rain forest trail with easy descent leads to a long expanse of sand and pebble beach. Time down-about 10 minutes; up-about 15 minutes. A beach walk from here to Jordan River is about 3 km one way.

JORDAN RIVER RECREATION SITE (WFP Ltd.)

At the mouth of the Jordan River, about 90 minutes' drive from Victoria, Western Forest Products Ltd. has provided a parking and picnic area large enough to accommodate campers and trailers, with park facilities including fire pits and picnic tables. Any day that the "surf's up" you can watch surfboarders and kayakers just off the beach.

A brochure "Visitor's Guide to Jordan River Area" with information on this whole area is available from Western Forest Products Ltd. Jordan River Forest Operation, River Jordan, BC   V0S 1L0 (phone 646-2031); or in person at their Jordan River office, 8 am-4:30 pm weekdays.

When Sub-Lt. Manuel Quimper of the sloop *Princesa Real* (the confiscated British *Princess Royal*) explored this area, he named the river after Alejandro Jordon, who accompanied Lt. Francisco Eliza to Nootka, in 1790, as chaplain.

MAP 39: PORT RENFREW / SAN JUAN AREA

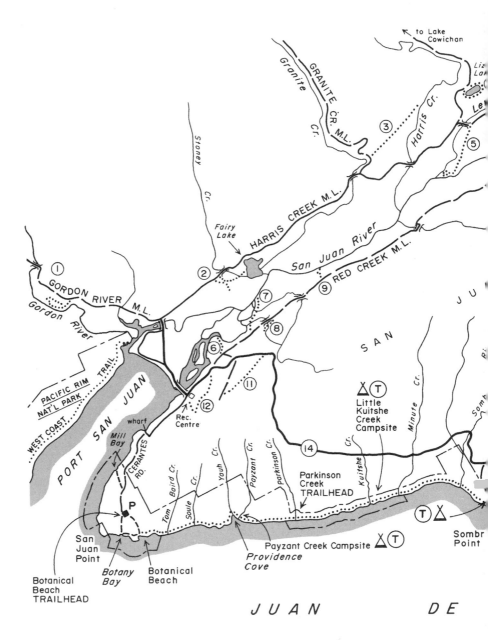

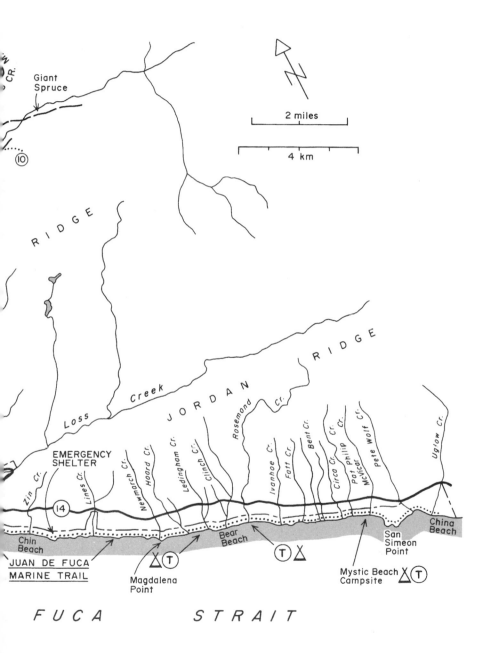

FUCA   STRAIT

JUAN DE FUCA PROVINCIAL PARK and JUAN DE FUCA MARINE TRAIL (MAP 39)

This new Provincial Park was created as part of the Commonwealth Nature Legacy when Victoria hosted the 1994 Commonwealth Games. It takes in four previously existing parks (China Beach, Loss Creek, Parkinson Creek and Botanical Beach) and adds Sombrio Beach and a strip of coastal parkland to provide for the 47-km Juan de Fuca Marine Trail. There are only four trail access points for now: China Beach, Sombrio Beach, Parkinson Creek and Botanical Beach; a fifth trailhead is planned for Lines Creek, but is not open as of 1997. Be prepared for wet, muddy sections and for difficult creek crossings after heavy rainfall. Suspension bridges have been installed at Pete Wolf Creek, Loss Creek, Sombrio River, and Minute Creek. Although most of the Juan de Fuca Trail has been constructed inland, some sections do take you out onto the beach. These beach/trail access points are marked by fluorescent orange balls hanging from tree limbs. See our section-by-section descriptions below to identify these sections; some of these beaches are impassable for short periods at high tide, so plan ahead. Remember that storms and high winds can greatly affect the high tide mark. Stay on designated trails (no shortcuts); pack out your garbage; no vehicles, bikes or horses; pack fresh water; no harvesting of shellfish, plants or animals; no fires (use portable camp stoves).

Notes:
- There is no camping at the two main trailheads: China Beach and Botanical Beach
- The Juan de Fuca Trail does not connect directly to the West Coast Trail.
- See also our cautions about **dangerous waves and surf**: Botanical Beach section, page 202; and about **bears and cougars:** Hints and Cautions section, pages 13-14.

CHINA BEACH Section:

From the Jordan River Bridge it is 4 km to the ample China Beach parking lots. A good trail, fairly steep, but well-graded and suitable for family hikers, leads down through rain forest to a long sandy beach. There are toilet facilities but no camping is permitted. Time down-15 minutes; up-about 25 minutes. With the creation of the new Juan de Fuca Marine Trail, there are now two parking lots, one for day visitors to the beach and the other at the trailhead. Tide charts are posted at the information kiosk, but if you are taking the Trail, you should carry your own copy. Remember to adjust by one hour during Daylight Saving Time.

If you spot any whales, porpoises, dolphins, elephant seals or fur seals (dead or alive) please call the **Whale Hotline**, toll-free at 1-800-665-5939, or write to **Marine Mammal Research Group**, Box 6244, Victoria, BC V8P 5L5.

From CHINA BEACH (km 0) to SOMBRIO BEACH east (km 27) and SOMBRIO (km 29):

This section has numerous creek crossings and steep changes in elevation, especially between Bear Beach and Loss Creek. Hiking difficulty is rated as "moderate" from China Beach to Hoard Creek, "most difficult" from Hoard Creek to Chin Beach, and "difficult" from Chin Beach to Sombrio Point. Newmarch Creek to Loss Creek is described as "wet and muddy". Bear Beach offers two campsites, with toilets, about 2 km apart. The trail section between them (**km 8.7**) is impassable at tide levels above **3 m**, so hikers must consult their tide tables and plan accordingly. Similarly, 0.5 km west of Zin Creek, **km 20.6 to 21.3** is a beach walk that is impassable at tide levels higher than **2.75 m**, with no alternate trail. An **emergency shelter** is located at the east end of Chin Beach. Closer to Sombrio, the beach at **km 28.05** can only be traversed at tides below **3 m**, and **km 29.3 to 29.9**, at tides below **2.6 m.**

The old **Mystic Beach Trail** is now closed; the new access is along the Juan de Fuca Trail from China Beach. Similarly, the **Rossalan, MacInnes, and Sea Lion** trails have been absorbed by the new park. Access is via access road 7, the first logging road to your left after Loss Creek.

The suspension bridge over Loss Creek is spectacular, and well worth the effort of a day trip. The old **Sombrio East Trail** from access road 8 is now closed.

SOMBRIO BEACH TO PARKINSON CREEK Section: 9 km

Sombrio Beach is about 85 km (2 hr) from Victoria. Over the years a number of squatters settled here, but with the creation of Juan de Fuca Provincial Park, they were asked to vacate by the end of January, 1997. Access to the Sombrio Beach trailhead is via access road 9, 19 km west of China Beach. The gravel road is steep and rough. Parks facilities are planned for the future. Wilderness camping is available at the extreme east end of Sombrio Beach; camping on the beach is recommended; wilderness camping is also available at Little Kuitshe Creek. From Sombrio to Parkinson Creek the trail is in generally good condition, with some muddy sections, and is rated as moderately challenging. The beach at **km 30.15** can only be negotiated at tides of less than **3 m.**

PARKINSON CREEK TO BOTANICAL BEACH Section: 10 km

The Parkinson Creek trailhead is 29 km west of China Beach, with access via the Minute Creek Forest Service Road (access road 10). Parks facilities are planned. This is the easiest section of the trail, which is in generally good condition but with some muddy sections. Camping with toilet facilities is available at Payzant Creek.

BOTANICAL BEACH Section: MAP 39

Access to Port Renfrew as below. Just before reaching the Port Renfrew Hotel and government wharf (public phone here), turn left on Cerantes Road (rough, gravel), 1.5 km to the park boundary. If you haven't visited Botanical Beach for some time, you are in for a pleasant surprise. The access road has been rebuilt, giving all vehicles access to new, large parking lots, a picnic area, pit toilets and information kiosks. Just .8 km inside the park boundary there's an information kiosk (tide tables posted) and a parking area for the Mill Bay Trail, a 15 min/1 km easy hike down to the beach (no facilities). Don't let the initial steepness of the trail deter you; the rest is easy going. Time your visit for low tide to explore the cave at one end of the beach. One km beyond the Mill Bay trailhead and you're in the main parking area. From here the Botany Bay Trail (.5 km) and the Shoreline Trail (1 km) are easy hikes. The Shoreline trail is actually along the cliffs overlooking the beach, affording visitors a safe opportunity to be mesmerized by the pounding surf. The Botanical Beach Trail (1 km) leads to the beach and the trailhead of the Juan de Fuca Trail. Since a very low (1.2-metre or 4-foot) tide is most desirable for viewing tidepools, check tide tables when planning your visit. Obtain "Pacific Coast Tide and Current Tables" Volume 5 and refer to tides at Tofino, using correction for Port Renfrew. This booklet is available from marine chandlers or on loan at local public libraries.

The unique beach area, with tidal pools filled with a variety of marine life, is of particular interest to marine biologists and other naturalists. Dr. Josephine Tildon chose it as the site of the University of Minnesota's marine station in 1900. Access at that time was by steamship from Victoria to Port Renfrew, then on foot along a muddy track. This difficult access was a contributing factor in the station's closure in 1907. The Nature Conservancy of Canada has purchased two ha at the original site of the marine station; this is now part of the park. When the area became Botanical Beach Provincial Park in 1989, universities continued to use the beach for research, but under a Park-Use permit. In 1994 Botanical Beach Provincial Park was incorporated into the new Juan de Fuca Provincial Park.

PLEASE NOTE: NO COLLECTING OR HARMING OF ANY MARINE SPECIES (whether it is alive or not).

To ensure a safe and "low-impact" visit, please remember:

- You are in a wilderness area: be prepared to be self-sufficient. You should be properly equipped with suitable outerwear and footwear. The shoreline is very rocky and slippery and first aid is not readily available.

- There are no garbage facilities, so pack out what you pack in. We do not want the bears to become familiar with human garbage.

- We repeat that you are in a wilderness area, home to **black bears and cougars**. Leave your pets at home and keep small children close by at all times. Please read the comments on wild animals in our Hints and Cautions, pages 13-15.

- **Caution: Dangerous waves and surf:**
  We cannot overemphasize the danger posed by the force of the waves. Periodically and unpredictably an unusually large wave (a rogue wave) or a series of large waves will hit the beach. These waves can pull an unsuspecting park visitor into the water. NEVER ALLOW CHILDREN TO PLAY NEAR THE SURF. Be extra careful when crossing surge channels. As we go to press in October of 1997, three tourists have just lost their lives at Long Beach in nearby Pacific Rim National Park after being swept off the rocks by a rogue wave.

- And finally, let's keep this wilderness area as we find it. Camping and fires are not permitted at Botanical Beach.

(17) PORT RENFREW / SAN JUAN AREA (MAP 39)

Port Renfrew is located on the west coast of southern Vancouver Island. From Victoria via Sooke and Jordan River along Highway 14 (the West Coast Road) is about 110 km on a paved road- about 2 hours' driving time; the alternative is to drive in from Cowichan Lake on mostly gravel roads. Highway 14 is now paved all the way, but it is subject to washouts during periods of heavy rain. Yield to oncoming traffic on the numerous one-lane bridges. Port Renfrew telephone listings are located at the end of the white pages in the BC Tel Victoria telephone directory.

The Spanish presence on this coast, 1790-91, included Francisco de Eliza in the *San Carlos*, Jose Maria Narvaez of the *Saturnia*, and Sub-lieutenant Manuel Quimper commanding the *Princesa Real* (the British sloop *Princess Royal*, seized by the Spanish at Nootka in 1789, and returned in 1791 at the Sandwich Islands). In 1788, Captain Meares had named this harbour Port Hawkesbury, after the then president of the British Board of Trade, but, in 1790, Quimper renamed it Puerto de San Juan o de Narvaez. The port was surveyed by Lt. Commander James Wood on the *Pandora* (see Roche Cove) in 1847. Port San Juan it remained until 1895, when the settlers, tired of having their mail sent to the San Juan Islands, named the post office Port Renfrew, after Lord Renfrew, who had at one time plans for Scottish settlement in the valley.

SAN JUAN VALLEY TRAILS

Hiking Through History-Trails of the San Juan Valley is the intriguing title of a booklet that was produced by the Port Renfrew Community Association in 1993. A dozen trails, varying in length from 0.5 to 6 km, take you to river sandbars, a waterfall, lakes, a grove of ancient trees and an old railway logging camp. The history of logging in the San Juan Valley is featured in visits to an old timber road, a plank road and a railway grade. The booklet, containing maps, trail information, historical photographs and stories, is now out of print, so we include these hikes in our book for the first time. For further information on recreation in the San Juan Valley area please contact the **Port Renfrew Community Association**, General Delivery, Port Renfrew, BC V0S 1K0.

The Community Association has accepted responsibility for many of the trails below, under the Adopt-A-Trail program of the Federation of Mountain Clubs of BC (see page 221).

① **Deacon / Beauchene Trail:** round trip 1.9 km - 30 min

Access: From the Recreation Centre, cross the bridge over the south arm of the San Juan River. Drive through the Indian Reserve and cross the bridge over the north arm of the San Juan. Turn left onto the Gordon River Mainline. After 3 km look for the trail sign on the left. Trail is subject to flooding in wet weather.

A short distance in from the trailhead, keep left at the fork and head out to and along the river sandbars. A holly tree amongst non-native locust trees is your cue to turn inland and pick up the trail again. The trail then swings in an arc through the site of the Deacon homestead before rejoining the access trail. The trail is named for Emily and Alfred Deacon, who, with their daughter, Violet, were among the original homesteaders in the valley, arriving around 1889. Ten years later, Art Beauchene appeared on the scene. He worked with Alfred to log the land, then he married Violet, and they built their own home here. If you spot what appear to be large cattle hoofprints in the mud, they were not made by the ghost of Violet's milk cow, drowned in a winter flood. They belong to one of 16 Roosevelt elk, transplanted here from Cassidy (south of Nanaimo) in January, 1993. Funding was through the Habitat Conservation Fund (BC Environment, Parliament Buildings, Victoria, BC V8V 1X5). For information on elk management on Vancouver Island contact the Wildlife Section of BC Environment in Nanaimo or any Conservation Officer with BC Environment. Elk hunting is not permitted. Report infractions to local RCMP or Wildlife at 1-800-663-9453 (663-WILD).

For a pleasant side-trip, continue a further km or so along the Gordon River Mainline to the bridge over the Gordon, which is named after Commander (later Admiral) George Thomas Gordon, of HMS *Cormorant* in 1846 and HMS *Driver* in 1850. A steep trail leads down to the river for swimming and kayaking.

②**Fairy Lake Nature Trail:** return trip 2 km - 40 min

Access: As above, but after crossing north arm of the San Juan River, turn right onto the Harris Creek Mainline. About 2 km along, look for the trail sign on the right, opposite the rock quarry.

Welcome to an open-air forest laboratory of second-growth timber. The trail runs from the Harris Creek Mainline to TimberWest's Fairy Lake Recreation Site. About 100 m short of the campground you'll encounter Stoney Creek, which flows into Fairy Lake. In the summer months you can cross the creekbed but in the wet season you'll need to retrace your steps. Turning right onto the old logging road you crossed on your way in provides an alternate route out. Close to the creek look for young trees growing in straight lines, as if planted as a hedge, where they've sprung up along a single nurselog.

Note:

If you are camping at TimberWest's Fairy Lake campsite, heed the warning about rapidly-rising waters. In February of 1994 the water level in the campsite rose by two metres overnight, trapping a couple in their camper. (They crawled out via the top hatch, swam for help and enjoyed the hospitality - and the ribbing - of the local residents.)

③ **Harris Creek Camp II Trail**: return trip 6 km - 3-4 hr

Access: As above but continue past Fairy Lake for a further 6 km. Cross the Granite Creek bridge and turn left onto the Granite Creek Mainline. Stop and check the sign for entry restrictions. If the road is open, you'll soon come to a gravel pit, where you can park off the road; the trailhead is just beyond. Shortly after setting out you must cross a tributary of Harris Creek, so your way may be blocked during the wettest months.

This, truly, is hiking through history, as you follow the route of an old railway grade into the site of Cathels and Sorenson Logging's Camp II in the days of railway logging in the valley.

④ **Lizard Lake Nature Trail**: round trip 1.5 km - 35 min

Access: As above. After crossing the Granite Creek bridge, continue a further 6 km on the Harris Creek Mainline (the road to Lake Cowichan). You'll cross Harris Creek and keep left at the next intersection (Lens

Creek Mainline) to reach the Lizard Lake Recreation Site where TimberWest and the BC Forest Service have provided camping spots, pit toilets, and a dock for fishing. Just beyond the recreation site look for an old logging road (blocked) on the right. Park well off the road. There are numerous picnic sites above the lake. The trail starts to your left - look for red and blue markers.

This rough, zig-zagging trail circles the lake, but at some distance from it, so it can be quite dark. It leads you round to the newly-developed campsites to the west of the lake before coming out onto the Harris Creek Mainline again.

If you choose to leave the Port Renfrew / San Juan area via Lake Cowichan and Duncan, we have one more treat in store for you. Nearly 8 km beyond Lizard Lake on the Harris Creek Mainline you come upon the signposted trail to the **Harris Creek Spruce Tree**. Though its girth hardly makes it a competitor against the other giant spruce trees in this area, its height, at a lofty 82 m, is clearly head and shoulders above the rest. The short access trail, built by the Pacheenaht Crew and TimberWest, provides wheelchair access on crushed gravel.

(5) **Lens Creek Trail:** round trip 3 km - 1 hr

Access: As above but 2 km past the Harris Creek bridge turn right onto the Lens Creek Mainline (gravel) and cross the bridge. Look for the trail sign on your right and park well off the road.

A 20-minute easy walk brings you to Chester's Grove of truly monumental trees on the banks of the San Juan River. Your naturalist's guidebook will help you identify the following species: western red cedar (*Thuja plicata*), Sitka spruce (*Picea sitchensis*), western hemlock (*Tsuga heterophylla*) and black cottonwood (*Populus trichocarpa*). A ten-minute walk downstream takes you to Ben's Beach and more huge trees, mostly spruce. The gravel bar here is accessible even in winter.

If you are still in the mood for big trees, return to your vehicle and continue on along the Lens Creek Mainline. Keep right at the triangular intersection and ignore the minor cross- roads. Immediately after crossing the new truck bridge over the San Juan (parallel to the old suspension bridge) turn left into the clearing at the base of the Sitka spruce giant with the following impressive dimensions: 3.7 m diameter and 57.9 m tall although the main trunk is broken above 53 m. The shade of a huge fern-festooned maple and the sound of the river make one long for a hammock and a long summer afternoon. If you were to visit the Red Creek Fir in the morning and this San Juan spruce in the afternoon, you would have travelled close to 40 km and almost wound up where you started: the Red Creek Tree is about 2 km to the southwest of where you are now.

(6) **Sandbar Trail:** return trip 1.5 km - 30 min

Access: From Highway 14, 2.4 km east of the Rec. Centre, turn left and descend to the junction with the Red Creek Mainline. The trailhead (signposted) is straight ahead.

This is an easy, level walk out to the river's edge. Plan your visit for low tide, or bush-bash your way through the salmonberry bushes out to the sand bars. Close to the water the trees are heavily hung with moss and ferns - this feels like a rain forest.

(7) **First and Second Creek Trail**: return trip 3.2 km - 2 hr

Access: as above, then a further km along the Red Creek Mainline (narrow; rough gravel). Look for the trail sign on the left.

This area is at its best when the spring flowers, including the pink fawn lilies (erythronium revolutum), burst forth. Remember to "wear your Wellies" (rubber boots) when you visit this low-lying, often-flooded river delta.

(8) **Falls Creek Trail**: return trip .4 km - 10 min

Access: as above, then over the bridge. Watch for the trail marker on the right.

In dry weather you can easily walk across the creekbed, but through the wet season you'll need high, waterproof boots to ford the stream. When you reach the canyon, admire the green-on-green of maidenhair ferns gracing green slate. The gravel bar not far from the road offers a cool spot for a summer picnic.

⑨ **Riverbank Trail:** Return trip 750 m - 20 min

Access: as above, then a further 2.4 km. Look for the trail sign on the left.

The trail is not well-defined, so watch for the red trail markers in the trees. Wooden stepping blocks and a boardwalk make this trail accessible even in winter, but the river sandbars at your destination are a summer-only treat.

⑩ **The Red Creek Fir:** return trip 1 km - 30 min.

Access: As above; follow the Red Creek Mainline about 12 km to a small parking area.

The signposted trail takes you on a good climb, past the Three Guardsmen (three large western red cedars) and up to the big tree. Until 1996, this was Canada's largest known Douglas-fir tree, with these impressive dimensions: circumference at chest height: 12.6 m; diameter 4 m; height to its twice-broken top, 74 m. Its age is estimated to be between 900 and 1000 years. Its record as the tallest known Douglas-fir in Canada has now passed to a towering giant in the watershed of the Coquitlam River on BC's mainland. The 94.3 m-high newcomer is taller, but slimmer, a mere 8.07 m in circumference. It's younger, too, at around 800 years. In its prime, the Red Creek Fir probably outstripped both the Coquitlam tree and the giant Sitka spruce in the Carmanah Valley. Even now, it may contain a greater board measure of timber than the mainland upstart. The Douglas-fir (*Pseudotsuga menziesii*) is named after botanist David Douglas, an early visitor to this coast. The name is hyphenated because it is not a true fir (*Abies*). For information on the Red Creek Fir and other remarkable trees, consult Randy Stoltmann's "Hiking Guide to the Big Trees of Southwestern British Columbia", published by the Western Canada Wilderness Committee. (In 1994, Randy Stoltmann died in an avalanche in northern BC. A grove of Sitka spruce trees in the Carmanah Pacific Provincial Park has been dedicated in his name.)

⑪ **Stan Harrison Plankboard Trail**: return trip 3 km - 1 hr

Access: 3.5 km east of the Rec. Centre look for the trail sign on the right. Parking is just beyond, on the opposite side of the road.

Climb a set of wooden stairs and take yourself back to the early 40s. This really is hiking through history. Imagine riding downhill, in a fully-loaded logging truck, on a misty morning when the planks were slick with rain.

⑫ **John Quinn Trail**: return trip 4 km - 1.5 hr

Access from the west: off a gravel road 1 km east of the Rec. Centre
Access from the east: behind the Rec. Centre
The trail follows an old timber road from the early '30s. John Quinn came to Port Renfrew in 1926, where he established a shingle mill. High in the hills above the town, cedar shingle bolts (and pulpwood cants from hemlock, spruce and balsam) would be cut into 4-foot lengths. They would ride down log chutes to the bottom of the hill, where they would be collected onto trucks and driven along the timber road to the mill at the government wharf.

SAN JUAN RIDGE

In cooperation with Western Forest Products, Pacific Forest Products and Fletcher Challenge, the Kludahk Outdoors Club is developing an 80-km-long San Juan Ridge trail from Leechtown to Botanical Beach, to eventually connect the Galloping Goose Trail with the Juan de Fuca and West Coast trails. Much of the work of building the trail has been completed, using volunteer labor and some money from the Forest Renewal Fund, but much work remains in preparing the trail, and the public, for safe, responsible use of this wilderness environment. Until this final, important phase of development is complete, the Kludahk Outdoors Club is asking that people refrain from accessing the trail, which passes through Ecological Reserve 83. Kludahk means "home of the elk."

For more information please contact:

The Kludahk Outdoors Club
2037 Kaltasin Road,
R R 1 Sooke, BC   V0S 1N0
642-4342 (Phoebe Dunbar-after 6 pm)

⟨18⟩ WEST COAST TRAIL (MAP 39): 75 km

We include the West Coast Trail in HikingTrails I because its southernmost (Gordon River) trailhead is in the Port Renfrew area; the Trail is also included in our Hiking Trails II because the Nitinat and Bamfield area trailheads are accessible from that part of Vancouver Island.

The West Coast Trail is part of **Pacific Rim National Park Reserve**. It is an arduous wilderness experience recommended for experienced backpackers only. You must be fit, experienced and well-equipped before attempting this challenge. The trail is only open from April 15 to September 30; it is closed during the hazardous off-season. A quota system limiting use is in place and reservations, though optional, are highly recommended. **Reservations** (for the current year only) can be made after March 1st and are available by phone only at the numbers listed below. Currently (1997) the Reservation Fee is $25.00 Cdn per person, including GST (payable only by Visa or MasterCard) and provides each hiker with a guaranteed start date and place, the West Coast Trail Preparation Guide, and a detailed, waterproof trail map. Hikers must be at the trailhead no later than 12 noon on the day they are scheduled to hike. Your hiking space will be forfeited if you are late. There are no refunds in the event of a cancellation. Start dates can only be changed if spaces are still available for the requested new start date.

Trail Use Permits, to be displayed on the outside of each hiker's pack, are mandatory for all park/trail users, even for kayakers approaching by water. This regulation is strictly enforced. Only 60 Trail Use Permits will be issued per day for the 3 trail access points: 26 at the Pachena Bay Trailhead (north end, near Bamfield); 26 at the Gordon River Trailhead (south end, near Port Renfrew), and 8 at the Nitinat Visitor Centre at the head of Nitinat Lake. (Nitinat Narrows, the mid-point of the trail, is at the outlet of long, narrow Nitinat Lake, so to start or finish at mid-point along the trail, you need to take a water-taxi from the Visitor Centre to the Narrows.) At 12:30 pm each day, any unreserved or unclaimed permits from the daily quota are assigned on a first-come, first-served basis from a wait-list. You must place your name on the wait-list in person. Although this avoids the $25 Reservation Fee, demand is high, especially during

July and August, and you could face a 2 or 3 day wait (or longer) for your name to come up on the list. The Trail Use Permit Fee is payable at the three trailheads only, on the day you start. Peak season fee (May 1 - September 30): $60.00 per person; shoulder season (April 15 - April 30): $30.00 per person (1996 rates). The fee is non-refundable and is payable by Visa, MasterCard, cash or travellers cheque (exact amount). At the time of registration you must pre-pay the ferry charges (as they apply) for the Gordon River and Nitinat Narrows crossings (about $15.00). Extra water-taxi fees are applicable if you cross Port San Juan or start/finish at Nitinat Narrows. Any large group should contact Pacific Rim National Park office early in the trip planning process: maximum group size is ten people. All hikers must register at their chosen trailhead and then take a 1-hour orientation before their Trail Use Permits are issued.

Access to Port Renfrew for the Gordon River Trailhead from Victoria via Sooke and Jordan River on Highway 14 (West Coast Road) is about 110 km on a paved road (about 2 hours). The alternative is to drive in from Cowichan Lake on mostly gravel roads. From Port Renfrew you need water-taxi service to the Gordon River Trailhead.

Access to the Nitinat Visitor Centre Trailhead starts from Duncan via Lake Cowichan (Highway 18, paved) then on gravel roads (about 1½ hours). It is also possible to drive in from Port Alberni on gravel roads. From the Visitor Centre you will need a water-taxi down Nitinat Lake to the Nitinat Narrows. Nitinat Lake Visitor Centre and water-taxi: (250) 745-8124.

Access to the Pachena Bay Trailhead, near Bamfield, is on gravel logging roads from Port Alberni or Duncan (about 3 hours). In 1997 alternative transportation is available as follows: West Coast Trail Express Bus from Victoria or Nanaimo; Alberni Marine Transport Ltd. Ferry from Port Alberni; Western Bus Lines from Port Alberni. You can drive or hike from Bamfield to the Pachena Bay Trailhead.

Caution: Parks Canada recommends that you do not hitchhike.

Information: Pacific Rim National Park Reserve
Box 280, Ucluelet, BC V0R 3A0
250-726-7721

West Coast Trail Information Centres: (Open daily from 9 am to 5 pm, May 1 to September 30 only.)

Pachena Bay	(250) 728-3234
Port Renfrew	(250) 647-5434

Trail reservations: West Coast Trail Reservations: line open 7 days a week, 6 am - 6 pm PST/PDT

Greater Vancouver:	(604) 663-6000
within Canada and the USA:	1-800-663-6000
outside Canada and the USA:	(250) 387-1642

Air Service:

Pacific Spirit Air	(250) 537-9359
Aero Air	(250) 656-7627

Bus Service: (Schedules vary throughout the year.)

Port Alberni to Bamfield: Western Bus Lines   (250) 723-3341

Victoria or Nanaimo to Bamfield or Port Renfrew: West Coast Trail Express Bus   (250) 477-8700.

Port Renfrew-Nitinat-Bamfield (3 hours): Pacheenaht First Nation Bus Service   (250) 647-5521.

Ferry Service: Port Alberni-Bamfield on the M.V. Lady Rose: Alberni Marine Transport, Box 188, Port Alberni, BC   V9Y 7M7 (250) 723-8313; fax (250) 723-8314. Reservations required from mid-June to mid-September.

Port Renfrew-Bamfield: Trailhead Charters Boat Service (5 hours): (250) 647-5468

Helpful Books and Maps:

A special waterproof topographical map of the West Coast Trail (scale 1:50,000) is available from Maps BC (see page 222) and is included in the trail reservation package.

The West Coast Trail Preparation Guide is included in the trail reservation package, or it may be ordered from Pacific Rim National Park Reserve, as above. A video is also available for $22.79.

The Canadian Tide and Current Tables: Volume 5, published by the Canadian Hydrographic Service.

Guide to the Forest Land of Southern Vancouver Island (1992) compiled by the Lake Cowichan Combined Fire Organization.

MacMillan Bloedel TFL 44 Recreation and Logging Road Guide (East Map).

West Coast Trail and Carmanah Pacific map (1:50,000) published (1992) by ITMB Publishing Ltd for World Wide Books.

Adventuring in British Columbia (1991) by Isabel Nanton and Mary Simpson has a section on the West Coast Trail and an account of a trip to Bamfield on the MV Lady Rose.

Blisters and Bliss, A Trekkers Guide to the West Coast Trail (revised edition, 1991) by David Foster and Wayne Aitken, illustrated by Nelson Dewey, is a practical and often humourous guide to the West Coast Trail (B&B Publishing, Victoria and Cloudcap Press, Seattle).

Island Adventures, An Outdoors Guide to Vancouver Island (1989) by Richard K. Blier, details logging road travel to both the Port Renfrew and Pachena Bay trailheads and contains a section on the West Coast Trail. Separate chapters describe canoeing the Nitinat Triangle and Nitinat Lake.

More Island Adventures, An Outdoors Guide to Vancouver Island (1993) by Richard K. Blier, gives an account of an off-season hike from Pachena Bay to Tsusiat Falls.

The Pacific Rim Explorer (1986) by Bruce Obee, includes information on the Nitinat Triangle, the Broken Island Group, Barkley Sound and the coastal area up to Hot Springs Cove (Whitecap Books, Vancouver).

The West Coast Trail and Nitinat Lakes (7th revised edition, 1992) by the Sierra Club of Western Canada has detailed descriptions and maps for the West Coast Trail and canoeing trips to the Nitinat Triangle (Douglas and McIntyre Press).

⟨19⟩ MALAHAT AREA

The undulating hills of the Malahat area acquired their native name, meaning "caterpillared," after a particularly devastating infestation of tent caterpillars.

Goldstream Provincial Park is your gateway to the famous Malahat Drive north to Mill Bay, Shawnigan Lake, Cobble Hill, Duncan and beyond. This section of the Island is covered in our *Hiking Trails II: Southeastern Vancouver Island.* Although Goldstream Park (see page 76) lies within the boundaries of Langford municipality, we include it with the Highlands area because it is immediately south of, and readily accessible from, the major Highlands park: Gowlland Tod Provincial Park.

SPECTACLE LAKE PROVINCIAL PARK AND OLIPHANT LAKE (MAP 40)

On Highway 1 travelling north past the first Shawnigan Lake cutoff, continue .8 km then turn left onto Whitaker Road - signposted to Spectacle Lake park (65 ha). About 1 km more brings you to the parking lot (about 30 km total from Victoria). There are parks facilities for day use; no camping is permitted. It is open year-round, free of charge. The toilets and the trail along the east side of the lake are wheelchair-accessible.

Spectacle Lake (so named as it resembles a pair of spectacles) is a pretty little lake, good for swimming, and a walk around it takes under an hour. It is said to have eastern brook trout in it. It's also one of the best spots near Victoria for open air ice skating in winter.

A good hike is possible from here to Oliphant Lake which is harder to find, as for the most part it is not visible from its eastern side. Follow the trail on the east side of Spectacle Lake and continue north on a pleasant woodsy trail① ascending gradually for about 30 minutes to a T junction ②.

MAP 40:
SPECTACLE LAKE PROVINCIAL PARK,
OLIPHANT LAKE

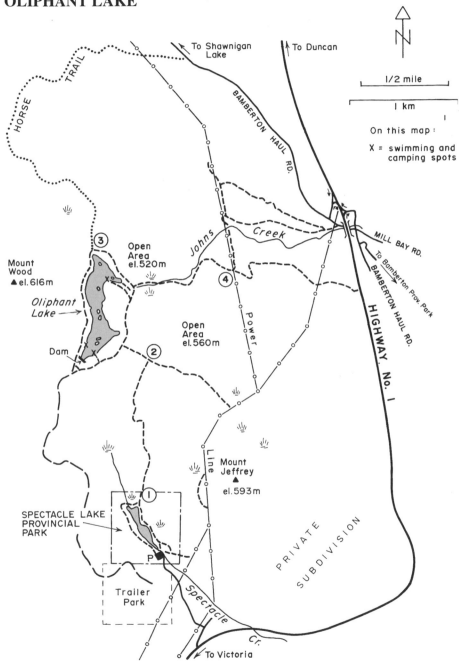

On this map:

X = swimming and camping spots

1/2 mile

1 km

To Shawnigan Lake

To Duncan

HORSE TRAIL

BAMBERTON HAUL RD.

Johns Creek

MILL BAY RD.

To Bamberton Prov. Park

BAMBERTON HAUL RD.

HIGHWAY No. 1

Mount Wood
▲ el. 616m

Oliphant Lake

Open Area el. 520m

Open Area el. 560m

Dam

Power Line

Mount Jeffrey
▲ el. 593m

SPECTACLE LAKE PROVINCIAL PARK

Trailer Park

Spectacle Cr.

PRIVATE SUBDIVISION

To Victoria

About a 10-minute hike to your left will bring you to a rough road. A right or left turn will lead you to the trails around Oliphant Lake. There is access to three good swimming and camping spots as shown on our map. At the north arm of the lake③ a horse trail continues north, then west, and then veers north-east crossing the power lines nearly 2 km north of Johns Creek. Just south of the creek at④ there is an excellent view of the Saanich Inlet. Other pleasant views can be found by picking your own route up to the open areas shown. **Mount Wood** is the highest point of the Malahat Ridge.

If returning via the powerline, you might miss the trail leading back to the T junction②, but the power line will lead you back to the Spectacle Lake parking lot. Crossing the creek is sometimes difficult, but there is a little trail to the right leading to the main trail.

The route via① ② ③ ② ① with a side trip to the viewpoint at the north end of the lake takes about four hours.

A rough road (4-wheel drive vehicles only) leads south from Oliphant Lake back to Spectacle Lake via the trailer park.

The rare Mountain Quail may be seen along the power line. In summer, wild strawberries are a treat.

This is the only destination in this book that is outside the Capital Regional District. The Cowichan Valley Regional District, with cooperation from BC Hydro, is planning trail expansion in this area, including a trail to the summit of **Mount Jeffrey**. For information please contact the CVRD Planning Department (see page 222).

TRAIL SYSTEMS and GREENWAYS

GREENWAYS

Greenways are "green" corridors that link parks with other community open space such as schoolyards, golf courses, beaches and forests. The Provincial Capital Commission (PCC) has established a grant program to encourage local greenways initiatives. The goals of the program are:

1. Development of a network of pathways, bikeways, highway corridors, waterways or undeveloped green corridors.
2. Preservation of significant heritage resources and natural corridors for ecosystem protection and wildlife movement.
3. Development and preservation of visual corridors to protect scenic quality.
4. Fostering of partnerships for the stewardship of natural areas, landscapes and linear green spaces.
5. Promotion and education regarding the benefits of a greenways system.
6. Maintenance of characteristic landscapes and sea views.

For information contact the Provincial Capital Commission office (see page 222).

GREEN / BLUE SPACES STRATEGY

The Capital Regional District and the Provincial Capital Commission are working together to prepare a plan for the protection of green space (both public and private lands) and blue space (bodies of fresh water or ocean). Public open houses were held in the fall of 1996 to review the draft strategy. For information contact the CRD or PCC (see page 222).

CAPITAL REGIONAL DISTRICT (CRD) REGIONAL TRUNK TRAIL SYSTEM

Imagine a continuous trail from the tip of the Saanich Peninsula all the way to the start of the West Coast Trail near Port Renfrew-others have, and many of them have served as members of the Regional Trails Coordinating Group (RTCG), a body that addresses matters dealing with planning, acquiring land, and developing just such a trail. The RTCG advises the CRD and local municipalities on how best to link up major parks and sites of scenic and historical interest along local trails. Many of the trails described in this book are part of this Regional Trail system including, most obviously, the Lochside Trail and the Galloping Goose Regional Trail. VITIS is a member of the RTCG.

VICTORIA-COWICHAN TRAIL

The Ministry of Transportation and Highways has entered into leasing agreements that would allow the Capital Regional District (CRD) and the Cowichan Valley Regional District (CVRD) to convert sections of the abandoned CNR line into a recreational corridor to extend from the present end of the Galloping Goose Regional Trail near Leechtown all the way to Lake Cowichan. This part of the route is as yet undeveloped and is not enthusiastically recommended. Heading north from Leechtown, after about 3 km the right-of-way soon becomes overgrown, blocked and difficult to follow around missing trestles. However, hikers and cyclists can, for the time being, follow the adjacent gravel highway 117 which follows the shore of Sooke Lake to Shawnigan Lake. For vehicles to complete a through trip from Sooke to Shawnigan Lake via Boneyard Main and highway 117 involves fording the river at Leechtown. Special note: On the approximately 13 km of this road within the former Greater Victoria Water District (now CRD Water Commission land) one is required to stay on the road at all times. The route is scenic but is not one of the more pleasant hikes, particularly when the road is dry and dusty. Carry water; leave nothing along the roadside; do not leave the road. This is in the interest of water quality and fire risk and there are no exceptions. As of 1997, highway 117 is posted for imminent closure. A re-routing of this trail away from the water supply catchment areas was one of the recommendations of the Perry Commission on the GVWD. From the west side of Shawnigan Lake the route continues north to Deerholme, where a spur runs east to Duncan. This 25.7-km stretch includes the condemned wooden Kinsol trestle over the Koksilah River. The name Kinsol comes from King Solomon Mine, an old copper prospect in the area. From Deerholme west the route roughly follows the Cowichan River for 22.5 km.

VANCOUVER ISLAND BACKBONE TRAIL

Earlier this decade, the Mid-Island Branch of the Western Canada Wilderness Committee had a vision of a continuous north-south hiking route for Vancouver Island, to link the areas near Sooke, Cowichan Lake, Nanaimo Lakes, Port Alberni, Comox Lake, Tahsis, Woss Lake and on to Port McNeill. Much of this route retraces the steps of William Washington Bolton who in 1894 was the first white explorer to travel the north/south route. The grand opening was to have coincided with the Commonwealth Games in Victoria in 1994. With sponsorship from Mountain Equipment Co-op in Vancouver, a brochure did get produced, and some sections of the trail have been built. For information please contact:

Mid-Island Branch, Western Canada Wilderness Committee
Box 1153, Station A, Nanaimo, BC   V9R 6E7
phone (250) 716-9292

CENTENNIAL TRAILS TRUST

Many trails in BC were built in the 1960s and early 70s to commemorate the 100th anniversary of the union of the Crown colonies of Vancouver Island and British Columbia in 1866, the 100th anniversary of Canadian Confederation in 1967, and the 100th anniversary of BC becoming a Canadian province in 1971. Early in the 90s, the Centennial Trails Trust was formed as a non- profit provincial organization responsible for linking these and other trails to create BCs portion of the **National Trail of Canada,** from Victoria to Banff, Alberta. Starting in Victoria, the trail would follow the Galloping Goose Regional Trail to Leechtown, then the Lake Cowichan route described above. Trails or logging roads would complete the route to Nanaimo and the ferry to Horseshoe Bay. On the West Vancouver side, the proposal links up with some historic trails as it runs along the Centennial Trail, through Manning and Cathedral Parks, along the Dewdney Heritage Trail and on to Fort Steele and Palliser Pass. For information please contact:

The Centennial Trails Trust
#203 - 1646 West 7th Ave., Vancouver, BC   V6J 1S5

TRANS CANADA TRAIL / SENTIER TRANSCANADIEN

Once into Alberta, the trail described above links with the Trans-Alberta Trail section of the National Trail of Canada, and could take you coast-to-coast, all the way from Victoria, BC to St. John's, Newfoundland. A north-south spur will run from Calgary through the Yukon to Tuktoyaktuk, NWT. Plans are to have a 15,000-km trail for hikers, equestrians, skiers and non-motorized vehicles (with snowmobiles where desired) in place by the year 2000. The total cost is projected to be $432 million. Funding is to come from corporate and private sponsors ($36 buys you a metre of trail); amenities are to include toilets, campsites and hostels. Our own Galloping Goose Regional Trail was the first registered section of the Trans Canada Trail. The remaining decision to be made in Victoria is how to link the Selkirk trestle with Mile Zero. For information please contact:

Trans Canada Trail Foundation	or:	Trails BC
837 Second Ave. S W		393 5158 48th Ave.
Calgary, AB T2P 0E6		Delta, BC V4K 5B6
phone (403) 731-9195		phone (604) 940-1803
or 1-800-465-3636		or 1-888-908-7245
website: http://www.tctrail.ca		fax: (604) 946-2317
e-mail: info@tctrail.ca		e-mail: jsapple@msn.com

RAILS TO GREENWAYS

This national volunteer organization was founded in 1991 with the aim of converting Canada's abandoned railway corridors into a nation-wide public network of recreational, heritage and nature trails. As with our two main railways themselves, the CPR and CNR, the movement began in the east and has spread westward. Prince Edward Island has purchased all 440 k of its abandoned railway corridor, and in New Brunswick trail networks will eventually link with the Appalachian Trail and with Quebec.

CLUB ADDRESSES

Many hiking groups welcome non-members on scheduled outings. Any hiking group wishing to have its name appear in future revisions of this book should contact:

Vancouver Island Trails Information Society
c/o Orca Book Publishers
1030 North Park St.
Mail: PO Box 5626, Stn. B, Victoria, BC V8R 6S4
e-mail: ahunter@vanisle.net

Outdoor Club of Victoria:

The OCV was formed in 1942 by a group of Victorians interested in hiking together so they could share the companionship of others with similar interests and pool their knowledge of places to go. There are hikes every Saturday and Sunday throughout the year and monthly evening meetings with entertainment programs. The current issue of the hiking schedule (The Groundsheet) with telephone numbers as to who to contact is available at the Greater Victoria Public Library (see page 222).

Alpine Club of Canada, **Vancouver Island section**: contact the Greater Victoria Public Library.

Club Tread: contact the Greater Victoria Public Library.

Island Mountain Ramblers

PO Box 691, Nanaimo, BC   V9R 5M2

The **Alpine Club** and the **Ramblers** have district representatives.

The Federation of Mountain Clubs of British Columbia has information on other hiking clubs on Vancouver Island:

336 - 1367 West Broadway, Vancouver, BC   V6H 4A9
phone (604) 737-3053
or 1-888-892-2266; fax (604) 738-7175
e-mail: fmcbc@istar.ca
website: http://home.istar.ca/~fmcbc/fmcbc.htm

Victorienteers Orienteering Club

Mail to: c/o 7268 Veyaness Road, Saanichton, BC   V8M 1M2
Maps from: Diana Hocking, phone (250) 477-7624

USEFUL ADDRESSES

BC Parks, South Vancouver Island District
2930 Trans-Canada Highway
Victoria, BC   V9E 1K3
phone (250) 391-2300
BC Parks campground reservation service: 1-800-689-9025
     (March 1-Sept 15; see page 17.)

Capital Regional District Parks
490 Atkins Road
Victoria, BC   V9B 2Z9
phone (250) 478-3344; fax (250) 478-5416
24-hr recorded message: (250) 474-7275
website: http://www.crd.bc.ca/parks/index.htm

Cowichan Valley Regional District
137 Evans Street
Duncan, BC   V9L 1P5
phone (250) 746-2500

Greater Victoria Public Library
735 Broughton Street
Victoria, BC   V8W 3H2
phone (250) 382-7241; fax (250) 382-7125

Maps BC
1802 Douglas Street
Victoria, BC V8V 1X4
phone (250) 387-1441

Provincial Capital Commission
613 Pandora Avenue
Victoria, BC V8W 1N8
phone (250) 386-1356; fax (250) 386-1303

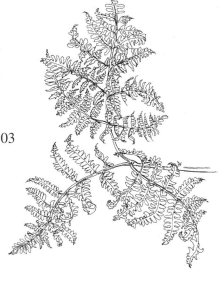

ACKNOWLEDGEMENTS

In addition to all the contributors to the original volume and the many revisions over the years, we are indebted to the following individuals and groups who have assisted with this revision:

BC Parks, South Vancouver Island District (Debby Funk, Don McLaren, Rick Whetter, Ross Dawson, Bob Austad, Selma Low)

CRD Parks (Trisha Bland, Christine Morissette, James Mulchinock, Brad Drew, Joel Ussery)

Municipal staff in North Saanich, Sidney, Central Saanich, Highlands, Saanich, Oak Bay, Victoria, Esquimalt, View Royal, Langford, Colwood and Metchosin

Representatives of clubs and organizations who have verified information

Arnold Fraser, for his patience and precision

Hemlock Printing, for their advice and expertise.

INDEX

Note: **Bold print** indicates a **map reference.**

Acknowledgements	9, 223	
Addresses	221, 222	
Agate Park		**100**
Albert Head Lagoon Regional Park	167	**169**
Anderson Hill Park	124	**123**
Arbutus Cove	120	
Aylard Farm	182	**185**
Ayum Creek watershed	192	**191**
Backbone Trail	219	
Banfield Park	141	**129**
Barnard Park	139	**129, 144**
Baynes Peak	33	**29**
Bayside lands	142	
Bazan Bay Park	45	**43**
BC Ferries	19	**42, 49**
BC Parks	17, 222	
Beacon Hill Park	131	**129**
bears	13, 198, 202	
Bear Hill Regional Park	94	**96**

Beaver Lake (see Elk/Beaver Lake Regional Park)		
Beaver Point Provincial Park	31	**29**
Beckwith Park	104	**101**
Benvenuto Avenue, Hill	62	**61**
bikes	10	
bike racks on buses	167, appendix	
Blenkinsop Lake Park	99	**101**
Blinkhorn Lake	173	**171**
Blueberry Hill	124	
Blue Heron Park	44	**42, 49**
Bluffs Park	19	
Bob Mountain Park and Trail	175	**171, 176**
Bodega Ridge	19	
Botanical Beach	198, 200	**196**
Boulderwood Park	103	**100**
Bow Park	116	**101, 117**
Bowker Creek Walkway	122	**123**
Braefoot Park	116	**101, 117**
bridle trails	10	
Brighton Avenue	127	**123**
Broadmead	102	**101**
Brodick Park	116	**101, 117**
Bruce Peak	27	**29**
Brydon Park	108	**110**
Buckbrush Swamp Park	175	**171**
Butterfield Park	57	**59, 61**
Buxton Green	143	**144**
bus routes	166, appendix	
Cadboro Bay	121	**123**
Caleb Pike / south access to Gowlland Tod Provincial Park	71	**73**
Camp Thunderbird	189	**191**
Canwest Shopping Centre	156	
Capital Regional District Parks (see CRD Parks)		
Carnarvon Park	123	
Cattle Point	122	**123**
Cecelia Ravine Park	140	
Cedar Hill Golf Course Trail	118	**117**
Cedarvale Park		**156**
Centennial Park (Central Saanich)	53, 56, 57, 60	**57, 61**
Centennial Park (Saltspring Island)	25	
Centennial Park (Victoria)	135	
Centennial Trails Trust	219	
Central Saanich area	56	**55, 61, 63**
Channel Ridge	36	**28**
Charters River watershed	192	**191**
China Beach	198, 199	**5, 197**
Chinatown	136	
Chinese cemetery, Harling Point	126	**123**
Christ Church Cathedral	137, 138	
Christmas Hill	115	**101, 117**
Clover Point	132	**129**

club addresses	221	
Coles Bay Regional Park	45	**47**
Colquitz River Linear Park	108-111	**110**
Colwood	155	**157**
Colwood Creek	164	**157**
Colwood Creek Park	165	**157**
Connector Park	175	**171**
Contents Map	5	
Copley Memorial Park	108	**110**
Cordova Bay Park	99	**100**
Corry Road trailhead, Mount Work Park	84	**83**
cougars	14, 198, 202	
Cowichan Valley Regional District	216, 218, 222	
Craigflower Farmhouse and School	114	
CRD Parks	16, 217, 218, 222	
CRD Regional Trail System	217	
Cuthbert Holmes Park	109, 111	**111**
cycling	10, 232	
Deacon / Beauchene Trail	204	**196**
Deep Cove		**46**
Deep Woods Trail	178	
Denham Till Park	44	**46**
Devonian Regional Park	173	**171**
Dionisio Point Provincial Park	19	
Dockside Lands	142	
Dominion Astrophysical Observatory	85	**88**
Donwood Park	99	**101**
Doris Page Park	99	**100**
Doumac Park	99	**100**
Drummond Children's Park	26	
Duck Creek	37	**28**
Dunsmuir Lodge	51	**43, 55**
Durrance Lake	70, 84	**72, 82**
Eagles Lake Park	84	
East Sooke area	180	**5**
East Sooke Regional Park	182	**185**
Ecological Reserves	15	
Edge Park	111	
Editor's Notes	7	
Elk / Beaver Lake Regional Park	94-98	**88, 97, 110**
Elk Lake (see above)		
Emily Carr Park	102	**101**
Esquimalt	143	**144**
Esquimalt Lagoon	162	**156**
Fairfield Hill	134	
Fairy Lake Nature Trail	205	**196**
Falls Creek Trail	207	**196**
Federation of Mountain Clubs of BC	204, 221	
Feltham Park	116	**117**
Fernwood area	130	
Finlayson Point	133	**129**

fires	13	
First and Second Creek Trail	207	**196**
Fisherman's Wharf Park	135	**129**
Fleming Beach	143	**144**
Fort Rodd Hill, Fisgard Lighthouse	160	**156**
Francis / King Regional Park	90, 154	**89, 93, 153**
Freeman King Park (see above)		
French Beach Provincial Park	195	**5**
Galloping Goose Regional Trail, text references	98, 112, 140, 149, 154, 159, 163, 165, 166, 179	
Galloping Goose Regional Trail, map references		**111, 148, 153, 156 169, 176, 181, 191**
Garry Oak Meadow Preservation Society	128	
Glencoe Cove	120	
Glen Cove Park	165	**156**
Glendale Lands	87	**89**
Goldstream Provincial Park	76, 158, 214	**73, 78**
Gonzales Hill Regional Park	124	**123**
Gore Nature Park	60	**61**
Gorge Park	114	**129, 144**
Gorge Waterway Park	114	**144, 148**
Government House	134	
Gowlland Range	71	**72**
Gowlland Tod Provincial Park	65, 70, 71, 76	**66, 72, 82**
Grant Park	99, 102, 103	**100**
Green / Blue Spaces Strategy	217	
Greenways	217	
Gulf Islands	19	**5**
Gulf View Picnic Site	52	
GVWD Non-Catchment Lands	193	**5**
Gyro Park, Cadboro Bay	121	**123**
Haldon Park	56	**55, 61**
Happy Valley	165	**157**
Hardy Park	60	**61**
Harling Point, Chinese Cemetery	125	**123**
Haro Woods	119	
Harris Creek Camp II Trail	205	**196**
Harris Creek spruce tree	206	
Harrison Trail	192	**191**
Hartland Landfill - Surplus Lands	84	**83**
Hatley Park (see Royal Roads)		
Haynes Park	122	**123**
Hazlitt Creek Park	69	**72**
Helmcken House	137	
Henderson Park and Recreation Centre	119, 122	**123**
Highlands	68	**5, 72, 82**
Highrock Cairn Park	145	**144**
Hints and Cautions	10	
Holland Point Park	132	**129**
Holmes Peak		**72**
Hope Hill Trails	27	**29**

Horth Hill Regional Park	50	**49**
horses	10	
Horticulture Centre of the Pacific	87	**88**
Hyacinth Park	109, 110, 116	**111**
Iroquois Park	39	
Island View Beach Regional Park	64	**63**
Jack Foster Trail, Southey Point	37	**28**
Jocelyn Hill (see cover photo)	75	**72**
John Dean Park	52, 56	**43, 54, 61**
John Quinn Trail	209	**196**
John Tod home	127	
Jordan River	195	**5**
Juan de Fuca Provincial Park and Marine Trail	198	**196**
Juan de Fuca Recreation Centre	159	**148, 156**
King George Terrace lookout	126	**123**
Kinsmen Gorge Park	115, 145	**144**
Kludahk Outdoors Club	209	
Knockan Hill Park	113	**111**
Konukson Park	121	**123**
Lambrick Park	116	
Langford	155	**156**
Langford Electoral Area	68	
Laurel Point Park	135	
Layritz Park	87, 90	**89, 110**
Legend	6	
Leechtown	150, 189	**190**
Lens Creek Trail	206	**196**
Lester B. Pearson College of the Pacific (see Pearson College)		
Library, Greater Victoria Public	222	
Lizard Lake Nature Trail	205	**196**
Lochside Drive Promenade	39	**40**
Lochside Park	62, 99	**63, 100**
Lochside Trail	62, 98, 112	**63,101**
Logan Park	86	**89**
Lone Tree Hill Regional Park	80	**80**
Loss Creek	198, 199	**197**
Macaulay Point	143	**144**
Malahat	214	**5**
Maps BC	222	
maps - list of	inside back cover	
maps - sample diagram of how maps interrelate	70	
Mariners Way	139	
Martindale Road, Flats	62, 64	**63**
Matheson Lake Regional Park	177	**171, 176**
McDonald Provincial Park	44	**42, 49**
McKenzie Bight Trail	70, 81	**66, 82**
McMinn Park	99	**100**
Metchosin	166	**168**
Metchosin Wilderness Park	175	171
Mill Farm Regional Park	30	**29**
Mill Hill Regional Park	154, 158	**148, 153**

Mitchell Park	173	**169**
Moor Park	108	**110**
Moss Rock Park	134	
Mouat Provincial Park	25	**28**
Mount Ball	177	**176**
Mount Douglas Park	99, 104-107, 116	**101, 107**
Mount Erskine	35	**28**
Mount Finlayson	76, 158	**73, 78**
Mount Jeffrey	216	**215**
Mount Matheson	180	**176**
Mount Maxwell Provincial Park	33	**34**
Mount Norman	19	
Mount Parke	19	
Mount Tolmie	118, 122	**117, 123**
Mount Tuam	30	**29**
Mount Wells Regional Park	165	
Mount Wood	216	**215**
Mount Work Regional Park	70, 81-84	**66, 72, 82, 88**
Musgrave Greenbelt	31	**29**
Mystic Beach Trail	199	**5**
Mystic Vale	119	
North Saanich	41	**42**
Nymph Point Park	44	**49**
Oak Bay area, Oak Bay Marina	122	**123**
Observatory, Dominion Astrophysical	85	**88**
Observatory, Gonzales Hill	124	**123**
Ogden Point	132	**129**
Old Cemeteries Society	135, 138	
Old Joe's Trail	108	
Old Town	136	
Oliphant Lake	214	**215**
Outdoor Club of Victoria	7, 221	
Outer Gulf Islands	19	**5**
Pacific Rim National Park	210, 211	**196**
Panama Hill	109	**111**
Parkinson Creek trailhead, Juan de Fuca Trail	198, 200	**196**
Parson's Bridge Park	147	**148**
Partridge Hills	65, 70, 84	**66**
Patricia Bay Park	50	**43**
Peacock Hill	130	
Pearson College	178	**171**
Pease Lake, Pease Creek	68, 70	**66, 72**
Pemberton Park	127, 128	**123, 129**
Perez Park	103	
Peter Arnell Park	33	**29**
Phyllis Park	121	**123**
Pioneer Square/ Quadra Street Cemetery	137	
Point Ellice House	142	
population	8	
Portage Park	147	**148**
Porter Park	134	

Portland Island	22	**23**
Portlock Park	26	
Port Renfrew	194, 203, 211	**196**
Princess Margaret Provincial Marine Park	22	**23**
Prospect Lake	87	**88**
Provincial Capital Commission	222	
Quadra Street Cemetery (see Pioneer Square)		
Quarry Lake (Central Saanich)	65	**66**
Quarry Park (North Saanich)	51	**43**
Quarry Drive Park (Saltspring Island)	36	**28**
Quick's Bottom	108	**89, 110**
Rails to Greenways	220	
Reay Creek Park	41	**40**
Red Creek Fir	207, 208	**196**
Reeson Regional Park	135	
Reginald Hill	26	**29**
Resthaven Park	39	**40**
Rithet's Bog	102	**101**
Riverbank Trail	208	**196**
Roche Cove Regional Park	180	**171, 181**
Ross Bay Cemetery	134, 135, 138	**129**
Royal Oak area	102	**101, 110**
Royal Oak Burial Park	103	**100**
Royal Roads, Hatley Park	162, 163	**156**
Ruckle Provincial Park	25, 31	**29**
Saanich area	85	
Saanich (south)		**117**
Saanich (west)		**88**
Saanich Historical Artifacts Society	62, 102	**63**
Saanich Spur, Galloping Goose Regional Trail	112	**117**
Saltspring Island	19, 24	**5, 28**
Sandbar Trail	207	**196**
Sandcut Creek Trail	195	**5**
San Juan Ridge	209	**196**
San Juan Sitka spruce	206	**197**
San Juan Valley trails	203	**196**
Saxe Point Park	145	**144**
Scafe Hill	68, 151	**73, 153**
Scenic Drive, Harling Point	125	**123, 129**
Seabluff Trail	173	**169**
Sea-to-Sea Greenbelt Proposal	192	
Section 28, Metchosin	178	**169**
Selkirk Waterfront	141	**129**
Shadywood Park	102	**101**
Sidney	38	**40**
Sidney Island	19	**5**
Sidney Spit Provincial Marine Park	19	**20**
Skirt Mountain	77	
Sombrio Beach	199, 200	**196**
Songhees Way	139	**129**
Sooke area	188	**191**

Sooke Hills Wilderness Regional Park	193	**5**
Sooke Mountain Provincial Park	192	**191**
Sooke to Port Renfrew: distances	194	
Sooke Potholes Provincial Park	189	**191**
Southey Point, Jack Foster Trail	37	**28**
South Prospect Lake Park	87	**88**
Spectacle Lake Provincial Park	214	**215**
Stan Harrison Plankboard Trail	208	**196**
Strawberry Knoll	86	**89**
Summit Park	128	**129**
Swan Creek Park/Trail	110	**111, 117**
Swan Lake Christmas Hill Nature Sanctuary	115	**117**
Ten Mile Point	121	**123**
Thetis Lake Regional Park	151	**89, 148, 152**
Thomson Park		**59**
Timberman Trail	68, 70	**82**
Tod Inlet / Partridge Hills	65	**66**
Tower Point	172	**171**
Trafalgar Park	125	**123**
Trail Systems	217	
Trans Canada Trail	140, 220	
Trevlac Pond	87	**89**
Tulista Park	39, 102	**40**
University of Victoria lands	119, 122	**123**
Uplands Park	122	**123**
Useful addresses	222	
Vancouver Island Backbone Trail	219	
Vancouver Island Trails Information Society (VITIS)	7, 221	
Victoria area	128	**129**
Victoria-Cowichan Trail	218	
Victoria Harbour Ferry	139	
Victorienteers	221	
View Royal, View Royal Park	146	**148**
Wain Park	44	**46**
Walbran Park	125	**123**
Wallace Drive / north access to Tod Inlet / Partridge Hills (Gowlland Tod Provincial Park)	65	**66**
Wallace Island Provincial Marine Park	19	
Waters Edge Walkway	147	**148**
weather	11	
West Bay Park and West Bay Walkway/Promenade	139, 145	**144**
West Coast Trail	210	**196**
Westsong Way	139	**129, 144**
Whale Hotline	199	
Whiffen Spit	192	**191**
Whitehead Park		**88**
Wildlife Trees	172	
Willows Park	122	**123**
Willow Way	53, 60	**61**
Windsor Park	122, 127	**123**
Witty's Lagoon Regional Park	170	**169, 171**

APPENDIX

HIKING TRAILS - How to Get There by Public Transit

Swartz Bay Ferry Terminal	70 Pat Bay Hwy
Horth Hill Regional Park	70 Pat Bay and walk
Town of Sidney	70 Pat Bay Hwy
Resthaven Park	70 Pat Bay Hwy
Reay Creek Park	70 Pat Bay Hwy
Sidney Island Ferry	70 Pat Bay Hwy
Coles Bay Regional Park	70 Pat Bay Hwy and long walk
John Dean Park	70 Pat Bay Hwy and short walk
Dunsmuir Lodge	70 Pat Bay Hwy and walk
Centennial Park	75 Central Saanich
Island View Beach	70 Pat Bay Hwy then walk
Tod Inlet from Wallace Drive	75 Central Saanich and walk
Logan Park	21 Interurban via Viaduct and walk
Elk/Beaver Lake Regional Park	70 Pat Bay Hwy
Cordova Bay Park	31 Glanford via 32 Cordova Bay
Lochside Park	31 Glanford via 32 Cordova Bay
Grant Park	32 Cordova Bay and walk *
Mount Douglas Park	28 Majestic and short walk
Glencoe Cove	27 Gordon Head
Braefoot Park	24 Cedar Hill or 25 Maplewood, walk
Beckwith Park	6 Quadra and short walk
Cedar Hill Golf Course	24 Cedar Hill
Cedar Hill Recreation Centre	24 Cedar Hill
Swan Lake/Christmas Hill Nature Sanctuary	26 Crosstown or 70 Pat Bay Hwy
	/75 Central Saanich, then walk
Quick's Bottom	30 Carey
Copley Park	30 Carey
Hyacinth Park	21 Interurban
Tillicum Mall	10 Gorge/21 Interurban/22 Burnside
Cuthbert Holmes Park	10 Gorge and short walk
Knockan Hill Park	22 Burnside
Gorge Waterway Park	10 Gorge
University of Victoria	14 University, 51 UVic, 39 UVic,
	4 Mt.Tolmie, 11 Uplands,
	26 Crosstown, 7 Foul Bay
Mount Tolmie	14 University
Henderson Recreation Centre	14 University or
	4 Mt. Tolmie and short walk
Uplands Park	11 Uplands
Willows Park	1 Willows
Oak Bay Marina	2 Oak Bay and short walk
Oak Bay Recreation Centre	11 Uplands, 7 Foul Bay
Pemberton Park	1 Richardson
Oak Bay Village	2 Oak Bay / 1 Willows
Windsor Park	2 Oak Bay
Gonzales Hill Regional Park	2 Gonzales and walk
Anderson Hill Park	1 Richardson and walk /
	2 Oak Bay and walk
Walbran Park	1 Richardson and walk

Summit Park	25 Maplewood
Ross Bay Cemetery	2 Gonzales
Beacon Hill Park	5 South Fairfield / Beacon Hill
Odgen Point breakwater	30 / 31 James Bay
Johnson Street Bridge	24 Colville, 25 Munro, 6 Esquimalt
Barnard Park	6 Esquimalt / 25 Munro
Saxe Point park	25 Munro
Fleming Beach	25 Munro
Highrock Cairn Park	24 Colville
Kinsmen Gorge Park	10 Gorge and short walk
West Bay Walkway	24 Colville / 25 Munro / 6 Esquimalt
Portage Park	14 Craigflower
Banfield Park	14 Craigflower
View Royal park	14 Craigflower
Parson's Bridge	50 Goldstream
Thetis Lake Park	50 Goldstream and walk
Goldstream Provincial Park	50 Goldstream to 58 Langford Meadows
Mill Hill Regional Park	50 Goldstream
Juan de Fuca Recreation Centre	50 Goldstream
Fort Rodd Hill	50 Goldstream - short walk
Esquimalt Lagoon	50 Goldstream, short walk / 52 Wishart *
Hatley Park	52 Wishart / 61 Sooke *
Canwest Mall	50 Goldstream
Albert Head Lagoon	55 Happy Valley
Seabluff Trail	50 Goldstream to 54 Metchosin or 55 Happy Valley
Devonian Park	50 Goldstream to 54 Metchosin or 55 Happy Valley
Metchosin Wilderness Park	50 Goldstream to 54 Metchosin or 55 Happy Valley
Witty's Lagoon Regional Park	50 Goldstream to 54 Metchosin or 55 Happy Valley
Matheson Lake Regional Park	61 Sooke / 54 Metchosin / 55 Happy Valley, all long walks
Roche Cove Regional Park	61 Sooke and walk *
East Sooke Park	61 Sooke and walk *
Sooke Potholes	61 Sooke and walk *
Town of Sooke	61 Sooke

* check for direct service

For more information and schedules please call BUSLINE at 382-6161. A brochure, ***Explore Victoria by Bus,*** is available at the **BC Transit** office, 520 Gorge Road East.

In the fall of 1997, **bike racks** were added to the low-floor accessible buses on the Western Communities bus routes. All accessible trips on bus routes with numbers 50 or higher will now be able to carry two bikes. These trips are highlighted in the ***Rider's Guide* transit schedule**. An information pamphlet is available on board buses, at cycling shops, and from the Transit office, where demonstrations of the bike racks are available.